REDISCOVERING
JESUS

An Introduction to Biblical, Religious
and Cultural Perspectives on Christ

DAVID B. CAPES, RODNEY REEVES
AND E. RANDOLPH RICHARDS

IVP Academic

An imprint of InterVarsity Press
Downers Grove, Illinois

InterVarsity Press
P.O. Box 1400, Downers Grove, IL 60515-1426
ivpress.com
email@ivpress.com

InterVarsity Press® is the book-publishing division of InterVarsity Christian Fellowship/USA®, a movement of students and faculty active on campus at hundreds of universities, colleges and schools of nursing in the United States of America, and a member movement of the International Fellowship of Evangelical Students. For information about local and regional activities, visit intervarsity.org.

Scripture quotations, unless otherwise noted, are from the New Revised Standard Version of the Bible, copyright 1989 by the Division of Christian Education of the National Council of the Churches of Christ in the USA. Used by permission. All rights reserved.

While any stories in this book are true, some names and identifying information may have been changed to protect the privacy of individuals.

Cover design: Cindy Kiple
Interior design: Beth McGill
Images: Head of Christ by Antonio Allegri Correggio at J. Paul Getty Museum, Los Angeles, USA, Bridgeman Images
  torn paper: © kay/iStockphoto

ISBN 978-0-8308-2472-4 (print)
ISBN 978-0-8308-9856-5 (digital)
Printed in the United States of America ∞

Library of Congress Cataloging-in-Publication Data
Capes, David B.
 Rediscovering Jesus : an introduction to biblical, religious, and cultural perspectives on Christ / David B. Capes, Rodney Reeves and E. Randolph Richards.
   pages cm
 Includes bibliographical references and index.
 ISBN 978-0-8308-2472-4 (casebound : alk. paper)
 1. Jesus Christ--Person and offices. I. Title.
 BT203.C35 2015
 232—dc23
                          2015014882

P 23 22 21 20 19 18 17 16 15 14 13 12 11 10 9 8 7 6 5 4 3 2 1

Y 34 33 32 31 30 29 28 27 26 25 24 23 22 21 20 19 18 17 16 15

To our students

who want answers to questions

scholars tend to ignore

Contents

PREFACE

Since many have undertaken to set down an orderly account (as Luke noted in his preface long ago), why add another? There are a lot of great textbooks on Jesus. We are particularly keen on the ones by Mark Strauss, Bruce Fisk, Darrell Bock and Craig Blomberg. As teachers, though, we found that our students often asked questions these books did not address. Whether spurred by Dan Brown's *The Da Vinci Code*, a headline spied on a grocery store tabloid, or a thoughtful documentary on *The History Channel*, inquiring minds want to know. We decided to write a textbook with a different approach to complement these other works.

We begin by looking at the biblical Jesus. We examine Mark's Jesus and each of the other three Gospel portraits, allowing each Gospel writer to tell his own story of Jesus. Then each section of the New Testament is allowed to describe its portrait of Jesus, whether Paul, Hebrews, the General Epistles or Revelation. In the second half of the book we look at some images of Jesus outside the New Testament that have been formative to our modern Western view of him. The Gnostic Jesus, the Muslim Jesus, the Jesus of the Enlightenment, the Mormon Jesus, even the American Jesus and the Jesus of film—each is given a voice. Although we do not believe that these extrabiblical voices are authoritative, they have influenced how all of us see Jesus. When we look back to the New Testament, we often look through rather than around these images of Jesus. Rediscovering Jesus requires hearing all the voices that have colored our perceptions of him.

Each chapter has three parts. First, we ask what a particular picture of Jesus looks like. We play off Jesus' question at Caesarea Philippi when he asked his disciples, "Who do people say that I am?" This is still a very important question. So, for example, we ask, "Who does Mark say that Jesus is?" "Who does Revelation say that he is?" "Who do the Mormons say that he is?" Second, each chapter will ask how this picture of Jesus is different. What are the distinctives of Mark's Jesus? How is the picture of Jesus in Hebrews different? We try to highlight the more unique elements and emphases that this portrait of Jesus contains. Third, each chapter will ask, "What if this were our only portrait of Jesus?" This is, admittedly, a creative exercise, but it is helpful to ask, "What if Mark's Jesus were our only Jesus?" For some Christian communities in the first few centuries, this likely was their only Jesus. What if the American Jesus were our only Jesus? For many Americans, this may be true. For some of you, there may be an "Aha!" moment in this section.

Each chapter also has some text boxes called "What's More . . . ," which contain additional information or ideas that might be helpful to you. Also, every chapter has several boxes labeled "So What?" These call-out boxes are in honor of our students who have always been faithful to assist us as professors to "keep it real." Asking why something matters in the life of a believer today can be very helpful. We hope that these boxes kick-start that discussion in your own life.

Chapters end with two elements. First, we list additional resources. These are not exhaustive lists but rather books or articles that might help the reader who is curious to read more about that subject. We also end each chapter with some discussion questions.

You have noticed by now that we have used the word "we." Three good friends joined together to write this book. We share a common viewpoint as evangelicals who take the story of Jesus very seriously and as teachers who want our students to follow Jesus as a lifelong journey. This book, though, is not a compilation of independently written essays. One of us made the initial attempt at a first draft for a chapter, but then we wrote on top of each other, discussed each paragraph in videoconferences, debated in personal visits, and rewrote together several times. Each chapter, in the end, is not the work of one of us but all three of us. We cannot even separate out who is responsible for the wording on any given page. An illustration started with one of us, hence the "I" in the story, but we decided not to try to clarify which author first told that story. By this time, all three of us have read the story so many times that each of us feels ownership of the story. We want our readers to know that these stories we tell are true, but it does not matter who first experienced it.

For good reason, authors often end their prefaces by thanking their families, and so do we. We three are intensely grateful to our wives and children. As husbands and fathers, our prayer has always been that they would follow Jesus.

Abbreviations

Alleg. Interp.	Philo, *Allegorical Interpretation*
Bar	Baruch
2 Bar.	*2 Baruch (Syriac Apocalypse)*
1 En.	*1 Enoch*
2 Esd	2 Esdras
4 Ezra	*4 Ezra*
4QFlor (4Q174)	4QFlorilegium
Gos. Mary	*Gospel of Mary*
Gos. Pet.	*Gospel of Peter*
Gos. Thom.	*Gospel of Thomas*
Gos. Truth	*Gospel of Truth*
Herm. *Sim.*	Shepherd of Hermas, *Similitude*
Hist. eccl.	Eusebius, *Historia ecclesiastica*
LXX	Septuagint
m. Sanh.	Mishnah, *Sanhedrin*
2 Macc	2 Maccabees
P.Oxy.	Oxyrhynchus Papyri
Pss. Sol.	*Psalms of Solomon*
Soph. Jes. Chr.	*Sophia of Jesus Christ*
Treat. Seth	*Second Treatise of the Great Seth*
Wis	Wisdom of Solomon

"My Jesus"

I was sitting in the seminary cafeteria, enjoying a cup of coffee, and reminding myself that Jesus wouldn't mind if I skipped chapel that day. After all, didn't Jesus himself withdraw from the crowds for a little "down time"? I was sitting there with some fellow seminary students. A colleague was waxing eloquently about Jesus turning the water into wine, joking that if Jesus had been a Baptist, he would have turned the wine back into water. One of my tablemates wasn't enjoying the joke as much, judging from his stern look of disapproval. He reminded us that Jesus was a teetotaler. When someone else pointed out that Jesus drank wine, he informed us that the wine that Jesus drank was nonalcoholic. This caught my attention, and I asked him where Jesus would get such wine. He announced with righteous indignation, "I don't know, but *my* Jesus would not drink alcoholic wine." The discussion was over, but I was left wondering if my Jesus was the same one as his.

We recognize that not everyone in the world sees Jesus the same way as we do, but in our heart of hearts, each of us believes that "my Jesus" is closest to the real Jesus. Others also have the real Jesus, *if* they have a Jesus that doesn't differ significantly from mine—that is, only minor differences, which really means as long as the differences involve issues that don't overly concern me. Although I will concede that at other times and in other places people have misinterpreted Jesus, I am fairly confident that I have Jesus somewhat "right." Jesus tells the story of a slave owner who commands his slave to serve him even when the slave is weary (Lk 17:7-10). I have baggage from my American history that makes me uncomfortable with Jesus talking about real slaves. Surely, Jesus is referring to some sort of spiritual slavery, I posit. At the very least, I want my translation to change the word from "slave" to "servant." Or perhaps this is some minor illustration that Jesus was making, and I am best served by skipping over that story. I feel certain that it would misrepresent Jesus for us to highlight that parable. Although Luke included the story, we would not list it as one of our top ten favorite parables.

We are all aware that others reinterpret Jesus, reading Jesus through their own cultural and religious lenses. Tolerance is highly regarded in our society. I don't like the story where Jesus equates a woman with a dog (Mt 15:21-28). My Jesus wouldn't offend anyone—unless it was a bad person. My Jesus didn't really mean it when he said, "Woe to you who are rich, for you have received your consolation" (Lk 6:24). Even though I live comfortably, my Jesus was talking about someone far richer than me, and, I reason, someone who probably got rich by oppressing honest folks. However, deep down inside, I believe that I don't have an interpreted Jesus; I am simply "reading" the Bible or taking the Bible "literally." I have the "real Jesus."

Not only do I have a misinterpreted or reinterpreted Jesus, but also my Jesus is commonly a composite Jesus—a Jesus we can't find in any *one* of the Gospels. He ministers in a composite world that I have created by joining together the stories and characters that I think belong together. For example, my Jesus, the real Jesus, cared about the rich young ruler, but actually no Gospel identifies the man that way. He is rich in Mark 10, a rich young man in Matthew 19, and a rich ruler in Luke 18. Only by combining all the stories do we conclude that he is a rich young ruler. Likewise, often we think that Mary, the sister of Lazarus, was a sinful woman. We conclude this only by combining stories across Gospels. In Luke 7 we are told that a sinful woman anointed Jesus. In John 11–12 we read that Mary anointed Jesus, so we conclude that Mary was a sinful woman (rescued by Jesus). We may be slandering Mary's character. So, my Jesus often is the product of combined stories. In Christmas plays, the shepherds and the magi visit the newborn Jesus in the manger on the same night. These composite accounts require us to gloss over differences in order to combine the stories. According to

Matthew, the magi actually visit the toddler Jesus, who was living in a house. The rich ruler in Luke 18 insists that he had been keeping all the commandments ever since he was young. When we create a composite Jesus, we risk losing Luke's Jesus or Matthew's Jesus, leaving us a Jesus of the lowest common denominator or, worse, a Jesus made up of the parts I like.

My Jesus is often a smorgasbord Jesus, a Jesus who doesn't look like the one in the Bible. Just like a buffet in the cafeteria, where I go through the line and pick out what I want, I read through the Gospels, pulling out the stories I like. I see Brussels sprouts. I know that they're good for me, but I don't like them, so I skip past them. So likewise, this smorgasbord Jesus doesn't hurl epithets at women or make demands of slaves. In the cafeteria buffet, I like dessert. I likewise want a sweet, agreeable Jesus, one who likes what I like and hates what I hate. Everyone agrees that child trafficking is bad, so let's talk about a Jesus who loves children. But I'm uncomfortable with a Jesus who might disapprove of my purchase of the latest hi-tech gadget when there are millions of children who don't have enough to eat, so I avoid sayings of Jesus that might suggest that. Frankly, my Jesus isn't overly concerned with the things I'm not overly concerned about.

But we can see that it can't be all about me. The British rock band Depeche Mode sang about "my personal Jesus." Yet, I know it cannot just be about my personal experience with the risen Christ. So, how do we rediscover the real Jesus? We suggest first allowing each picture of Jesus to speak for itself. As evangelicals, we believe that it was the inspiration of the Spirit that led to producing four portraits of Jesus rather than a single composite one. Although each of our Gospels probably arose in its own community, why didn't early Christians bring the four stories into one, at least when they were gathering writings into a collection? An early church father, Tatian (ca. A.D. 120–180), thought it would be better just to have one Gospel, so he wove our four together. The result is his book the *Diatessaron* (meaning "through four"). Collecting all the unique stories and blending the shared stories creates what is called a "harmony of the Gospels." Early Christians rejected Tatian's well-intended efforts—although, in practice, we still combine stories. Having different images of Jesus is somehow better. So, we are going to look at the New Testament Jesus from a number of angles. Clearly, we privilege the four canonical Gospels, but the New Testament has other pictures of

Jesus as well. Beyond the New Testament, individuals and groups through the ages have also interpreted Jesus. As much as we would like to think otherwise, we have been influenced by how Jesus has been viewed before us. We also no longer have the luxury of pretending that white Western males are the only ones whose opinions matter. Could African and Asian voices help us to see Jesus better? Those outside our faith also have interpretations of Jesus: righteous angel, rightly guided prophet, enlightened sage, darling of heaven. When Jesus asked his followers, "Who do people say that I am?" he wasn't just curious about what his followers believed; he wanted to know what the crowds were saying. In effect, he set up a question that can be and must be asked by all peoples down through the ages.

As each chapter in this book explores a different view of Jesus, we will ask first, "What does this picture of Jesus look like?" For example, in chapter three we pose the question "Who does Luke say that I am?" narrowing the focus of Jesus' famous question. In other words, we are going to look at each story individually, what Mark Strauss calls reading "vertically," from top to bottom—without looking "horizontally" to other Gospels—to discover the meaning of Jesus in each Gospel, on its own terms, from beginning to end. Strauss contends that since each Gospel has a story to tell (and since the Holy Spirit chose to inspire four and not just one), "we should respect the integrity of each story."[1] Looking at Mark's Jesus allows us to see the picture that Mark wanted us to see, from how he introduces Jesus, to the rise of followers and opponents and the seemingly inevitable conflict, to God's grand resolution.

The second section of each chapter looks at how a particular portrayal of Jesus differs from other images or even from the composite image that we have of Jesus. So, we will ask, for example, "How is Luke's Jesus different?" Luke paints a different image than John does. That statement might make some uncomfortable, but even a casual reader can see that it is immediately true. We need to see the distinctives of each picture of Jesus. The dangers of Tatian's approach of reading harmonistically are that we blend stories and we lose uniqueness, both of which distort the message. For example, most of us are familiar with the "Seven Sayings of Jesus on the Cross." Yet, there

---

[1]Mark L. Strauss, *Four Portraits, One Jesus: An Introduction to Jesus and the Gospels* (Grand Rapids: Zondervan, 2007), p. 32.

are seven only if one collects the sayings from the four Gospels.[2] When we add all of them together, however, we miss the emphasis of each writer. Mark's Jesus utters only one line from the cross: "My God, my God, why have you forsaken me?" (Mk 15:34). In Mark, the crucifixion is an ominous and dark moment. But Luke's Jesus speaks to the crowds around him, offering warnings as he carries his cross, "Do not weep for me, but weep for yourselves and for your children" (Lk 23:28); and to one person he offers forgiveness and encouragement from the cross, "Today you will be with me in Paradise" (Lk 23:43). From the cross John's Jesus makes sure that his mother will be taken care of, and then he announces, "It is finished" (Jn 19:30).[3] When we harmonize Luke's Jesus who is talking to the crowds with John's Jesus who is talking to his family, we miss Mark's picture of despairing isolation. It is important to look at each picture of Jesus separately first. How will this help us rediscover Jesus? Well, Luke's readers, for example, may have had only Luke's Gospel. They felt that it was enough. Churches arose. Christians grew in faith following Luke's Jesus. When we blend our pictures of Jesus too quickly, we can lose the distinctives of each. Worse, we can create a Jesus of the lowest common denominator or a Jesus overshadowed by the picture that we most prefer.

The third section of each chapter asks, Who would we say that Jesus is if this were the only picture of Jesus that we had? If we had only Mark's Jesus, what would Christmas and Easter look like (if we celebrated them at all)? What would our preaching sound like? Well, if we followed Mark's Jesus, we would preach, "The kingdom of God is near," and not John's message, "Believe in Jesus and you'll have eternal life." Or if we only had Luke's Jesus, what would our churches be doing? Luke's Jesus cares for the marginalized. Or consider Matthew's Jesus, who tells us that the greatest in the kingdom are the ones who practice and teach the commandments (Mt 5:19). And what about Paul? For Paul, the main thing is that Christ died for our sins and rose on the third day (1 Cor 15:3-4). Churches that emphasize Paul's Jesus will know exactly why Jesus died but will tend to compress the story of Jesus to

---

[2]In fact, the saying "Father, forgive them; for they do not know what they are doing" (Lk 23:34) doesn't appear in the oldest manuscripts, leading many scholars to conclude that it was added by scribes to create "seven sayings."

[3]For this insightful point we are indebted to Strauss, *Four Portraits*, pp. 33-34.

his death, burial and resurrection. And what about the Revelation of John? The apocalyptic Jesus is hardly the gentle savior, meek and mild, whom we read about in Luke. Consequently, this third section of each chapter helps us to clarify what that particular image of Jesus says to us. Looking directly at the question "What if this were our only Jesus?" will help us see first what this picture of Jesus is emphasizing. Maybe we need Mark's Jesus to remind us that Jesus was bringing in the kingdom *before* the cross. Or when we prefer Paul's Jesus to the neglect of James' Jesus, we forget that faith without works is dead. It matters what we do. When did you last hear a sermon that demanded, "Cleanse your hands, you sinners, and purify your hearts" (Jas 4:8)? While we love *abiding* in John's Jesus, Peter's Jesus reminds us to "make every *effort* to support your faith with goodness, and goodness with knowledge" (2 Pet 1:5).

This is what we need to do: take in the entire New Testament, and let each biblical writer teach us about Jesus. Rather than rely upon our favorite parts, our preferred picture of Jesus, we need to rediscover the "whole" Jesus— every portrait, every picture, every single verse. By looking at many different images of Jesus, even the ones outside the Bible, we might be in a better position to rediscover Jesus beyond our preferences, challenging our prejudices and enhancing our faith. Jesus asked his first disciples what others thought of him. Then he asked the question that matters just as much, or even more: "But who do *you* say that I am?" (Mk 8:29). Some might think that these are two, separate questions, and that you can answer the first and ignore the second, or you can answer the second as if you are unaffected by the first. We think that Jesus asked one question two ways. Indeed, you can't answer one without the other, for it seems that everyone has an opinion about Jesus, and no one can figure him out alone. In fact, we believe that this twofold question still deserves a good answer because Jesus' question still stands today. It's a question asked of every person. We hope that this book will help you find the answer.

PART I

Introduction

Jesus in the Bible

Iattended the funeral of Daniel, a fine Christian gentleman, whom I didn't
know all that well. The church was packed. It was a testament to a long
life, well lived. Clearly, Daniel was much loved and admired. Several people
stood up to share their memories of how Daniel had touched them. Some
stories were humorous, some quite serious. Some were told by close friends,
others by business associates. One person knew Daniel only as a young man,
another only when Daniel was old. In the reception time afterwards I heard
other stories. Sometimes I heard the same event told by different people with
different perspectives. Each story helped flesh out the man. Even though
each person spoke truthfully, every speaker helped me to see more. The
more stories I heard, the better I understood Daniel. It didn't lead me to
believe that there were many Daniels, but rather I began to see a more
complex Daniel, with rich overtones.

Likewise, four Gospels lead us to see not four Jesuses but rather a fuller
portrait of the one Jesus. One person's perspective doesn't tell the whole
story. Each New Testament image of Jesus enriches our understanding of
him. Yet, we tend to gravitate toward the pictures that we like the best or are
the most familiar. Thus, we in the modern West tend to spend our time with
the Jesus of Paul and John. In fact, when I was in seminary, a very popular
course was titled "The Theology of Paul and John." After all, wasn't that all
we really needed? When we say it so bluntly, we know immediately that it

isn't true. We know that we need the entire New Testament; yet, we often pull our image of Jesus from only select parts. In part one we will look at biblical portraits of Jesus.

However, we look not only at the common pictures of Jesus from the Gospels but also at the Jesus we find in Paul's letters, Hebrews, 1 Peter and Revelation. For example, we will ask the Jesus question "Who does James say that I am?" After looking at what James says, we will ask another important question: "How is James's Jesus different?" It is often in looking at what James says (and doesn't say) that we find the uniqueness of James's picture. Finally, we'll ask, "What if James's Jesus were our only Jesus?" How would our evangelism or worship be different? How would we even speak of evangelism if we don't have Romans to pull verses from? Instead of just assuming that we would have a truncated gospel, we will seek what treasures we can find in this other perspective of Jesus. What would our churches do if all we had were James's Jesus? Instead of just thinking about what we wouldn't have, such as not knowing about the parable of the good Samaritan, we should think about what we would be doing. For James, it matters that our deeds match our words. For James, the gospel of Jesus is about taking care of widows and orphans; it is about giving food and clothing to those who need them, and not merely spouting words of encouragement.

Taking in the full picture of the biblical Jesus will mean having ears to hear every story, both the familiar and obscure, and having eyes to appreciate every perspective, from the first book to the last. After all, since we believe that the entire New Testament was inspired by God, we want to know everything it says about the one we claim to follow.

1

MARK'S JESUS

Have you ever wanted to travel back in time to witness firsthand some important event in history? In the early days of television Walter Cronkite hosted an educational series titled *You Are There*. The program took us "back in time" and reenacted key events in American and world history. After a brief setup by Cronkite from his studios in New York, the announcer says, "The date is October 14, 1912, and the place is Milwaukee, Wisconsin, and *You Are There* for the attempted assassination of Teddy Roosevelt."[1] The scene immediately shifts to the past. News reporters, in modern dress, cover the events of the day and interview the people involved just as they do modern events. The half-hour show concludes with Cronkite in New York with these words: "What sort of day was it? A day like all days, filled with those events that alter and illuminate our times. And you were there."

CBS News understood the power of drawing the audience in by portraying past actions in a vivid, up-to-the-minute way. They wanted us to sense that we are there at the moment when these extraordinary events are taking place. Mark used a similar technique in his Gospel, writing the story as if "you were there": his Greek text switches from past to present tense at key moments of a story to highlight the critical action (e.g., Mk 4:35-41), with the effect of bringing Jesus' time into our own. Mark used several techniques to bring his audience face-to-face with Jesus.

---

[1]Episode 10, first broadcast on June 2, 1957.

WHO DOES MARK SAY THAT I AM?

And who is this Jesus? He is the Messiah (Christ) and Son of God—that is, God's end-time agent whose task is to liberate the world from evil, oppression, sin, sickness, and death. The world that Jesus enters is hostile and contrary to the human race. The Messiah appears in order to claim all that God has made on behalf of heaven. In Mark's account Jesus moves quickly along "the way" challenging and disrupting demonic powers, disease, religious authorities, storms and, ultimately, the power of Rome itself.

But Jesus does not appear from nowhere; prophets such as Malachi and Isaiah have written of him long ago. They foresaw his coming, and John the Baptizer arrived right on schedule to prepare his way. If John is God's messenger (Mal 3:1) and the voice crying out in the wilderness (Is 40:3), then surely Jesus is the "Lord" whose paths must be made straight (Mk 1:2-3). But the word "Lord" here is no polite address to an English country gentleman or a simple affirmation of a person in authority; it is the way Greek-speaking Jews uttered the unspeakable name of the one, true God of Israel. Jesus the Christ is no ordinary man, for the very name of God—a name protected by the Ten Commandments—belongs rightly to him. As Mark's story unfolds, it is apparent why this is so.

When Jesus heard that a prophet had again appeared in Israel, he left Nazareth to see for himself. As he entered the Jordan River to be baptized, onlookers would have thought that Jesus was becoming a disciple of John. But it was what Jesus heard and saw next that dramatically changed his life. He saw a vision: the heavens were ripped open, and the Spirit descended on him like a dove. Then he heard a voice from heaven: "You are my Son" (Ps 2:7) and "with you I am well pleased" (Is 42:1). Whether or not anyone else saw or heard what was going on in the heavens that day is unclear. Mark tells us only that Jesus saw and heard; perhaps Jesus' special sonship was a secret that needed protecting for a while. But it was enough for Jesus to see and hear it, because it was about him and him alone. He knew what he must do next. He must leave behind Nazareth and the anonymity of the workshop for a public life in Galilee and beyond. He must trade a builder's tools for the skills of a traveling rabbi.

THE MESSIAH IN ACTION

The Spirit sends—actually, drives—Jesus into the wilderness, where he battles with Satan for forty days and is served by angels, a hint of things to come. When John is arrested (another hint), Jesus returns to Galilee to begin the

---

WHAT'S MORE . . .

What Is a Gospel?

Scholars do not often agree on much, but the majority of scholars today agree on this: the New Testament Gospels belong to a genre of literature known as "biographies" (*bioi*). In the middle of the twentieth century many scholars challenged this notion, arguing that the Gospels were totally unique compositions. But more recently scholars such as Richard Burridge and David Aune have made compelling cases that ancient biographies provide clear evidence that the Gospels ought to be read as a biography of a recent person. They point to analogies in Plutarch's *Lives*, Tacitus's *Annals* and Suetonius's *Lives of the Caesars.*

Modern biographies are different from ancient ones. We prefer dates and events in sequential order. Ancient biographies often are arranged in thematic or topical order rather than chronological. Moreover, they generally are not concerned with describing physical traits; instead, the true greatness of people is measured in what they did and what they said, and especially in how they died. In addition, ancient writers felt free to paraphrase (and usually abbreviate) a person's speeches as long as they stayed true to the essence of what was said. Finally, ancient biographies functioned in a variety of ways; they were entertaining, of course, but writers often chose their subjects because their lives provided inspiring examples worthy of imitation. We see many of these same dynamics at work in the New Testament Gospels.

---

next phase of his life with a profound message: "The time is fulfilled, and the kingdom of God has come near; repent, and believe in the good news" (Mk 1:15). The essential message of Jesus had to do with the kingdom of God. If we fail to understand that, then we will fail to understand Mark's Jesus. Jesus did not come so that people might go to heaven when they die. As important as that may be, that is not the center of his message. The crux of it is that God's reign on this world is about to begin, so get ready. It is not too far-fetched to understand everything that Mark's Jesus does and says has to do with the kingdom. So understanding what the kingdom of God means for Jesus and his first hearers is crucial. Simply put, the kingdom of God is the time and place in history when God's will is done on earth as it is in heaven.

There is ambiguity in Jesus' statements about the kingdom, beginning with his initial proclamation: "The kingdom of God is near." What does Jesus mean? Is the kingdom already here (present), or has it not yet arrived (future)? For Mark, the focus appears to be the future, but the future has already begun, in the present. The ambiguous nature of the kingdom's present-future or "already but not yet" aspect gains clarity in reference to Jesus. For Mark, it is impossible to talk about the kingdom apart from Jesus. Where the king is, there is the kingdom.

The claim that God's reign is about to begin on earth does not sit well with the powers that be. Satan and dark forces line up against Jesus. Powerful people—some religious, some not so much—band together against Jesus in order to silence him. In Mark's Gospel Jesus is a deeply polarizing figure. He is either loved or hated. He is either a devil who deserves to be destroyed or God's Messiah, the Son of God, who has come to serve and give his life "a ransom for many" (Mk 10:45). Mark does not leave room for an ambiguous response to Jesus. He never meant to.

Signs and wonders. Mark's portrait of Jesus emphasizes miracles in the cities and villages of the Galilee. As he travels, Jesus encounters people in great need; some are demonized, sick, hungry and dying. They come alone and others with large masses because they wish what we all wish: to be whole and well.

Yet there is some ambiguity regarding the relationship of faith to Jesus' miracles. Where faith exists, Jesus is portrayed as able to do mighty deeds unhindered. The leper who approaches Jesus confident that the Nazarene can make him well is soon healed and sent to procure the priest's confirmation (Mk 1:40-45). When Jesus encounters the disabled man carried by four friends, he sees the faith of his friends and heals him (Mk 2:1-12). Jesus also heals the woman with a bleeding disorder and sends her home with this encouragement: "Your faith has made you well" (Mk 5:34). He says the same thing to the formerly blind beggar Bartimaeus in Jericho (Mk 10:52). Unbelief, however, seems to have impeded Jesus' healing ministry at home in Nazareth. Although he did perform a handful of healings, "he could do no deed of power there" (Mk 6:5), due apparently to unbelief. This may explain passages such as Mark 1:32-34, where the locals in Galilee brought to Jesus "all" who were sick and oppressed, and Jesus healed "many." On the other hand, faith must have been full in Gennesaret the day Jesus embarked there, for all who touched the fringe of his garments were healed (Mk 6:53-56).

WHAT'S MORE . . .

Four Types of Miracles

Jesus performs four kinds of miracles. Each demonstrates something of his authority.

1. Exorcisms: Jesus has authority over evil.
   - the man in the synagogue at Capernaum (Mk 1:21-28)
   - the man from Gerasa (Mk 5:1-20)
   - the boy with an unclean spirit (Mk 9:14-29)

2. Healings: Jesus has authority over disease.
   - the leper (Mk 1:35-39)
   - the paralytic (Mk 2:1-12)
   - the blind man in Bethsaida (Mk 8:22-26)

3. Nature miracles: Jesus has authority over nature itself.
   - he stills a storm (Mk 4:35-41)
   - he walks on water (Mk 6:45-52)
   - he feeds a crowd of five thousand (Mk 6:30-44)

4. Resuscitations: Jesus has authority over death.
   - Jairus's daughter (Mk 5:21-43)

For Mark, the miracles that Jesus performs are not just individual acts of benevolence, good deeds done to deserving persons. Rather, properly understood, the miracles are manifestations of the reign of God in the world. They demonstrate the priorities of the kingdom and what kind of world there will be when the world to come eclipses the present evil age. Evil will no longer oppress. Disease will no longer ravage. Nature will no longer be contrary. Death will no longer claim. The reign of God looks much different from this age, and the miracles pull back the veil to reveal the world as God had always intended it.

Parables. Although Jesus is often addressed as "Teacher" in Mark's Gospel (e.g., Mk 4:38; 10:17; 12:14; 13:1), we encounter only a little of his formal teaching. Seldom in Mark does Jesus sit down or stand before a crowd to teach. When he does (Mk 1:21-28), we're not told what he says, for the point of the story lies beyond the lesson of the day. For Mark, Jesus teaches by example, evident in his daily interactions with the sick, sinners, nature, opponents and disciples. When he does sit before the crowds, he speaks in parables designed to conceal as much as they reveal (Mk 4:1-20). For insiders, the parables reveal the true nature of the kingdom of God; for those outside, the parables merely conceal it.

THE MESSIAH IN CONFLICT

When Jesus performs miracles, he stirs things up. Demons recognize him. Crowds grow. Questions are asked: "What is this? A new teaching—with authority!" (Mk 1:27). People are amazed at his authority. But Jesus' kingdom message and actions also stir up his opponents. Mark wants his readers to see how quickly Jesus' message rubbed the self-appointed guardians of culture the wrong way. So he lays out for his audience a series of controversies that swirled around Jesus. Jesus meets each challenge with a clarifying word—a pronouncement—about his mission and ministry. How he answers these charges reveal the heart of the Markan Jesus.

Blasphemy. Opponents charge Jesus with blasphemy for claiming to forgive the sins of the paralyzed man (Mk 2:1-12). No one can forgive sins except God alone, they grumble. Jesus answers by appealing to his favorite self-designation. The "Son of Man" has not usurped God's right; indeed, he exercises properly heaven's authority to forgive sins on earth. He punctuates the pronouncement by healing the man and sending him home.

Friend of sinners. Opponents charge Jesus with befriending notorious sinners. Jesus responds with a pronouncement: "Those who are well have no need of a physician, but those who are sick; I have come to call not the righteous but sinners" (Mk 2:17). Jesus seems more comfortable in the company of sinners than of those who think that they are righteous.

Violating the traditions of the elders. Opponents charge Jesus with not following the traditions handed down from the elders (Mk 2:18; 7:5). Jesus responds not by declaring an end to all tradition but by appealing to the moment. Now is not the time to fast; now is the time to feast because the bridegroom (Jesus himself) is present. When the bridegroom is taken away—a cryptic reference to Jesus' arrest and execution—it will be time to fast. With parables about mending garments and making wine Jesus hints that the newness of the kingdom requires new traditions to contain it.

Breaking Sabbath law. Jesus' opponents watched him carefully, scrutinized his every move, and were quick to accuse him of breaking God's law regarding the Sabbath. So Jesus appealed to Scripture and compassion. If someone is in need of food or healing or some other good thing on the Sabbath, it is lawful to provide them. He pronounces, "The sabbath was made for humankind, and not humankind for the sabbath; so the Son of Man is lord even of the sabbath" (Mk 2:27-28).

In league with the devil. Opponents claim that Jesus casts out demons because he is in league with the devil. Ironically, they never challenge his ability to perform these exorcisms; they claim that Jesus received his power from the devil (Beelzebul) himself. Jesus responds with a bit of common sense. How can Satan cast out Satan? A house divided cannot stand. But it is the parable that Jesus tells next that sheds the greatest light on how he understood his role: "But no one can enter a strong man's house and plunder his property without first tying up the strong man; then indeed the house can be plundered" (Mk 3:27). What are we to make of such a cryptic lesson? Who is the strong man? Who is the robber who dares to break in, tie up the strong man, and plunder his world? The world that Mark's Jesus enters has been co-opted by Satan, dark forces and rulers. Satan is "the god of this world," working contrary to the will of heaven. So Satan is the strong man; he acts like he owns the house and all its goodies. That makes Jesus the robber. For Mark, it was the miracles of Jesus, particularly his exorcisms, that constituted Jesus' sustained attack on the dominion of darkness. Through his miracles Jesus corrected the horrible results of the evil one's pretentious reign. The Master's miracles were binding the devil, restricting him to the point that Jesus could take back the house that rightly belonged to God. So Mark's Jesus is an apocalyptic Jesus. As the Son of Man, he has come from above bearing the name of the one, true God, directed and empowered by the Spirit, to take on Satan and the world that he rules.

WHAT'S MORE . . .

Jesus at War

Although Mark portrays Jesus at war, often Christians avoid this image. Notice in the famous hymn by Folliott S. Pierpoint (1835–1917) how the world is all rosy and undefiled and all in the universe are friends:

> For the beauty of the earth,
> for the beauty of the skies,
> for the love which from our birth
> over and around us lies:
> Lord of all, to thee we raise
> this our grateful hymn of praise.
> For the beauty of each hour
> of the day and of the night,
> hill and vale, and tree and flower,
> sun and moon, and stars of light:
> Lord of all, to thee we raise
> this our grateful hymn of praise.
> For the joy of human love,
> brother, sister, parent, child,
> friends on earth, and friends above,
> Pleasures pure and undefiled:
> Lord of all, to thee we raise
> this our grateful hymn of praise.

Mark's Jesus seems less likely to sing about love, beauty and flowers. He's at war.

THE MESSIAH REJECTED

As Jesus' baptism is a major point in his life, the episode in Caesarea Philippi is the watershed moment in Mark's story. The readers of the Gospel have known from the beginning that Jesus is the Messiah, the Son of God (Mk 1:1). Likewise, demons and dark forces have recognized Jesus as the Holy One of God and recoiled in terror in his presence (Mk 1:24, 34). The religious leaders who opposed him understood the threat that he posed to their comfortable existence. Now, finally, the disciples have the opportunity to stake their claim. Peter, speaking for the rest, says what they all have come to believe: "You are the Messiah" (Mk 8:29). Immediately, Jesus warns them not to speak of this to anyone else.

More than any other Gospel, Mark underscores the need to keep Jesus' true identity a secret, at least at first. We see this at work in several ways. Jesus appears to have been the only one to see the vision and hear the voice of the Father at his baptism: "You are my Son" (Mk 1:11). Demons recognize him and are told to be silent (Mk 1:24-25; 3:11-12). Those made well by Jesus' miracles are instructed to keep the good news to themselves (Mk 1:44; 5:43; 7:36). Now he warns his disciples to tell no one what they have come to believe about him. Much has been made of what is now called the "messianic secret" in Mark's Gospel. Some consider it Mark's clever cover-up for the fact that Jesus never claimed to be the Messiah. Others regard it as Jesus taking care not to allow hostile forces to compromise his mission and bring it to a premature end. What seems clear is that Jesus wanted to define his messianic destiny for himself as the Suffering Servant (see Is 52:13–53:12). Regardless of Mark's purpose for this "secret," after Caesarea Philippi the secret is out.

Peter's insightful confession that Jesus is the Messiah is left hanging in the air, nearly forgotten by the sting of Jesus' rebuke. As soon as Peter confesses the disciples' belief, Jesus predicts that the Son of Man must suffer, be rejected by their leaders, be crucified and then be raised on the third day. But "the Rock" (the meaning of Peter's nickname) will have none of it, so Peter rebukes Jesus in private. To Jesus, Peter's rebuke sounds like the voice of Satan tempting him to avoid the suffering to come. So Jesus returns the rebuke for the rest of the disciples to hear: "Get behind me, Satan! For you are setting your mind not on divine things but on human things" (Mk 8:33). As their reactions will show in the short time remaining, none of the disciples have a clue that "the way" destined for Jesus will be a way of suffering.

So we see that the disciples in Mark play an ambiguous role. Although they can display great faith and insight, they often fail to understand what Jesus is trying to tell them, especially when it comes to his suffering. They act out of pride and self-interest. They lack faith. They seem ignorant of the basics of discipleship. Other New Testament Gospels sometimes portray the disciples in a somewhat negative light, but Mark takes it to a whole new level. He has no interest in rehabilitating the disciples' image. Judas, one of the Twelve, betrays him. Peter, one of the inner circle, denies him. When Jesus is arrested, the disciples scatter and abandon him. At what may well be the end of Mark's story, the women who find the tomb empty run away in terror. For Mark, the disciples are not worthy of imitation, but Jesus is. He is the ideal disciple. His faithfulness to God stands in contrast to the faithlessness of the disciples. He alone is worthy to be followed and imitated, for he understood that the path to glory must not bypass suffering.

The purpose of that suffering is described in Mark 10:45: "For the Son of Man came not to be served but to serve, and to give his life a ransom for many." This pronouncement echoes the Servant Songs of Isaiah, particularly Isaiah 52:13–53:12. In these poetic lines the Servant of Yahweh (the Lord) is rejected by the people yet suffers for their sins. It is the will of God to crush him and make his life an atoning sacrifice; this is why the Servant pours out his life and bears the sins of "many." In these words Mark's Jesus

WHAT'S MORE . . .

Reading Stories Together

Mark intends many of his stories to be read together, each lending meaning to the other. Some episodes are tied by shared words. Jairus's daughter is twelve years old; the woman with a bleeding disorder had suffered it for twelve years. Jairus falls at Jesus' feet, as does the healed woman. Both women are termed "daughter." Other stories in Mark are tied by their position to each other. In Mark, the story of the cursing of the fig tree is split in half, with the clearing of the temple in between. Mark intends us to use the fig tree to interpret the temple incident. Jesus didn't hate trees. Rather, like the fig tree, the temple was full of life but bearing no fruit. So Jesus curses the fig tree and condemns the activities in the temple.

finds the meaning and focus of his life; suffering and rejection are "the way" set aside for him.

This is not to say that Mark fails to provide positive examples of faith and faithfulness other than Jesus. He does. He finds them in the leper who confidently asks Jesus to make him well (Mk 1:40-45). Mark finds them in the friends of a disabled man who peel back the roof of a house in Capernaum to gain access to Jesus (Mk 2:1-11). Mark utilizes a literary technique known as "framing" to weave together the healing of Jairus's daughter and of a woman suffering from a bleeding disorder. In both cases Mark discovers great faith (Mk 5:21-43).

Jesus finds extraordinary faith not among the religious leaders, but rather among the sick of Gennesaret (Mk 6:53-56), in the Syrophoenician woman (Mk 7:23-30), in blind Bartimaeus (Mk 10:46-52), and in the widow who gave two small coins (Mk 12:41-44). Perhaps the greatest irony, however, lies in the confession voiced by the Roman centurion in charge of Jesus' crucifixion. When Jesus drew his final breath, the officer said, "Truly this man was God's Son!" (Mk 15:39). The confession made by this Roman soldier matches the testimony of God the Father as it echoed from heaven at Jesus' baptism and transfiguration; it accords completely with what the disciples had come to believe—on one of their better days—about who Jesus is. Indeed, the faithful are like the seed growing secretly (Mk 4:26-29); the poor, the blind, the lame, and the sick are the fertile soil where the gospel is taking root and will one day fill the garden (Mk 4:1-20).

How Is This Jesus Different?

Mark's Jesus arrives on the scene as an adult. We know little about him other than he was the son of Mary, a descendant of King David, and a carpenter from Nazareth in Galilee (e.g., Mk 6:1-6). No account of his birth or childhood fills out the portrait or helps to explain what he is about to do. Jesus, it seems, is just a man who arrives at the Jordan curious that a desert prophet is announcing God is up to something new.

In Mark's account Jesus is not a warm, fuzzy fellow; he is a man driven by the Spirit. He moves quickly from place to place, pressed into conflict with spiritual and political powers. Here is a Jesus who acts more and teaches less, for when he does teach, no one seems to get it. Here is a son and brother whose family is concerned for his safety and sanity (Mk 3:19b-21). After John's arrest and death, it is up to him and him alone to make straight the way. As the Messiah and Son of God, his every word and action is calculated to put the present-future kingdom on full display. Mark describes how Jesus becomes angry at those who place religious correctness above people. Mark's Jesus extends mercy and shows compassion to the sick and lost (e.g., Mk 3:1-6). He is a model of righteous indignation.

On the eve of his death this Jesus experiences deep distress and anxiety (Mk 14:33-34). Even though Jesus predicted this day, he recoils from the prospect and prays, "Abba, Father, . . . remove this cup from me" (Mk 14:36). Nevertheless, the day comes, and Jesus is nailed to a Roman cross. For reasons not altogether clear, Mark details the hours of Jesus' suffering: at 9:00 a.m. they hung him on the cross; at 12:00 noon darkness covered the land; at 3:00 p.m. Jesus cried out the words of Psalm 22 and then breathed one last time.

On the Sunday following Jesus' execution something amazing happened. The rock-hewn tomb where they laid the body of Jesus is found empty. Inside, a young man dressed in white proclaims to the women, "He has risen." He tells them the risen one is heading for Galilee, and they will see him there. But unlike the other Gospels, Mark relates no account of Jesus himself appearing to his followers. It ends—rather oddly, according to some—with those same women running from the tomb, gripped with fear and amazement.

Mark's account of Jesus ends as it begins, in dramatic fashion. In this fast-moving, hard-hitting Gospel Mark wants his readers to see the

---

SO WHAT?

Should Christians Fear Death?

We often hear people say that Christians facing death should "have more faith." Popular Greek philosophers in Jesus' day welcomed death as a friend that freed the soul from the prison of the body. Christian faith teaches that death is the last enemy of God (1 Cor 15:26). We should admit that death is real. Even Jesus prayed that God would remove the cup of suffering from him. A desire to avoid suffering and death does not signify a lack of faith.

life of Jesus from his baptism to his resurrection as the beginning of the good news. This strategy invites his audience to see their lives as the next installment of the good news. For Mark, God was on the move in remarkable ways through Jesus, ways only the prophets could have imagined; and God was still on the move when the churches gathered to read Mark's Gospel.

WHAT IF THIS WERE OUR ONLY JESUS?

It's difficult to say what is different about Mark's Jesus, since 90 percent of his Gospel appears in Matthew and Luke. So, let's conduct a thought experiment. If we were to pretend that Mark's Jesus were the only Jesus, what would we believe about him? What would the church look like today? With no account of the virgin birth, no shepherds in the field keeping watch over flocks, and no magi following the star, we would likely not celebrate Christmas at all. Likewise, with only an empty tomb and no resurrection appearances, we would have much less to talk about at Easter.

Given Mark's emphasis upon Jesus as a healer and exorcist, our gatherings would feature fewer sermons and more exorcisms. When we did sermonize on Jesus' teachings, we would have little to say about forgiveness, nothing to say about turning the other cheek, and no one would have ever heard of the "golden rule" (Do to others what you would have others do to you).

SO WHAT?

WWJD:
What Would Jesus Do?

This is the kind of question that Mark's Jesus encourages, rather than "What does Jesus teach?" In fact, you cannot ask "What would Jesus do?" until you know "What did Jesus do?" That is why reading the Gospels is so crucial to our faith. Our churches wouldn't be about coming, sitting and listening to a sermon; they'd be about confronting the moral decay in our neighborhoods. Mark's Jesus wouldn't convene a prayer meeting to discuss the problems of the inner city; he'd be walking the streets and confronting the darkness with light. Does such talk make modern religious leaders squirm and worry how the local authorities will react? What would Mark's Jesus do?

Like Jesus, we would have more interest in the kingdom of God than in going to heaven after we die. We would view our mission in more aggressive terms than most modern Christians find comfortable. We would accommodate less and confront more. We would see ourselves locked in conflict with evil, oppression, death and disease. We may build hospitals in his name, but we would name them "Victory Care" rather than "Good Samaritan Hospital."

Since Mark never uses the word "church," our gatherings may go by a different name. With Jesus' rebuke of Peter still ringing in their ears and Peter's denials of Jesus unaddressed, it is not likely anyone would have thought Peter a good candidate to succeed Jesus. Apostolic succession, in general, probably would be considered a bad idea, given how badly Jesus' followers behaved. Thomas, however, would never have been branded "doubting Thomas."

Without the Sermon on the Mount (Mt 5–7) encouraging us to be peacemakers, Christians might be turning over more tables. We wouldn't shrink from conflict, for our Master never did. In fact, he seemed to relish taking the battle to God's enemies. With so little instruction on prayer in Mark, there would be nothing distinctive about Christian prayer and perhaps little interest in it. Without the mandate to make disciples of the nations and baptize others (Mt 28:16-20), it is not clear whether Christ fol-

---

SO WHAT?
. . . .
Turning Over Tables

Angry Christians often appeal to Jesus' behavior in the temple, citing his "righteous indignation." Indignation is actually pretty easy; it's the righteous part that's the challenge. How often is our anger really righteous? One instance from Jesus' ministry shouldn't justify weekly outbursts from us.

Jesus clearly was a polarizing figure and found himself in conflict with others. Christians may also find themselves in conflict with those around them. But we need to assess whether the conflict arises because we are standing up for what is right or because we are being vindictive, judgmental or condemning. Rather than defend ourselves, perhaps we should recognize there will always be conflict for those who follow Jesus, but there are no heavenly (or earthly, for that matter) rewards for being a jerk. There is a difference.

lowers would have founded universities and seminaries or engaged in modern missions; baptism itself may be something that Jesus did but not that we do.

If Mark's Jesus were our only Jesus, the Dutch master Rembrandt never would have created the famous painting *The Return of the Prodigal Son*, now hanging in the Hermitage Museum in Saint Petersburg, Russia. Nor would Italian Renaissance artists have captured the story of the annunciation and birth of Jesus so memorably on canvas and wood.

Mark provides us with a memorable portrait of Jesus. At one point, early in Christian history, there were communities located in the Mediterranean basin that had only one Gospel, the Gospel of Mark. They read it and recited it when they gathered for worship. They copied it and shared it with others. This Gospel shaped their lives and gave them all they knew about Jesus.

READ MORE ABOUT IT

Burridge, Richard. *What Are the Gospels? A Comparison with Graeco-Roman Biography.* 2nd ed. Grand Rapids: Eerdmans, 2004.

Henderson, Suzanne Watts. "Mark, Gospel according to." In *The Oxford Encyclopedia of the Books of the Bible*, edited by Michael Coogan, pp. 42-56. Oxford: Oxford University Press, 2011.

Lane, William L. *The Gospel According to Mark.* New International Commentary on the New Testament. Grand Rapids, Eerdmans, 1974.

Martin, Ralph P. *Mark: Evangelist and Theologian.* Grand Rapids: Zondervan, 1973.

Perrin, Nicholas. "Mark, Gospel of." In *Dictionary of Jesus and the Gospels*, edited by Joel B. Green, Jeannine K. Brown and Nicholas Perrin, pp. 553-66. 2nd ed. Downers Grove, IL: IVP Academic, 2013.

DISCUSSION QUESTIONS

1. What do the titles "Lord" and "Son of God" mean for Mark? How do these titles relate to the Old Testament?

2. The central message of Jesus has to do with the kingdom of God. What did Jesus' disciples take away from that message? How do his miracles fit the message?

3. Why is Mark's presentation of the disciples primarily negative?

4. For Mark, what does it mean to "follow Jesus"?

5. If Mark were the only Gospel we had, what would we know about Jesus? What would we not know? What difference would it make?

6. What does Mark add to our understanding of Jesus?

2

MATTHEW'S JESUS

By Roman standards, Matthew's Jesus was a loser. Anyone who claims, "The meek will inherit the earth," is a fool. Watch and see, they'd say, it's the rich, the powerful, the ruthless who will inherit the earth. Rome's expansion had proved that well enough. And more than that: anyone crazy enough to claim to be a king as long as Rome is in charge will inherit the lash and the rough wood of a cross. Strike the shepherd, and the sheep will be scattered—or so they say.

Matthew's Jewish audience experienced life under Roman rule. Imagine standing by powerlessly as a troop of Roman soldiers escorted a tax collector from your farm with too much of your harvest in tow. You and your family will go hungry this winter while Roman soldiers eat their fill of your grain. Jesus said what? Go the second mile? Love and pray for your enemies? You must be kidding.

SO WHAT?

The Meek Will Inherit the Earth?

Appearances deceive. When Jesus said, "The meek will inherit the earth," the Galilean countryside was dotted with silos full of grain, while Jesus' hearers were hungry. Roman soldiers stomped freely about the land. We now know that the Romans didn't inherit the earth, but in Jesus' time his hearers imagined it impossible for the meek to do so. We cannot trust our eyes when it comes to the kingdom of God. It's like yeast working in flour.

Jesus was a scandalous character, scandalous by both Roman and Jewish standards for different reasons. That is why, they argued, he must be opposed, dishonored and stopped. What Jesus says and does, however, reverse the bogus world that they have inherited from their ancestors and sets it on a new course. Matthew understood how and why so many had stumbled because of Jesus. He was determined to set the record straight for those with ears to hear.

Who Does Matthew Say That I Am?

Matthew begins his Gospel with a bold claim: Jesus is the Messiah, the son of Abraham, the son of David (Mt 1:1). Each of these titles addresses something unique and important about Jesus. Each reinforces and redefines the other. Each ties into a broader story of covenant and redemption that had begun centuries earlier. Matthew's Jesus provides God's answer to any and all unresolved promises. In truth, the title "Messiah" (or its Greek equivalent, "Christ") meant a lot of things to a lot of people; there were even those for whom the title meant next to nothing. The word in Hebrew means "anointed," and for many, "Messiah/Christ" carried strong political associations (e.g., *Pss. Sol.* 17–18). But Matthew uses it unapologetically and then lets the story that he tells unpack its meaning. For Matthew, "Messiah" refers to God's chosen (anointed) agent whose task is to liberate the world from disease, death, sin and oppression in all forms, Roman and religious included. "Son of David" is a specialized messianic title that reminds any competent Jewish reader or hearer of God's millennium-old covenant with David (2 Sam 7:12-16). "Son of Abraham" likewise takes the hearer/reader back to God's promises to make Abraham a great nation and bring blessing to all the nations through him (Gen 12:1-3). For Matthew, Jesus is no run-of-the-mill son of Abraham. He is *the* son of Abraham, whose mission extends God's blessings to the nations. Jesus embodies the ideal Israel, the true Jew, the one chosen by God to fulfill his promises.

Jesus' Family Tree

Matthew follows up his opening line with a carefully constructed genealogy that begins with Abraham and ends with Jesus. For many modern Westerners, genealogies are boring, but for many others, especially those in Jesus' time and place, this genealogy connects Jesus to reality. His isn't a "once upon a time" story. So, before your eyes glaze over, remember that Matthew's audience would not have heard this as a list of meaningless names; they would have known these people as their physical and spiritual ancestors. To them, it would be like opening up the family photo album.

Matthew capitalizes on certain names and episodes from the past. At a time when genealogies typically did not include women—despite their obvious significance to begetting children—Matthew includes the names of five women to signal a new role for women in the kingdom of heaven. Matthew's genealogy also refers intentionally to moments when scandal rocked the people of God—for example, when Tamar poses as a harlot and is impregnated by her father-in-law, and when David fathers Solomon through the wife of another man. Matthew could have avoided these shameful moments; instead, he highlights them to show that Jesus' family had a checkered past too. If Jesus' line includes such reckless behavior and flawed people, then there is hope for all of us. Finally, Matthew's genealogy also includes the names of outsiders (e.g., Rahab and Ruth) who become part of Abraham's family. If the blood of the nations already is running in Jesus' kin, then surely the blood of the new covenant must extend to the nations. After seeing how Matthew presents the family tree of Abraham and David, the

WHAT'S MORE . . .

God's Covenant with David

Nearly one thousand years before Jesus was born, God made a series of promises to King David through the court prophet Nathan (2 Sam 7:12-16). It is often referred to as the "Davidic covenant":

- I will continue your dynasty through your (David's) son.
- Your son will build the temple (a house for my name).
- I will establish a father-son relationship with your son.
- I will see to it that your throne lasts forever.

These promises to David become the basis of God's covenant with the king and his royal line. The messianic hope is based on this covenant.

reader is ready to hear the story of Joseph, Mary and Jesus, which in hindsight does not seem so strange.

Emmanuel. The scandal begins with Jesus' virgin birth: "'Look, the virgin shall conceive and bear a son, and they call name him Emmanuel,' which means, 'God is with us'" (Mt 1:23 [fulfilling Is 7:14]). Matthew frames his entire Gospel around the Emmanuel theme. He uses the prophecy of Isaiah to introduce the idea. Emmanuel, the God-with-us One, enters our world in a most unusual fashion. He leaves behind a small group of followers with a most unusual promise: "I am with you always" (Mt 28:20). The Emmanuel motif is unique to Matthew and provides a coherent narrative shape to the Gospel. Everything in the Gospel can be read against these two defining moments: Jesus enters as the God-with-us One and leaves with the promise to be with us always. Historic Christianity has had no problem affirming the God-ness of Jesus, and most Christians today confess it as central to their faith. But Matthew's Jesus faced real opposition when he began to speak and act in ways to suggest he is God-with-us.

Before you think that Matthew is all about names and titles, read a bit more carefully. Matthew's Jesus cannot be contained in titles or concepts regardless of their rich pedigree or expression; the Messiah's true identity can be worked out only through the story itself. It is what he says and does that reveal the rich truth of his nature. Matthew's Jesus is from above. His Jesus is an occurrence of God.

This is expressed in various ways in the story. Again, in the words of Isaiah (Is 40:3) Jesus is "the Lord," whose way is prepared by John (Mt 3:3). The word "Lord" translates the divine name ("Yahweh") and associates Jesus closely with the unspeakable name of the one, true God. Jesus speaks as if his teachings are as authoritative as Scripture (e.g., "You have heard that it was said [in the Scriptures] . . . But I say to you . . ." [Mt 5:21-22]).

Jesus acts in ways that seem right only for God. He forgives sins (Mt 9:2-8) and declares that he will sit in judgment of the nations on the last day (Mt 25:31-46). Jesus speaks of himself as having an intimate relationship with God (Mt 11:27) and promises to be with even two or three disciples who gather in his name (Mt 18:20), a pledge that makes sense only if Jesus is no ordinary fellow. From time to time people come to Jesus in a posture of worship and are not rebuffed (Mt 2:1; 20:20; 28:9, 17). Indeed, Matthew presents Jesus as a teacher of wisdom with unusual authority perhaps even as the very embodiment of God's wisdom (Mt 11:19, 27-30; 12:42). Taken together, these words and deeds flesh out what it means to call Jesus "God-with-us."

WHAT'S MORE . . .

Having Ears to Hear and Eyes to Read

To those who could read, such as scribes, Jesus said, "Have you never read . . . ?" (Mt 21:16). To the crowds, who couldn't read, Jesus said, "You have heard . . ." (Mt 5:21). Regardless of how Jesus' audience encountered Scripture, he announced, without condescension, the good news of the kingdom to all who were willing to listen.

"For just such a time as this" (with apologies to Esther). For Matthew, the scandalous claim that the virgin-born Jesus is none other than God-with-us "fulfills" the earlier Scriptures. At the most basic level this means that Jesus doesn't do or say anything to contradict what the law, prophets and writings have set in motion, despite what his critics claim (e.g., Mt 5:17). Positively, it means that all the promises and hopes in the Hebrew Scriptures converge at one point, in the man of history, Jesus of Nazareth. Sometimes this promise-fulfillment scheme is highlighted in a formulaic way—for example, "All this took place to fulfill what had been spoken by the Lord through the prophet" (Mt 1:22)—at other times it lies subtly beneath the surface, ready to be uncovered by the competent reader.

Matthew uses "fulfillment" in ways broader than modern readers might think. In some cases "fulfillment" refers to a prediction that has come true. Jesus' birth in Bethlehem, for example, fulfills what Micah said centuries earlier about the origin of a ruler and shepherd of Israel (Mt 2:6, quoting Mic 5:2). In other cases "fulfillment" appears to be Matthew's way of demonstrating that Jesus is listening to and directed by Scripture. After John is arrested, Jesus returns to Galilee and settles in Capernaum, fulfilling the words of Isaiah (Mt 4:15, quoting Is 9:1-2). Is Jesus' return to Galilee a happy coincidence, or is he taking direction from Scripture? Jesus' Scripture-shaped ministry has a particular logic. The northern territories were the first to fall to Assyrian cruelty (in Isaiah's day); they will be the first to experience the light of renewal (in Jesus' day).

WHAT'S MORE . . .

Mountaintop Experiences

Have you noticed how many key events in Matthew's Gospel take place on a mountain?

- The third temptation of Jesus occurs on a mountain (Mt 4:1-11 [cf. Lk 4:1-13]).

- Jesus preaches the Sermon on the Mount (Mt 5–7 [cf. Lk 6:17-49]).

- After encountering the Canaanite woman, Jesus ascends a mountain for a time of teaching and healing (Mt 15:29-31).

- Jesus is transfigured on a mountain (Mt 17:1-8).

- Jesus gives the Great Commission on a mountain in Galilee (Mt 28:16-20).

So why does Matthew emphasize the mountain? Mountains are common enough in Galilee, but there appears to be a theological point in Matthew's telling. Mountains are extraordinary places. There is a feeling of awe and transcendence when you ascend a mountain and take in the vistas. Temples and altars are built on mountains precisely because they share in a feeling of sacredness; they represent the nexus of heaven and earth. The evangelist knows this and leverages it in his account of Jesus' life. If Jesus is Emmanuel, it makes perfect sense that Matthew would want to make note of all the times when the God-with-us One ascended the mountain to bring heaven to earth.

Still, the word "fulfill" is not always necessary to make the point. From prison John sends his disciples to ask Jesus, "Are you the one who is to come, or are we to wait for another?" Jesus responds, "Go and tell John what you hear and see: the blind receive their sight, the lame walk, the lepers are cleansed, the deaf hear, the dead are raised, and the poor have good news brought to them" (Mt 11:3-5). Without pointing out the obvious, Matthew sees the prophecies of Isaiah (Is 29:18-19; 35:5-6; 42:18; 61:1) as fulfilled in the miracles and preaching of Jesus.

Much of Matthew's "fulfillment" involves typologies. Typology is a strategy for pointing out the correspondence between two (or more) of God's acts. The earlier act is described as the type (from the Greek *typos*, meaning "model") of the latter (antitype). When Matthew uses typology, he points out the ways in which the antitype (the second) is like the type (the first). When the antitype transcends or escalates the type, we say that the latter "fulfills" the other. This appears to account for Jesus' statements in Matthew 12: (1) "something greater than the temple is here" (Mt 12:6); (2) "something greater than Jonah is here" (Mt 12:41); and (3) "something greater than Solomon is here" (Mt 12:42). It also explains why Matthew says that the flight of Joseph and his young family to Egypt fulfills the words of Hosea: "Out of Egypt I have called my son" (Mt 2:15, quoting Hos 11:1). Hosea is looking back to how God rescued Israel, "my son," from Egyptian slavery. The exodus from Egypt was a saving event like no other. Hosea wasn't predicting a second exodus. Jesus' return from Egypt is a typological fulfillment rather than a prophetic fulfillment. Jesus' return is an antitype of how God saved his people from bondage. Young Jesus and his parents will retrace the steps of Israel from bondage to promise, and as an adult Jesus will go on to ratchet-up God's salvation through the cross for all nations.

Matthew works out themes of new exodus and new Israel throughout his Gospel. He often relates them with other, associated themes (e.g., new Moses) to complement and subvert the earlier stories found in the Scripture:

- Like Moses, Jesus is imperiled by the decree of a king.
- Like Moses, Jesus and his family return from Egypt.
- Like Moses, Jesus ascends a mountain to bring God's teaching.

But Matthew often turns the earlier narratives on their head:

- Unlike Israel, Jesus lives in a manner well pleasing to God.
- Unlike Israel, Jesus refuses to put God to the test and bow down to non-gods.
- Unlike Israel, Jesus (and his family) finds Egypt a land of refuge.

The evangelist adds to scriptural images like these various other associations as part of his fulfillment strategy:

- Jesus grows up in Nazareth (Mt 2:23), fulfilling Isaiah 11:1 (?).
- Jesus directs his ministry to Galilee (Mt 4:12-16), fulfilling Isaiah 9:1-2.
- Jesus heals the sick (Mt 8:17), fulfilling Isaiah 53:4.
- Jesus performs signs (Mt 11:2-6), fulfilling Isaiah 35:5-6; 61:1.
- Jesus exercises the role of the Servant (Mt 12:15-21), fulfilling Isaiah 42:1-4.
- Jesus speaks in parables (Mt 13:14-15), fulfilling Isaiah 6:9-10.
- Jesus enters Jerusalem on a donkey (Mt 21:4-5), fulfilling Zechariah 9:9.
- Jesus is betrayed for thirty pieces of silver (Mt 27:9-10), fulfilling Zechariah 11:12-13.

So it is clear that Matthew intends for his audience to be well versed in all the ways Jesus speaks and acts to fulfill the Scriptures, both prophetically and typologically. The better you know the Old Testament—the Bible of Jesus and Matthew—the better you will be able to understand Matthew's Jesus and his significance.

Ironically, many of Jesus' opponents claim that he was set on abolishing God's law and raising up disciples to do the same (Mt 5:17-20). They accuse him of violating the Sabbath, failing to fast appropriately, and generally neglecting the tried-and-true traditions that marked off the Jews as God's covenant people. Matthew's Jesus refuses to back down and denies these charges vehemently, giving us the most law-centered Gospel in the New Testament. Jesus comes dotting every "i" crossing every "t" of the law and requires his followers to take the path of greater righteousness based on the law. Whereas the disciples of the scribes must not murder, Jesus' disciples must not even harbor anger (Mt 5:21-22). Whereas the disciples of the Pharisees must not commit adultery, Jesus' disciples must not even entertain lust or seek easy divorces (Mt 5:27-28, 31-32). Whereas the disciples of the scribes give alms with great fanfare, Jesus' disciples are told not to let the left hand know what the right is doing (Mt 6:1-4). Essentially, Jesus does not abrogate the law; he asks his followers to internalize it. Jesus focuses more on heart than action, more on motive than deed. If the heart is true, so too will the action be. This pits him against other Jewish teachers on matters such as marriage and divorce, fasting, and keeping kosher. Paradoxically, this means that Jesus will welcome sinners while being very tough on those Jews closest to him theologically. This is why so many woes are pronounced against Pharisees and why "hypocrite" seems to be their middle name (Mt 23:13-36).

WHAT'S MORE . . .

"Rabbi Jesus"?

As a teacher, Jesus is familiar with different styles of rabbinic exegesis and argumentation. He makes ample use of a technique known as *qal wahomer*, which involves arguing from a minor premise to a major one ("how much more . . ."). So, for example, in the Sermon on the Mount Jesus urges his followers not to worry about the necessities of life (Mt 6:25-27), for if the heavenly Father feeds the birds of air, will he not also feed them? (If God cares for birds, "how much more" will he care for us?) Utilizing a different technique known as *binyan av*, Jesus links two foundational scriptural texts to answer a question implied by another. So when Jesus is asked whether a husband can divorce his wife for any cause (based on Deut 24:1-4), he links two prior, foundational texts in Genesis (Gen 1:26-27; 2:24) to show that all the way back in Genesis God was establishing the ideal of marriage for man and woman. Moses may have allowed divorce, but Genesis teaches that it was never the ideal.

As was hinted above, Jesus comes as a prophet like Moses (see Deut 18:18), inscribing his unique version of the law on the hearts of his disciples. He speaks with unusual authority, interpreting and reinterpreting the law in light of "your kingdom come." If Moses' law intended to curb cruelty, Jesus hoped to do away with it altogether (Mt 5:38-42). If the silence of Moses' law could be exploited to teach "hate your enemy," then Jesus plugged the silence with his own version: "Love your enemies and pray for those who persecute you" (Mt 5:43-44). From the outside this may have seemed like an insignificant Jewish squabble; from the inside it felt like a battle for the heart and soul of Israel—which it was.

Jesus, Son of God. Matthew employs the title "Son of God" for Jesus at key moments in his story. The title originated in the scriptural tradition: (1) angels are called "sons of God" (e.g., Job 1:6; Ps 29:1); (2) Israel is called "my firstborn son" by God (Ex 4:22; cf. Hos 11:1); and (3) a Davidic king may be called properly a "son of God" (2 Sam 7:14-16; Ps 2:7; 4QFlor 1 I, 10-11). With Matthew's obvious interest in Jesus as the true Israel and the Son of David, the latter two seem to be the most important for Matthew's portrait. But Matthew doesn't simply refer to Jesus as God's Son or have Jesus use it as a self-reference; he weaves the title throughout his account. It is spoken by a variety of "witnesses" in a variety of contexts. Each time something new is disclosed, and the portrait advances.

Upon being baptized by John, Jesus sees a vision of the heavens open and the Spirit of God descending on him as a heavenly voice addresses the crowd: "This is my Son, the Beloved, with whom I am well pleased" (Mt 3:17). The voice echoes the language of Scripture, linking royal psalms with prophetic verse (Ps 2:7; Is 42:1). Soon after this life-transforming event, the Spirit leads Jesus into the wilderness to be tempted for forty days and nights. The devil tempts Jesus by saying, "If you are the Son of God" (Mt 4:3, 6). At the high point of Jesus' ministry Peter makes a bold confession at Caesarea Philippi. When Jesus queries his disciples with the question "Who do you say that I am?" Peter responds, "You are the Messiah, the Son of the Living God" (Mt 16:16). On the mountain of transfiguration the heavenly voice returns to the story, echoing and expanding the words addressed at Jesus' baptism: "This is my Son, the

---

SO WHAT?

....

"I Will Build My Church"
(Mt 16:18)

The Messiah was to build a temple for the Lord. But Jesus envisioned a temple built not of stones and mortar, built not upon an actual rock as was Solomon's temple, but one built of people. The new temple would not be made with human hands. With Jesus as the cornerstone, believers are to come to him and make up this new temple "as living stones" (1 Pet 2:5). When we say, "That's my church," we need to be pointing at people and not at a building.

Beloved; with him I am well pleased; listen to him!" (Mt 17:5).

At Jesus' trial before the Sanhedrin the high priest presses him: "I put you under oath before the living God, tell us if you are the Messiah, the Son of God" (Mt 26:63). Jesus answers, "You have said so. But I tell you, from now on you will see the Son of Man seated at the right hand of Power and coming on the clouds of heaven" (Mt 26:64). The answer infuriates the high priest, who tears his clothes and charges Jesus with blasphemy. In other words, Jesus hands the high priest the charge that he is looking for. But what does Jesus say that is blasphemous? That he is the Messiah? No. It is not blasphemous to claim to be the Messiah. It is what Jesus said next that condemns him: the Son of Man—understood as a self-reference—will (soon) be seated at the right hand of Power and coming on the clouds of heaven. While "son of man" can mean simply a "human being" (as Ezekiel uses it), Jesus' assertion here clarifies what he meant by the title. He is the Son of Man, of whom Daniel spoke. Jesus' words allude to Psalm 110:1 and Daniel 7:13-14. Matthew's Jesus links the Messiah with heaven's power. The messianic Son of God will be vindicated and enthroned at God's right hand. The Sanhedrin may stand in judgment of him this day, but a day is coming soon when he will join God on his throne to judge them. The juxtaposition of the titles "Messiah," "Son of God" and "Son of Man seated at the right hand of Power" provides Matthew with a satisfying and accurate way of addressing Jesus' real significance.

The moment Jesus dies on the cross the Roman centurion who superintends his execution utters in fear, "Truly this man was God's Son!" (Mt 27:54). Finally, after his resurrection, Jesus appears to the eleven remaining disciples on a mountain in Galilee. Some disciples believe and worship Jesus; others doubt. In his parting words (in Matthew) Jesus claims that God has given him all authority and urges, "Go therefore and make disciples of all nations, baptizing them in the name of the Father and of the Son and of the Holy Spirit, and teaching them to obey everything I have commanded you. And remember, I am with you always, to the end of the age" (Mt 28:19-20).

In the end, Matthew's Jesus uses the title "Son of God" in two distinct but related ways (cf. Rom 1:3-4). On the one hand, the title indicates that Jesus is the Messiah or Christ by linking him with the Davidic covenant (Mt 8:29; 16:16; 26:63; 27:40; 27:54; cf. 2 Sam 7:12-16). In this way, like the titles

"Christ" and "Son of David," it emphasizes Jesus' full and complete humanity. But Matthew's Jesus also uses the title "Son of God" to express a transcendent aspect and quality to Jesus' sonship, a filial relationship with God expressed in Jesus' own words: "All things have been handed over to me by my Father; and no one knows the Son except the Father, and no one knows the Father except the Son and anyone to whom the Son chooses to reveal him" (Mt 11:27).

How Is This Jesus Different?

If Mark's Jesus is a healer and exorcist, Matthew's Jesus is the consummate teacher, a prophet like Moses who is superior to Moses in every way. Indeed, in Matthew's Gospel we don't have to speculate on what Jesus means like we do in Mark. Mark often forces us to infer Jesus' intentions by his actions. Matthew's Jesus tells us plainly what's on his mind: "You have heard it said. . . . But I say to you. . . ." And this "teaching Jesus" also happens to be the most Jewish Jesus we find in the New Testament. He insists that his followers keep the law as he lives and interprets it, and he flatly denies any charge that he secretly wants to do away with it. Likewise, the mission of Jesus seems directed primarily to the Jews. When Jesus sends his disciples to preach and heal, he sends them only to the lost sheep of the house of Israel (Mt 10:5-6).

Matthew's Jesus provides us with some of the most memorable teaching in the New Testament: the Beatitudes, the Lord's Prayer, unique parables, exhortations to love one's enemies and pray for those who persecute you. Pacifists tend to quote Matthew's Jesus more than any other because of his strong advocacy for nonviolence. In truth, the Sermon on the Mount sets the agenda for everything that Jesus comes to say and do. The kingdom vision that Jesus relates in the Sermon on the Mount is worked out primarily in a number of parables that Jesus tells. These stories are taken from events common to rural folk living in Galilee.

Finally, Matthew's Jesus is the Jesus of the Great Commission. Nothing quite like it exists in the other Gospels. The crucified, now risen Jesus meets the eleven remaining disciples on a mountain high over Galilee and announces that God has given him all authority in heaven and earth. He instructs the remnant to go and make disciples of all nations—not just the lost tribes of Israel—baptizing them in the name of the Father, the Son and the

---

WHAT'S MORE . . .

Is Matthew Anti-Semitic?

Jesus died on a Roman cross, under a Roman charge, condemned by a Roman governor, Pontius Pilate. Pilate had tried to distance himself from the verdict and washed his hands of the matter, but he was responsible for what took place. Perhaps, he was an unwitting tool of God, no different than the Assyrians and the Babylonians. Still, historical records inside and outside the Bible indicate that Jesus was executed by the Romans.

Unfortunately, Matthew's Gospel has been used by some to justify the mistreatment of Jews. These (mis)interpreters have routinely cited Matthew 27:25 as their warrant: "His blood be on us and on our children!" Anti-Semites have taken this as a blanket statement condemning all Jews. But who exactly is speaking? Who is taking the blame for what happened to Jesus? Well, in a word, Jerusalem. Jerusalem is to blame: not the stone and mortar architecture of the city, but rather the people in power. They were controlling the agenda and manipulating the crowds. It was the same bunch who corrupted the temple and turned God's house into a den of robbers. So when they say, "His blood be on us and on our children," they are calling down judgment on Jerusalem. In prophetic word and action Jesus himself had expressed the same message when he pronounced woe upon the city, cleared the temple, cursed the fig tree, and predicted the temple's demise. When the holy city was sacked and the temple destroyed in A.D. 70, the children and grandchildren of those who urged Pilate to crucify Jesus had to run for their lives. Then, from a distance, they could only watch as the distant rumble and smoke-filled skies announced the end of their beloved city.

Holy Spirit and passing on the teachings that he had taught to them during his time with him. He ends the charge with a promise based on the prophetic name bestowed on him as a result of his miraculous birth, "Emmanuel": "And remember, I am with you always, to the end of the age" (Mt 28:20).

WHAT IF THIS WERE OUR ONLY JESUS?

If Matthew's Jesus were the only Jesus, his followers would be far better students of the Old Testament than we are today, for Jesus plainly says that not one single bit of the law will be set aside. So we'd study it in depth and urge our leaders to do the same. We may call them "rabbi" rather than "pastor" and privilege teaching over other spiritual gifts. As we read through the law, prophets and writings, we would take note of all the ways Jesus fulfilled one aspect of it or another. Perhaps we'd out-Matthew Matthew in pointing out all the ways Jesus' life, words, death and resurrection fulfill God's earlier promises. We'd become experts in typologies and gematria (numerology). So "new covenant" would not necessarily mean a new canon. If the Old Testament was good enough for Jesus and Matthew, it probably would be good enough for us.

This means that we'd see Jesus as a rabbi, a teacher-expert in the law capable of rendering judgments of how the law is to be applied in this and that situation. As a result, his disciples would be living a Torah-observant brand of Christianity rather than a law-free gospel. All of us would be worshiping on Saturday rather than Sunday in order to keep the fourth commandment. We would be keeping the law Jesus' way. Christians would circumcise their sons on the eighth day for religious, not medical, reasons, as a sign of the covenant. Perhaps it is even possible that we would have sided with the Judaizers against Paul during the Gentile mission. But those who dig deeper realize that for Jesus, the law is truly a matter of the heart and not just about keeping rules.

When we realize the depth of sin in Jesus' family tree, we'd likely go easier on the lost sheep in our own families and the sins of others. In fact, we'd feel more comfortable in the presence of honest sinners than self-righteous saints. Perhaps our churches would be more welcoming to (even) notorious sinners and more leery of overtly professional, religious types. Our leaders would look more like fishermen and less like scribes. In fact, with Matthew's story setting the agenda, Peter, not Paul, would be our favorite apostle. Christians would no doubt consider Peter the first leader of the church, founded by Jesus himself. And, even though Gentile members would eventually overtake the church, we would never forget our Jewish roots. Indeed, we wouldn't even think of Christianity as a separate religion. Rather, as disciples continued to make disciples to the ends of the earth, faith in the Jewish Messiah, Jesus, would be seen as the fulfillment of all the promises God made to Abraham.

We would point to this "sect" within Judaism as proof that, indeed, Abraham had become the father of a multitude of nations.

Read More About It

Brown, Jeannine K. "Matthew, Gospel of." In *Dictionary of Jesus and the Gospels*, edited by Joel B. Green, Jeannine K. Brown and Nicholas Perrin, pp. 570-84. 2nd ed. Downers Grove, IL: IVP Academic, 2013.

France, R. T. *Matthew: Evangelist and Teacher*. Downers Grove, IL: InterVarsity Press, 1989.

Kingsbury, Jack D. *Matthew: Structure, Christology, Kingdom*. 2nd ed. Philadelphia: Fortress, 1989.

Strauss, Mark L. *Four Portraits, One Jesus: An Introduction to Jesus and the Gospels*. Grand Rapids: Zondervan, 2007.

Yang, Seung Ai. "Sermon on the Mount/Plain." In *Dictionary of Jesus and the Gospels*, edited by Joel B. Green, Jeannine K. Brown and Nicholas Perrin, pp. 845-55. 2nd ed. Downers Grove, IL: IVP Academic, 2013.

Discussion Questions

1. Matthew frames his entire story of Jesus around the Emmanuel (God-with-us) theme. Choose any story from Matthew, read it, and consider how Jesus' words and actions reveal the truth about the God-with-us One. Start with these: (a) Jesus' baptism by John (Mt 3:1-6, 13-17); (b) the "I say to you" passages (Mt 5:17-48); (c) the mission of the Twelve (Mt 10:1-42); (d) the Sabbath healings (Mt 12:1-14).

2. Why do many people consider Matthew's account of Jesus' life the most Jewish in the New Testament?

3. How does the Great Commission (Mt 28:18-20) pull together the great themes of Matthew's Gospel?

4. If Matthew were the only Gospel we had, what would we know about Jesus? What would we not know? What difference would it make?

3

LUKE'S JESUS

We all love to root for the underdog; it seems to be our national instinct. Rebels who take on "the man" are nearly always celebrated as heroes. Authority figures, on the other hand, become easy targets of our derision. Nobody wants to be "that guy," Mr. Responsibility, warning thrill seekers with paternal advice, "Remember: actions have consequences!" No. In our world, prodigals are held up as cultural icons. "Breaking the rules" is often considered a good thing to do. The rebel life is not only our birthright; we act like it's a blessing—which is why we miss the point of Jesus' parable about the prodigal son. Believe it or not, the rebel isn't the hero of the story.

The picture made the front page of newspapers around the world—a real-life parable of the prodigal son. There stood Pope John Paul II, the holy father of the Roman Catholic Church, and the rebel "son," a Nicaraguan priest and local hero, bowing at his feet. But this time, things were a little different. Rather than wait for the return of the prodigal, the "father" tracked down the rebel son, visiting the far-away country. This time there was no famine. This time the prodigal was unrepentant. This time the father wagged his finger at the son, scolding the prodigal for his rebel ways. The "prodigal son" of the Catholic Church was Ernesto Cardenal, a Jesuit who had accepted a position as minister of culture in the new government of Nicaragua established by the Sandinistas—a revolution supported by several Catholic priests who subscribed to "liberation theology." The recently elected pontiff decided to visit the region in 1983, in part as goodwill ambassador but also to see firsthand the results of this new theology that seemed to take root in Central America—a theological child born of the marriage of Marxist philosophy and a provocative reading of the Gospel of Luke. So, in this modern version of the famous parable who is the hero of the story? The pontificating father or the subversive son? Well, that depends upon how we understand Luke's portrayal of Jesus.

WHO DOES LUKE SAY THAT I AM?

Was Jesus a revolutionary? He was a poor man who brought the riches of God's reign to those who needed it the most. Was Jesus a liberator? He was a powerful man who conquered the devil by releasing those who were enslaved to evil powers. Was Jesus a hero? He was God's Son who was supposed to make good on every promise that his Father ever made to Israel and the world. In Luke's narrative world Jesus is called many things by all kinds. Angels call him "Savior" and "Son of the Most

SO WHAT?

What Do You Do with a Stubborn and Rebellious Son?

The law of Moses was clear: "If someone has a stubborn and rebellious son who will not obey his father and mother, who does not heed them when they discipline him, then his father and his mother shall take hold of him and bring him out to the elders of his town at the gate of that place. They shall say to the elders of his town, 'This son of ours is stubborn and rebellious. He will not obey us. He is a glutton and a drunkard.' Then all the men of the town shall stone him to death" (Deut 21:18-21).

This seems a bit harsh. How many of our sons would reach adulthood? The rabbis also felt this tension. They offered a way out. A son could not be condemned as stubborn and rebellious if his parents had certain physical impairments, for the Scripture says that they "shall take hold of him and bring him out" (so they cannot be maimed in the hand or lame) and "shall say . . . , 'This son of ours . . . will not obey us'" (so they cannot be mute, blind or deaf) (*m. Sanh.* 8.4). The rabbis sought to defang this stern commandment.

Jesus offered a different way to handle the stubborn and rebellious son: forgiveness. In Jesus' parable the prodigal (wasteful) son isn't stoned by the town elders but instead is received by his father. In fact, Jesus describes a father who is more "prodigal" than the son, lavishing (wasting?) forgiveness. The orderly world is turned upside down.

High." Demons growl that Jesus is "the Holy One of God." Prophets declare
that he is "a light for revelation to the Gentiles" and one who "will baptize
you with the Holy Spirit and fire." Bystanders blurt out, "A great prophet has
arisen among us." Peter confesses that Jesus is "the Messiah of God." A voice
from heaven boasts, "You are my Son, the Beloved." The placard on the cross
announces, "This is the King of the Jews." All sorts of opinions were flying
around. Even though other Gospel writers had tried (probably a reference
to Matthew and Mark), Luke claims that he will be the one to sort out everything that happened so that a man named "Theophilus" would know for
certain "the truth" about Jesus (Lk 1:1-4).

Mark started with John the Baptizer, Matthew with the birth of Jesus.
Luke begins his story earlier—before Jesus was born—in order to set the
stage for the arrival of "the Lord." In certain ways, it's a familiar beginning
to the old story of Israel: an elderly, righteous, barren couple waits faithfully
for God's promise to come true. A son will be born, and the hope of the
covenant will rest upon his shoulders. And yet, it's quite apparent that God
is doing something new. Sure enough, a son is born to a couple past child-
bearing years. John is special, a prophet of God baptized by the Spirit while
in his mother's womb. But, this is where the old story is eclipsed by the new.
Another son of promise will be born, to a virgin not an old woman. Another
story will be told, about a child who is more than a prophet. This child is the
very progeny of God. This son will inherit David's throne. This king will rule
in unexpected ways. The way Luke tells it, old things are passing away, and
everything is becoming new because the long-awaited Day of the Lord has
finally come.

Job description for a Messiah. At first, everyone seems to believe that it's
time. The events surrounding the birth of John and Jesus are undeniably
divine, just as Joel predicted: men and women prophesy, old men see dreams
come true, young shepherds see visions of angels (Joel 2:28). There is wonder
and amazement everywhere (Lk 1:5–2:52). The people of Israel are getting
the sense that something is about to happen, so that John's hardnosed
"repentance-is-more-than-words" message attracts rather than repels the
masses (Lk 3:1-18). Even ruthless tax collectors and hardened soldiers are
compelled to join the movement: "What should we do?" (Lk 3:10, 12, 14).
Therefore, after Jesus is baptized by the prophet and anointed by God's Spirit,

it comes as no surprise when the heavenly voice declares, "I am well pleased" (Lk 3:22). Up to this point, it seems as though God himself has orchestrated every event for the day of his visitation. Both the well-placed genealogy and predictable temptation narrative round out the momentum of the story so far: this son of Adam is the Son of God come to reverse the curse of sin and death because he is Israel's Messiah (Lk 3:23–4:13).

Despite such a fantastic beginning, after Jesus returns home to tell his good news, the story takes an ominous turn. Everyone can make claims about Jesus—angels, prophets, priests, parents—but as soon as Jesus owns his identity, there's trouble. Ironically, the problem was timing. Jesus acted as though Isaiah's vision of messianic blessing—good news for the poor, prisoners released, the blind seeing, the broken-hearted comforted (Is 61:1-4)—had already come true: "Today this scripture has been fulfilled in your hearing" (Lk 4:21). That caused quite a commotion. Who couldn't see this coming? Jesus certainly did: "Doubtless you will quote to me this proverb, 'Doctor, cure yourself!'" (Lk 4:23). Jesus was still a poor man; his fortunes hadn't changed one bit. The hometown crowd knew that better than anyone. Besides, how could Jesus claim that Isaiah's vision had come true when their fortunes hadn't changed either? Blind men were still begging in Nazareth, Roman taxes were still levied against God's people, and the poor were still

> ## SO WHAT?
> ·················
> *God's Kingdom Doesn't Have Me at the Center*
>
> The folks at Nazareth doubted Jesus' announcement that the kingdom was coming, because they weren't seeing it around them. Likewise, the Baptizer had doubts for the same reason. He wasn't seeing God's justice breaking into his situation. God doesn't always act according to my expectations. I cannot assess the kingdom's progress by measuring my personal comfort level or how my personal trials are resolving, any more than the people of Nazareth could.

serving time in the debtor's prison. If the year of the Lord's favor had already come, the people of Nazareth had missed out. Jesus seemed to rub salt into the wound by predicting that Gentiles would benefit from the kingdom more than his own people (Lk 4:25-27). It's no wonder the crowd kicked Jesus out of town and threatened to kill him—a sign of things to come.

This episode is crucial to Luke's Gospel; it reveals how Jesus saw himself. He's the Messiah of God who embodies the kingdom of God's blessing, "The Spirit of the Lord is upon me, because he has anointed [the Messiah] me" (Lk 4:18). Jesus saw himself as God's gift of the poor for the poor. The confrontation at Nazareth also reveals Jesus' messianic agenda: he will establish the reign of God on earth for those who need it the most. In fact, the way Luke has set up the story to this point, Jesus identifies with the meek, the poor and the disenfranchised because he was one of them. Rich with God's Spirit, Jesus embodies the Year of Jubilee, empowered to cancel debts, release prisoners, and share the wealth of God's kingdom. Of course, those who hold the debts—the strong, the wealthy, the powerful—would be threatened by the vision. The rulers feared what Mary hoped for: a day when they lose power, the hungry get good things, and the rich are sent away empty handed (Lk 1:52-53). Indeed, the prophets had warned of this day long ago: when the reign of God finally comes to Israel, it will come at the expense of wealthy rulers. As if on a seesaw, when God lifts up the poor, the rich are brought low. When God exalts the meek, the powerful are humiliated. By his life and by his words, Jesus would preach this gospel of the kingdom of God. Who will have eyes to see and ears to hear?

Blessed are the needy. In a rapid-fire sequence of episodes Luke makes it abundantly clear that the needy see and hear. Jesus found believers among the demonized, the sick, the paralyzed, the marginalized and the impaired (Lk 4:31–6:11). In fact, that's the way Jesus made disciples: he helped them, and they followed him. Unlike Mark and Matthew, in Luke's Gospel Jesus didn't find disciples first and then hit the road. Rather, Luke's Jesus moves around like a lone ranger, gathering followers as he brings the kingdom to them. The classic example is the story of the miraculous catch of fish (Lk 5:1-9). The reason these now famous fishermen (Simon Peter, James and John) end up following Jesus is that he was able to fill their nets with fish that they couldn't catch. And yet, ironically, the miracle convinces them to forsake their nets (and fish!) and follow Jesus (Lk 5:10-11). Indeed, according to Luke, Jesus attracted disciples, both male and female, before he chose them. That's why, after a while, Jesus ends up choosing "the twelve" from the crowd of disciples like a baseball coach choosing his starters (Lk 6:12-16). The same thing happens later, when the movement grows so large that Jesus appoints seventy disciples (Lk 10:1). All of this proved that Jesus was right: it was time for Isaiah's dream to come true. The blind will have eyes to see and the deaf will have ears to hear because the kingdom comes to those who need it. Conversely, those who didn't need it didn't get it.

WHAT'S MORE . . .

The Women Disciples of Jesus

Luke makes it plain that Jesus had women disciples, two of whom he even identifies by name, Mary and Joanna (Lk 8:2-3). Women played a prominent role in the kingdom work of Jesus: they supported him financially (Lk 8:3), they hosted meals for him (Lk 10:38), and "sat at his feet" and learned his teaching like any other disciple (Lk 10:39); and they faithfully followed him to the end, lamenting his suffering as he carried the cross (Lk 23:27), keeping vigil until he died (Lk 23:48-49), and preparing his body for burial (Lk 23:55–24:1). That's why Jesus gave special recognition to his female disciples—a rather scandalous thing to do in such a male-dominated culture. He held them up as models of wise discernment ("Mary has chosen the better part" [Lk 10:42]) and faithful devotion ("she has shown great love" [Lk 7:47]). It's no wonder the angels appeared to the women disciples of Jesus first so that they could report what they heard and saw. They had the honor of being the first witnesses of the resurrection of Jesus Christ, even though the apostles wouldn't believe them (Lk 24:1-11).

When the disciples heard Jesus' famous Sermon on the Plain, they got it (Lk 6:20-49). They knew that the poor were blessed. They were living proof of the kingdom. In Matthew's Gospel Jesus preached the similar Sermon on the Mount, after which the poor and the oppressed were drawn to him in hopes of God's blessing. In Luke's Gospel it worked the other way around: Jesus blessed the poor and oppressed by helping them, and the sermon was the exclamation point, promising even more. And, sure enough, Jesus promised that their hungry bellies would be filled, and it happened (Lk 9:12-17). He predicted that weeping would turn into laughter, and it happened

(Lk 7:11-16; 8:49-55). No wonder the crowds eventually turned into a stampede (Lk 12:1). Yet, even though Jesus promised more he also began to require more, making the Sermon on the Plain another significant turning point in Luke's story.

Promises to the poor and weak seemed to go hand in hand with warnings to the rich and powerful (Lk 6:24-25). And, blessings to disciples meant not only good times but also hard realities (Lk 6:22-23, 26-30). These ideas are linked in the sermon because Jesus anticipated that his disciples would be treated as he was. Since Jesus believed that in the kingdom the last becoming first would result in the first becoming last, he knew that he and his disciples would be treated harshly by those who are first. Such persecution might lead to doubts about the reality of God's reign on earth, which is why Jesus warned his disciples in advance. They would be hated because of him. They would be abused because of him. So, what were they supposed to do? Grin and bear it? Not in the least. Disciples of the kingdom do so much more: they love their enemies; they pray for their persecutors; they forgive rather than judge; they give rather than lend. They "count the cost" of following Jesus because they live for eternal rewards. And, since they knew all of this going in, Jesus predicted that the house of their lives would stand against the floodwaters of bad times (Lk 6:27-49). The kingdom of God is built upon a rock foundation that shall not be moved.

Jesus' warnings of impending persecution must have sounded like an exaggeration to the disciples in light of the events that immediately followed his sermon. The only opposition they faced came from demons and threatening storms, which Jesus handled without difficulty (Lk 8:22-39). He continued to heal the sick and raise the dead (Lk 7:1-17; 8:40-56). He even extended his gospel ministry through the Twelve, giving them power to defeat demons and heal sickness (Lk 9:1-6). A few had their doubts about Jesus (John the Baptizer and Simon the Pharisee [Lk 7:18-50]), but the Twelve appeared to be hanging on fairly well during the rollercoaster ride of the inbreaking kingdom of God. Three of them even got to see Moses and Elijah talk with a glorified Jesus about his approaching "exodus" (Lk 9:28-36). And yet, even though things were going well in Galilee—he used five loaves and two fish to feed over five thousand persons, certainly pleasing the crowds (Lk 9:9-17)—Jesus persisted with his talk of crosses and rejection (Lk 9:21-

27). In fact, it wasn't until after Jesus "set his face to go to Jerusalem" that his self-fulfilling prophecy began to come true when he and his entourage were rejected by the Samaritans (Lk 9:51-56). Unaccustomed to such treatment and forgetting what Jesus taught them during the Sermon on the Plain about forgiveness and loving enemies, the Twelve wanted to use their newly found powers to re-create the miracle of Elijah (1 Kings 18:37-38) as a pyrotechnic display of wrathful vengeance against the inhospitable people.

But Jesus knew that not finding a place to lay their heads for the night was only the beginning of sorrows—for him and for them (Lk 9:57-62). And this is when the story gets even more intriguing.

Jesus must die in Jerusalem. The next section of the Gospel—what scholars call the "travel narrative"—is where most of Luke's unique material appears (Lk 10:1–19:28). Of course, the entire account of Jesus' ministry could be called a "travel narrative" because he never stays in one place. Up to this point, there seems to be no particular destination to his travels. Jesus keeps moving around, going from one place to the next, without any direction. Then, for some unexplained reason (perhaps advice received during the transfiguration?), Jesus decides to "set his face to go to Jerusalem" (Lk 9:51). And yet, Luke's Jesus didn't

> ### SO WHAT?
> ....
> *Our Caustic Culture*
>
> We live in an age when it is customary to blast one's enemies. Rancor fills our retorts to those who are unkind to us. We resonate with Jesus' disciples when they found themselves unwelcomed. Although we might not call down fire upon our enemies, we may rain hate speech on them. Jesus suggests forgiveness, not so that we will be welcomed but because we are his disciples. When we still find ourselves with no place to lay our heads, it shouldn't surprise us. Perhaps when we encounter the same inhospitality, rather than offer a hateful response, we should remind ourselves that this is what happens to those who are following Jesus.

go straight to Jerusalem. Instead, Luke traces Jesus' movements along a meandering path, filled with vague geographical references, as Jesus moves from Galilee to a village near Jerusalem (Lk 10:38), circles back to Herod's kingdom (Galilee or Perea [Lk 13:31]), travels "through the region between Samaria and Galilee" (Lk 17:11), passing through Perea once again (Lk 18:35), and finally arriving just outside of Jerusalem (Lk 19:29). Obviously, to "set his face to go to Jerusalem" didn't mean taking a direct route to the holy city. Luke wasn't offering a geography lesson in Jesus' travels; rather, this episodic narrative implies that Jesus' purposeful journey had theological design. "Follow me" becomes more prominent for the Twelve since Jesus had already warned them to bring a cross because they were headed for Jerusalem (Lk 9:23). Indeed, following Jesus toward his final destination resulted in a meandering path with a clear destiny for the disciples, reminiscent of Israel's trek to the promise land.

During the journey to Jerusalem, Jesus told several parables that paint one picture: the way of the kingdom is a world turned upside down (a "good" Samaritan, a "foolish" rich man, the exalted humbled, the cursed blessed, the prodigal celebrated, the dishonest commended, a "tormented" man of luxury, a "righteous" collector of taxes). And, it's during this stretch of narrative where Jesus seems especially guarded ("Whoever is not with me is against me" [Lk 11:23]), countering his opponents who are openly attacking him, all the while doling out most of his notoriously "hard sayings" for disciples (e.g., the unforgiveable sin, selling off possessions, hating family). His teaching was so rough, his perspective so disorienting, that even Peter had to ask, "Lord, are you telling this parable for us or for everyone?" (Lk 12:41), a

SO WHAT?

The Christian Life as a Pilgrimage

Christianity is not just a journey; it also has a clear destination: not to heaven but to our Jerusalem. When Jesus says, "Follow me," he isn't telling us how to get to heaven when we die. Instead, just like the Twelve, we are to follow Jesus to Jerusalem to die. He's teaching us how to carry the cross to the city of peace ("Jerusalem" means "city of shalom"). The Christian life is "the Way"—a way of life that brings the kingdom of God to our city, that brings heaven to earth, that brings peace to our world. The way of the cross is not a means of escape from this life; rather, the cross of Jesus is the only way peace comes to this life.

question that Jesus ignored because to ask the question is to miss the point. Every episode of the travel narrative—parable, miracle, diatribe—tells the same subversive story for everyone. The topsy-turvy reign of God inverts the world order; the social map of the status quo is turned upside down. The rich need to be saved from their impoverished state too (Zacchaeus [Lk 19:1-10]). The binary world of religious extremes collapses into one divine kingdom when pious categories are ignored. Even the unclean need a holy God (the ten lepers [Lk 17:11-19]). What was evident before comes into sharp relief during Jesus' long trip to Jerusalem: enacting the favorable year of the Lord would result in a revolution.

WHAT'S MORE . . .

The Divine Reversal

When Jesus looked at the world, he saw that it was completely out of whack, off kilter, wrong side up. The good and beautiful world that God created was marred by sin. Therefore, when the reign of God comes to earth, all things must be made right, justice must come to all people, the world must be turned right side up. But, when the lowly are exalted, those in power must be humbled. As if on a see-saw, the hungry will get something to eat when the rich have been "sent away empty" (Lk 1:53). What looks like subversion is in fact correction. This is what Mary sang about in the Magnificat (Lk 1:46-55). This is what Jesus taught in his parables, such as the stories of the rich man and Lazarus (Lk 16:19-31), and the Pharisee and the tax collector (Lk 18:9-14). This is why Jesus kept emphasizing that when the kingdom comes, the exalted will be humbled but the humble will be exalted (Lk 14:11). Indeed, that is what Jesus was trying to teach his disciples, especially during the trip to Jerusalem. For when Jesus died, they would witness firsthand the ultimate divine reversal: the greatest will become the least (crucifixion), and the least will become the greatest (resurrection).

The way Jesus saw it, if Israel had obeyed the law and the prophets (Year of Jubilee), then the rich wouldn't wind up in hell and the poor wouldn't need to beg for God's mercy (Lk 16:19-31). And, if the sons of Abraham had humbled themselves, then the righteous would go to their houses justified because repentant sinners find God's forgiveness (Lk 18:9-14). This is why Jesus came: to liberate them all. But when the wealthy refuse to heed Jesus' warning and the righteous are justified in their own eyes, such as the rich ruler (Lk 18:18-25), it's no wonder that people asked, "Then who can be saved?" (Lk 18:26). What are the chances the rich will sell all that they have and give it away? What do the righteous have to repent of when there are so many sinners among us? Indeed, what Jesus envisioned regarding the kingdom of God bordered on the impossible (Lk 18:27). And, once Jesus and his disciples finally arrived in Jerusalem, preaching the same subversive message, the impossibility of the kingdom of God on earth seemed certain. The people in power made sure of it.

Talk of the reign of God coming to Jerusalem got people excited (Lk 19:11). Of course, the hope of God ruling the world from Jerusalem was as old as David's throne (Ps 110). So, as Jesus and his entourage got close to the holy city, many were expecting fireworks. And yet, even though Jesus tried to disabuse them of correlating his visit to Jerusalem with the arrival of God's kingdom ("Yes, I'm going to rule; but it won't happen for a while" [see Lk 19:12-27]), more than anyone else, Jesus seemed to be the one intent on lighting the fuses. He arranged the Zechariah-prophesied donkey ride into Jerusalem (Lk 19:29-40). He wept over God's inevitable judgment of the city (Lk 19:41-44). He moved into the temple as if it belonged to him, telling stories about a murdered son and rejected cornerstone (Lk 19:45–20:19). He predicted that Jerusalem was about to be destroyed by war (Lk 21:5-38). And, much to the chagrin of his disciples, Jesus repeated what he had said before, that he would suffer a horrible end too (Lk 18:31-34; 22:14-22). Such provocations were standard; Jesus agitated all kinds from the beginning. And yet, before he got to Jerusalem, the most that his opponents would do was threaten him with stones. This time, however, Jesus provoked the wrong people to wrath. Rural folk may run you out of town; city people are more likely to kill you when there's talk of God ruling the world without them.

Rulers and leaders, aristocrats and land owners lived in the city, protected by its walls. So, it was only a matter of time before Jesus was arrested for his rebellious behavior by the governing authorities, both Jewish and Roman. It was the perfect storm for such a catastrophe. Jerusalem was crammed with

Passover pilgrims. There was a long history of riots breaking out between Roman authorities and Jewish subjects during Passover, a holy day commemorating God's deliverance of Israel from a wicked ruler. So, the political fallout from Jesus' critique of the religious leaders—the temple and its priests—was predictable. The more Jesus challenged the leadership of the elites (the temple is corrupt, Jerusalem is not safe), the more popular he became among the people (Lk 19:47-48; 21:37–22:2). That the ruling council of the Jews (the Sanhedrin) took measures to silence his voice because they feared that the people would turn into an unruly mob made political sense, especially to the Roman procurator, Pilate (Lk 23:1-25). Peace at all costs made for dynamic political theater. But Luke maintains that what happened in Jerusalem was more than politics. This was a spiritual battle. And, the power behind the dramatic turn of events that led to Jesus' crucifixion was Satan (Lk 22:3, 31, 52-53).

The Messiah is not supposed to die; the Son of David must defeat all enemies. So, a suffering Messiah was a contradiction; it was completely unexpected. This explains why the disciples were confused even though Jesus had predicted his fate several times. Jesus seemed defeated by death, and the hopes of his followers were crushed. By every appearance, the enemies of Jesus had won. Rome kept the peace. Jewish leaders removed the threat of a blasphemous, false messiah. And Satan finished what he started during the temptation of Christ, finding the "opportune time" (Lk 4:13) to overthrow the kingdom of God by killing the heir to the throne. The wailing women helped Joseph, a man who "was waiting expectantly for the kingdom of God," to bury Jesus (Lk 23:27, 50-56). But, throughout this dark story Luke sprinkles dashes of hope. Jesus promised one of his partners in death, "Today you will be with me in Paradise" (Lk 23:43). Women returning to finish the burial of Jesus find an empty tomb and two strangers "in dazzling clothes" waiting for them with the message "He is not here, but has risen. Remember how he told you [that this would happen]?" (Lk 24:5-6). Later that day two men have a weird encounter with a fellow traveler who not only was completely unfazed by the atrocity of Jesus' death, but also mysteriously vanished during supper (Lk 24:13-32). It's not until Jesus appears to his disciples and shows them the final proof of his victory—a resurrected body and a lesson from the Scriptures that the "Messiah is to suffer and to rise from the dead on the third day"—that believers are made. In fact, it takes a resurrected Jesus ascending to the throne of God in heaven to seal the deal. The disciples will be witnesses of the power of God's reign from Jerusalem, the kingdom of God of repentance and forgiveness that will extend "to all nations"—a Gospel story that begins and ends in the temple (Lk 24:44-53).

How Is This Jesus Different?

It is fascinating to consider why the other Gospel writers believed that their stories were complete without a book like Acts. Or, to put it another way, why did Luke believe that his version of the Gospel would be incomplete without a sequel? There are a variety of scholarly opinions about the purpose of Acts. One seems certain: what Jesus started—the kingdom of God—his disciples continued because they were empowered by the same Holy Spirit. The burning question lingering on the lips of the disciples, "Is this the time?" (Acts 1:6), resonates with Luke's readers because we can't help but ask, "Did the reign of God come, yes or no?" And the answer Luke seems to give, necessitating his two-part work, is yes *and* no. Yes, the kingdom of God is already here because of the Spirit's work, evidenced by the fact the disciples perform the same miracles, preach the same message as Jesus. No, it hasn't come completely because the good news of God's reign through Jesus via the Spirit must expand to the end of the world. Thus, according to Luke, the kingdom of God doesn't happen all at one time or all in one place (Lk 17:20-21). Luke doesn't see the end of the world as one, huge, cosmic catastrophe when it all hits the apocalyptic fan. Rather, God's reign breaking into history comes slowly, deliberately, like leaven eventually overtaking a lump of dough called "earth." It will take a while before Jesus' disciples take the gospel to the ends of the earth. And Acts shows how that happens.

The second remarkable feature of Luke's Gospel is the so-called travel narrative to Jerusalem, which also features many of the unique parables of Jesus. What appears as a sideshow in Matthew and Mark (and is nearly absent in John)—the reversal of last and first—takes center stage in Luke. When God's reign comes to earth, everything is turned upside down or, more precisely, right side up, especially in the visionary world of Jesus' parables. The prodigal son's homecoming is celebrated, not the obedience of the elder son. A rich man winds up in hell, and a beggar goes to heaven. The shameful tax collector is honored, and the righteous ruler is condemned. The inverted order of God's heavenly kingdom brings disorder to earth; it is an unsettling picture, not only for the powerful but also for the disciples. The subversive world of God's reign is so disorienting that Jesus has to say things such as, "Let these words sink into your ears: The Son of Man is going to be betrayed into human hands" (Lk 9:44); and, "Do you think that I have come to bring peace to the earth? No, I tell you, but rather division!" (Lk 12:51). To make matters worse, Jesus even used Jewish symbols for sin, such as yeast, to talk about his work for God (Lk 13:20-21). He even says that his disciples are "evil," and he claims that no one but God is good (Lk 11:13; 18:19). Indeed, by the time Jesus gets to the holy city, he's offended almost everyone. Thus, what happens in Jerusalem, the death of Jesus, completes the picture of the scandalous, upside-down kingdom of God. Luke seems to relish the irony, for the cross is a strange place for Jesus to talk like a king and for a criminal to find paradise.

Finally, what makes Jesus a king in Luke's Gospel is different.[1] For example, this is not the story of a man who rises from obscurity to become king (Mark). Nor is this the story of a heavenly prince who becomes an earthly pauper (Matthew and John). Rather, Jesus is an earthy king from start to finish—a divine monarchy framed by the virgin birth and the ascension—a royal identity that never changes. So, the way Luke sees it, Jesus is born the Son of God because he is "the Lord." He is anointed by God's Spirit because he is the Messiah. He ascends to God's throne because he is the King. To be sure, Jesus must reign in heaven as he does on earth. But a shift in location occurs in Acts, where Jesus moves to heaven to continue his rule on earth.[2] That's why the ascension is indispensible to Luke; it's the last episode of the Gospel and the opening scene of Acts, the bridge that links the kingdom of God from the birth of Christ to the ends of the earth. Thus, the predictable plot of Luke's two-part Gospel story is the revelation of Jesus' true identity known from the beginning. And yet, it is the way the kingdom

---

[1]For a good survey of the various interpretations of Luke's Jesus, see H. Douglas Buckwalter, *The Character and Purpose of Luke's Christology,* Society for New Testament Studies Monograph Series 89 (Cambridge: Cambridge University Press, 1996), pp. 6-24.

[2]C. Kavin Rowe, *Early Narrative Christology: The Lord in the Gospel of Luke,* Beihefte zur Zeitschrift für die neutestamentliche Wissenschaft und die Kunde der älteren Kirche 139 (Berlin: de Gruyter, 2006), pp. 189-202.

comes—the subversive plot—that provides the dramatic twist. It is the way of the cross that brings heavenly power to earth (Lk 24:46-49).

WHAT IF THIS WERE OUR ONLY JESUS?

Think about how we would answer the question "What was Jesus' purpose?" if all we had was the Gospel of Luke. Setting aside Acts for the moment, what was Luke's Jesus trying to accomplish? It depends upon how we read Jesus' famous sermon at Nazareth and how we interpret Luke's theology of the cross. When Jesus claimed Isaiah's prophecy as his messianic agenda, did he expect the people to rise up and help him make it happen? In other words, when he pronounced that it was time for the favorable year of the Lord, time to cancel all debts, was he calling for a social revolution? When he talked about releasing prisoners, was he advocating anarchy, the overthrow of Herod and Rome? That is to say, should Jesus' agenda be taken literally or spiritually? He certainly made the blind see (literally and spiritually), but did he set prisoners free? John the Baptizer would say no. Indeed, he questioned Jesus' intentions (Lk 7:18-20). And who can blame him? If Jesus intended to break people out of prison, he apparently forgot about John. And yet, there are other places in Luke's Gospel where Jesus miraculously liberates prisoners, such as the Gerasene demoniac (Lk 8:29), the hunchback woman (Lk 13:16), and even Barabbas (Lk 23:18-25). Also, Jesus brought the wealth of God's kingdom to the poor, not only through miraculous feedings but also by a changed heart (Zacchaeus). So, did Jesus have a social agenda or not? When he preached about the kingdom of God, was he out to change "politics as usual" or was he speaking only about the spiritual realm of God's rule? For Luke, it seems to be both, for when it comes to the kingdom of God, the political and spiritual are indivisible.

The same is true for the death of Jesus. Some might say that Jesus' ultimate purpose was to die on a cross for the sins of the world. But that is not Luke's theme. In fact, nowhere in the Gospel does Luke interpret the death of Jesus as the necessary sacrifice to atone for sin. Whereas this theme in Matthew's version of the Last Supper is pronounced—"This is my blood of the covenant, which is poured out for many for the forgiveness of sins" (Mt 26:28)—and Jesus speaks of his approaching death as a ransom for many according to Matthew and Mark (Mt 20:28; Mk 10:45), Luke is practically silent about the efficacy of Jesus' death on a cross. Rather, when Luke's Jesus talks about his death as inevitable, either before the cross or after the resurrection, it is for different reasons: prophets must die in Jerusalem (Lk 13:33), and the Messiah must suffer to be glorified (Lk 24:26). The cross is the result of ignorant rulers and evil powers (Lk 22:3, 53; 23:34; 24:20). No doubt, "repentance and forgiveness of sins is to be proclaimed in his name" by Jesus' soon-to-be-empowered-from-on-high disciples, but that commissioned message has as much to do with the resurrection as the cross (Lk 24:45-49). In other words, for Luke's Gospel story, the importance of the cross is absorbed by and embedded in the resurrection of Jesus Christ.

So, if Luke does not spiritualize the death of Jesus as an atoning work—the cross looks more like a martyr's death triggered by political expedience—and the kingdom of God on earth sometimes resulted in social change, do we have a recipe for revolution in the Gospel according to Luke? Some think so, especially since Luke throws in the enigmatic teaching of Jesus about the necessity of purchasing swords (Lk 22:36-38). But, this is where we must read the whole Gospel to get the whole story. For example, it's quite obvious that Jesus didn't believe that the kingdom of God must come by force, for when one disciple did serious harm with a sword, Jesus rebuked such impulsive foolishness, repaired the damage, and chastised the temple police for brandishing their swords (Lk 22:49-53). Drawn swords draw out hidden swords—"Lord, should we strike with the sword?"—violence begets violence. The cross was supposed to teach them to die for their enemies, not kill them. They were supposed to see the upside-down world of the kingdom even when facing death. Perhaps it is no coincidence that a sword held up by the tip of the blade resembles a cross, the weapon of self-sacrifice. Indeed, Jesus knew all too well that, for him as well as for those who follow, the only way to save life is to lose it (Lk 9:23-24).

So, if Luke's Jesus were all we had, we would see the cross as a weapon of peace rather than as a symbol of the atonement. We wouldn't admire the death of Jesus; we would imitate him by carrying a cross. We would never be surprised when enemies opposed us, since Jesus predicted that it would be this way. We would always have our eyes on the margins of society, for that's where the kingdom of God is most evident. We would prefer the least, the last and the lost over the greatest, the first and the found. We would be wary of becoming wealthy for fear of not entering the kingdom of God. Rather than recognize veterans of war during Memorial Day worship services, we would remember the martyrs of our faith. Instead of emphasizing heaven as the goal of our salvation, we would fix our eyes on the prize of God ruling the earth. And, rather than pointing to our hearts and saying, "Jesus is here," we would point to the heavens and declare, "Jesus is there, at the right hand of God. And one day, he's coming back here to finish what he started." That's why Luke's Gospel ends with ascension, and why Acts begins with the disciples looking up to heaven, wondering when Jesus is coming back. For Christ was born to rule the world, and Acts tells the story of how that will happen: from Jerusalem, to Judea, to Samaria, to the ends of the earth.

Thus, Acts cannot be set aside when it comes to figuring out the significance of Luke's Jesus. Even though Luke seems to ignore the atoning work of Jesus' death in his Gospel, he makes it abundantly clear in the sequel that Jesus' death and resurrection resulted in forgiveness of sins for those who believed (Acts 2:22-39). Therefore, according to Luke's Gospel story in its entirety—parts one and two—Jesus taught his disciples to bring the reign of God to earth by using spiritual weapons that would result in political and social change. Luke's theology of liberation was neither a political manifesto for social engineering nor a spiritual strategy for escaping the problems of the world. Rather, Luke sees heaven and earth joined together in the gospel of Jesus Christ—a kingdom reign of heaven from Jerusalem to the end of our world.

READ MORE ABOUT IT

Bock, Darrell L. A *Theology of Luke and Acts: God's Promised Program, Realized for All Nations.* Grand Rapids: Zondervan, 2012.

Garland, David E. *Luke.* Zondervan Exegetical Commentary on the New Testament 3. Grand Rapids: Zondervan, 2011.

Green, Joel B. "Luke, Gospel of." In *Dictionary of Jesus and the Gospels,* edited by Joel B. Green, Jeannine K. Brown and Nicholas Perrin, pp. 540-52. 2nd ed. Downers Grove, IL: IVP Academic, 2013.

———. *The Theology of the Gospel of Luke.* New Testament Theology. Cambridge: Cambridge University Press, 1995.

Rowe, C. Kavin. *Early Narrative Christology: The Lord in the Gospel of Luke.* Beihefte zur Zeitschrift für die neutestamentliche Wissenschaft und die Kunde der älteren Kirche 139. Berlin: de Gruyter, 2006.

Sloan, Robert Bryan, Jr. *The Favorable Year of the Lord: A Study of Jubilary Theology in the Gospel of Luke.* Austin, TX: Schola Press, 1977.

DISCUSSION QUESTIONS

1. What do you admire about Luke's Jesus? Who should be offended by Luke's Jesus? Why?

2. Why was it so important to Jesus that the poor and oppressed experience the kingdom of God?

3. If the kingdom of God turns the world "right side up," what should it look like today? What is "upside down" in our world that Jesus would put right side up?

4. Is the kingdom of God political? Why or why not?

5. What is unique about Luke's Jesus? How has Luke changed your view of Jesus?

6. If Luke were the only Gospel we had, how would you describe the essence of Jesus' message and ministry? What would it look like if we followed Luke's Jesus today?

4

JOHN'S JESUS

Iᵗ's Sunday morning, and the first service is about to start. Most everybody knows everybody else, so the newcomer is more obvious. In she comes with several children in tow. To even a casual observer it seems obvious that the children have different fathers. Several frowning members note the current lack of a wedding ring. Oh, they know her kind. She is the conversation of the Sunday school class that meets after the first service. Disapproval spreads when one member who works at the bank knows more of her story. She has been married five times and is currently living with a guy down on Pine Street. What is she doing at church?

Since it's a Bible class, someone brings up the story of the Samaritan woman at the well. We all know the story: immoral woman, not too bright. If we were even less gracious, we might use words like "bimbo" or "loose woman." John's story of a scarlet woman who was met by a gracious and forgiving Lord has moved many modern readers to tears. The Sunday school class sits smugly when it was introduced. Here at least is one Bible story they know. Yet, do we really? John paints a different story. She's the hero. While Nicodemus, the male Jewish religious leader, is clueless about Jesus, this Samaritan peasant woman gets it. In John's Gospel the unnamed disciples are the heroes. How often do we misread John? He never calls the woman "immoral." "But," the class could object, "she was married five times and is now living with a man outside marriage!" Certainly, that qualifies as immoral! But the Samaritan woman easily could have been widowed that many times. If she was barren (and she seems to have no children to fetch water), she may have been divorced several times for failing to produce an heir. Romans also had forms of marriage (usually to protect inheritances from previous marriages) that Jews did not recognize as official marriage. This woman may be a victim of society, not a "loose woman." John's Jesus might caution the Sunday school class against hasty judgment.

John's Jesus has long been noted as different from the Jesus of the other Gospels. We use the term "Synoptic" (meaning "viewed together") to describe Matthew, Mark and Luke, who share a viewpoint on Jesus. John's Jesus seems at first glance to be a simpler story. His message appears more intimate, less like a sermon and more like the conversation afterwards. This Jesus sounds not like he's preaching to crowds but chatting with me. I was introduced to Jesus during a Billy Graham evangelistic rally. Billy Graham routinely gave new Christians a copy of the Gospel of John because it was "the easiest Gospel to understand." Although John's message might seem simple, he usually is talking at a deeper level as well, with a message filled with double meanings and often rich in irony. For example, when the transcendent Logos (Word), creator of the cosmos, storms into the world (in John 2), we expect a grander agenda than a family wedding. Really, he heads to a wedding? Rather than addressing the groanings of fallen creation, he hears family complaints about the catering.

Who Does John Say That I Am?

Setting the stage. The story of Jesus doesn't start with Mary and Joseph in Bethlehem. We are beckoned back to Genesis 1. "In the beginning was the Word" (Jn 1:1). This is a cosmic Jesus. More than that, Jesus is God ("and the Word was God" [Jn 1:1]), God incarnate ("and the Word became flesh" [Jn 1:14]), a very immanent incarnation ("We declare to you what was from the beginning, what we have heard, what we have seen with our eyes, what we have looked at and touched with our hands" [1 Jn 1:1]).

John's readers, both Jews and Gentiles, had heard about *logos*. Gentile Christians had heard Stoic preachers talk about *logos*. To say that something was alive was to say that it had a body and a "soul." Since the universe had a body (all that you see around you), it must also have a soul, the Stoics argued, calling it the *logos*, or mind or reason. But, it was with Jewish Christians that

John struck the best chord. Genesis describes God as speaking creation into existence ("And God said, 'Let there be . . . '"). Since wisdom was spoken, Proverbs paints the image of Woman Wisdom being at God's side as he created: "Does not wisdom call, and does not understanding raise her voice? . . . When he established the heavens, I was there, . . . when he marked out the foundations of the earth, then I was beside him, like a master worker" (Prov 8:1, 27, 29-30). In the centuries before Jesus Jewish writers debated where Wisdom "dwelt" after creation was finished.

WHAT'S MORE . . .

Where Did Wisdom Dwell?

Baruch argued,

Learn where there is wisdom. . . .
Who has found her place? . . .
No one knows the way to her. . . .
But the one who knows all things knows her. . . .
He . . . gave her to his servant Jacob
and to Israel, whom he loved.
Afterward she appeared on earth
and lived with humankind. (Bar 3:14-15, 31-32, 36-37)

Jesus ben Sira, however, insisted that Wisdom had not dwelt (pitched her tent) among humankind; rather, she lived in Jerusalem (probably meaning the temple):

Wisdom praises herself. . . .
"Then the Creator of all things gave me a command,
and my Creator chose the place for my tent [*skēnē*].
He said, 'Make your dwelling in Jacob.'. . .
And so I was established in Zion." (Sir 24:1, 8-10)

The writer of *1 Enoch* was more pessimistic. Wisdom was not to be found among humans at all:

Wisdom found no place where she might dwell;
then a dwelling-place was assigned her in the heavens.
(*1 En.* 42.1)

John tells his readers where Wisdom had actually come to dwell: "In the beginning was the Word [*logos*], and the Word was with God, and the Word was God. He was in the beginning with God. All things came into being through him. . . . And the Word became flesh and lived [*eskēnōsen*] among us" (Jn 1:1-3, 14).

John's Jesus is the transcendent Logos, the eternal Wisdom that all people should seek, whether Gentile or Jew. So, John's first chapter opens with elevated prose that reminds us of a poem or song, introducing themes that keep popping up in the Gospel: life, light, the world, judgment, water, the Spirit, and the disciples and their professions of faith. We are told, "In him was life, and the life was the light of all people" (Jn 1:4). Life—usually eternal life—occurs here where we are accustomed to hearing of the kingdom of God (Jn 4:36; 5:21-29; 17:3). Jesus is the life (Jn 14:6), but he is also the light of the world (Jn 8:12) that shines into the darkness (Jn 1:5). Not surprisingly, the Gospel notes that disciples come to the light (Jn 3:21), out of the night (Nicodemus [Jn 3:2]), while another leaves into the night (Judas [Jn 13:30]), loving "darkness rather than light" (Jn 3:19). John's Jesus talks a lot about light (Jn 1:4-5, 7-9; 3:19-21; 5:35; 8:12; 9:5; 11:9-10; 12:35-36) because "I have come as light into the world" (Jn 12:46). Yet, the opening chapter also warns us that some won't know and accept this light (Jn 1:10-11). God loved the world through the act of the cross (Jn 3:16), but believers are not to love the world (1 Jn 2:15), for the world hates them (Jn 15:19) because the world does not know believers just as it doesn't know him (1 Jn 3:1). To those who are not his disciples Jesus said, "You are of this world, I am not of this world" (Jn 8:23).

Where there is life, there is both light and water. Not surprisingly, then, water splashes around the first several chapters of John's Gospel. John the Baptizer comes "with water" (Jn 1:26); Jesus turns water into wine (Jn 2:1-12); Nicodemus must be born of water as well as of the Spirit (Jn 3:5); Jesus tells a Samaritan woman about living water (Jn 4:1-42); Jesus, not the stirring water, heals a man (Jn 5:1-9). Jesus walks on water (Jn 6:16-21) before finally announcing to the crowds in the temple, "Let the one who believes in me drink. As the scripture has said, 'Out of the believer's heart shall flow rivers of living water'" (Jn 7:38). He promises the Samaritan woman, "Those who drink of the water that I will give them will never be thirsty" (Jn 4:14), and the crowd that he fed, "Whoever believes in me will never be thirsty" (Jn 6:35); yet, ironically (in a Gospel filled with irony), Jesus says on the cross, "I am thirsty" (Jn 19:28). The wellspring of living water is spent; he has given all that he is on the cross.

Even the casual reader is struck by how carefully the Gospel weaves together stories. Although crowds want to see Jesus for his miracles, the reader is told, "But Jesus did not trust himself to them, because he knew all men and needed no one to bear witness of man; for he himself knew what was in man" (Jn 2:24-25 RSV).[1] The stories that follow illustrate that Jesus knows what is in the human heart. Nicodemus comes boasting of his knowledge, "We know that you are a teacher who has come from God" (Jn 3:2); yet, Jesus knows what is in his heart (Jn 3:3). In John 4 the Samaritan woman meets Jesus, who, she says, "told me everything I have ever done" (Jn 4:39). In John 5 Jesus knows the heart of the man healed by the pool (Jn 5:14). Jesus knows the heart of the crowd (Jn 5:40; 6:15, 26). It is even true of his disciples, as Jesus at one point was "aware that his disciples were complaining about it" (Jn 6:61).

For John's Jesus, the best disciples are not the Twelve or even the inner circle, not the named disciples but rather the unnamed ones.[2] The Gospel sets the stage for the departure of the Twelve. Although many might feel that the loss of the apostles, the eyewitnesses, would mark a decay in discipleship, John argues that the best disciples are not the famous ones. There is a clear contrast between the male Jewish religious leader Nicodemus and the Samaritan woman. John's Jesus inverts the normal paradigm. It is the Samaritan woman who recognizes who Jesus is; at this time, Nicodemus does not. It is not the leaders in the temple who understand and believe (Jn 7:48), but rather the man born blind who sits outside the temple who believes and worships (Jn 9:38). The leaders confuse the facts and make contradictory statements (Jn 7–8), while the man born blind makes the rhetorically irrefutable argument (Jn 9:33). They are blind, and he sees.

As the Gospel opens, John's Jesus invites prospective disciples (including the reader), "Come and see" (Jn 1:39). The Gospel ends with the same call.

---

[1]It is clearly tied together by the repetition of "man" (*anthrōpos*), including the next verse: "There was a man [*anthrōpos*] of the Pharisees" (Jn 3:1).

[2]See Rodney Reeves, *A Genuine Faith: How to Follow Jesus Today* (Grand Rapids: Baker Books, 2005), pp. 179-245.

After readers "see" what Jesus has been doing, John (and his community) calls again for them to come and see: "These are written that you may come to believe that Jesus is the Messiah, the Son of God, and that through believing you may have life in his name" (Jn 20:31). How is the reader to see? John argues for seven signs to point toward who Jesus is.

The Book of Signs. We often hear that "signs" is a synonym for "miracles." Because the "signs" that John picks are miracles, we equate the words. We miss John's point. A "sign" is just that. A sign points to something else. It identifies something; it clarifies; it explains. John argues that these miracles are not merely a matter of wonderworking. They are "signs" that point to who Jesus is.

So how is a miracle in John's Gospel a "sign"? Claiming to be the bread of life rings hollow in the ears of Israelites, unless you can upstage Moses and the manna that kept their ancestors alive in the wilderness. Jesus does just that, and then he rebukes them by pointedly reminding all that it was God, not Moses, who provided the manna (Jn 6:32). Claiming to be the light of the world makes you a crazy man, unless you can also heal a man born blind. Again, a superlative tag is attached. The blind man notes, "Never since the world began has it been heard that anyone opened the eyes of a person born blind" (Jn 9:32). Claiming to be the resurrection and the life is an empty boast, unless you can enliven a man who has been dead four days, which is exactly what Jesus did: "Lazarus, whom he had raised from the dead" (Jn 12:1). It is not boasting if you deliver on what you claim. In fact, the miracle points (like a sign) to the truth of the claim.

The seventh sign (the raising of Lazarus) is the definitive sign. If you don't see who Jesus is from that sign, you never will.[3] Ironically, this is the sign that turns Jesus' opponents against him (Jn 11:45-53).

And so in the second half of John's Gospel the glory of Jesus ("his glory, the glory as of a father's only son" [Jn 1:14]) is revealed, not in signs for all to see but intimately to his disciples. He is the Revealer. To those who are Jesus' sheep, John's signs are written to point to a true understanding of and faith in Jesus (Jn 10:25-27). Throughout the Gospel people are making professions

---

[3]Does the Lukan Jesus make this same point when he tells the parable of the beggar and the rich man? The dead rich man asks for Abraham's help, begging Abraham to send back someone from the dead to warn his brothers. Abraham refuses, stating, "If they do not listen to Moses and the prophets, neither will they be convinced even if someone rises from the dead" (Lk 16:31).

WHAT'S MORE . . .

The "I AM" Sayings

One of the most significant features of John's Gospel is a number of sayings spoken by Jesus. We call them the "I AM" sayings. Here are the seven most striking ones:

I AM the bread of life (Jn 6:35, 48)

I AM the light of the world (Jn 8:12)

I AM the gate for the sheep (Jn 10:7)

I AM the good shepherd (Jn 10:11)

I AM the resurrection and the life (Jn 11:25)

I AM the way, and the truth, and the life (Jn 14:6)

I AM the true vine (Jn 15:1)

In a few cases the "I AM" statements are absolute; that is, they stand alone without any modifier. For example, Jesus said to his Judean/Jewish opponents, "Before Abraham was, I am" (Jn 8:58); and at his arrest Jesus identified himself with "I am," and the arresting soldiers stepped back and fell down (Jn 18:6).

What are we to make of these remarkable claims and others like it? First, it is important to note that in several cases Jesus' "I AM" is closely associated with a sign. Jesus claims, "I am the bread of life" after feeding five thousand people (Jn 6:35). Further, Jesus says, "I am the light of the world" before bringing light to the eyes of the man born blind (Jn 8:12; 9:1-12). After the death of his friend Lazarus, Jesus told Martha, "I am the resurrection and the life" (Jn 11:25). Clearly, these signs point to the truth of the saying and Jesus' true identity. Together, the signs and the sayings paint a compelling picture of who John says Jesus is. The emphatic "I AM" links Jesus and his work to the unspeakable name of God revealed to Moses and Israel in the wilderness ("I AM WHO I AM" [Ex 3:14]). For John, to encounter Jesus is to encounter God in the flesh.

about who they think Jesus is, such as teacher (Jn 1:38; 3:2), Messiah (Jn 1:41; 4:25; 7:26; 11:27), the one "from God" (Jn 3:2; 9:33), the bridegroom (Jn 3:29), a prophet (Jn 4:19; 9:17), savior (Jn 4:42) and king (Jn 6:15; 12:13). The Gospel portrays each profession as accurate but ultimately inadequate until the reader reaches the final profession, made by Thomas: "My Lord and my God!" (Jn 20:28). Although John has emphasized the deity of Jesus from the beginning of his Gospel, he assembles a case for it, building the crescendo to this climactic moment. What the signs have pointed toward throughout the story is heard at the end on the lips of Thomas.[4] Then John tells us that we can always hear other things about Jesus ("Jesus did many other signs in the presence of his disciples, which are not written in this book" [Jn 20:30]), but what we needed to know John has told us. This was why he wrote, and this is the belief that will give his readers life in Jesus' name (Jn 20:31). While not explicitly anti-Jewish or anti-Rome, this profession still calls followers of Christ from their communities to join God's kingdom, which is "not from this world" (Jn 18:36). And since John is preparing the church for a day without apostles,[5] the Gospel commends this profession for "those who have not seen and yet have come to believe" (Jn 20:29).

How Is This Jesus Different?

Unlike Mark's man of action, John's Jesus performs fewer miracles but theologizes more about them.[6] All four Gospels mention the feeding of the five thousand, but in John we have a long discussion about its meaning and about Jesus as the bread of life. This Jesus likes discourses rather than parables and pithy statements. His explanations are long; his arguments are rhetorically complex. John's Jesus also has a much longer and more inclusive

---

[4]Thomas does not appear as a significant figure in other first-century traditions, notably the canonical texts. He appears four times in John's story (Jn 11:16; 14:5; 20:26; 21:2). John's portrayal of Thomas is not as negative as is often painted today, such as "a loyal but pessimistic follower of Jesus, ready to die with him if need be, but slow to comprehend and ready to say so" (G. R. Beasley-Murray, *John*, Word Biblical Commentary 36 [Waco, TX: Word Books, 1987], p. 384).

[5]When Jesus is lifted up, he will draw all people to himself (Jn 12:32); yet among the apostles it is only the Beloved Disciple who is drawn to the cross (Jn 19:26). He sees the empty tomb and believes (Jn 20:8). He is the first to recognize the risen Jesus (Jn 21:7). Thus, he is the one to tell the story to guide those who are to believe without seeing.

[6]The switch from a saying of Jesus to commentary by John is often smooth and sometimes hard to detect. For example, the commentary by John on Jesus' words in John 3:11-15 likely begins at John 3:16, whereas some see John 3:16-21 as further words of Jesus.

WHAT'S MORE . . .

"The Jews Were Looking for an Opportunity to Kill Him" (Jn 7:1)

John's Gospel mentions the Judeans, *Ioudaioi* (or "Jews," as we commonly translate it), twenty times more often than do the Synoptics. The occurrences in Matthew (5x), Mark (6x) and Luke (5x) are mostly in the trial of Jesus, whereas John mentions them ninety-eight times. Although modern readers may equate Jews and Israelites, John's readers would not have done so. Judeans ("Jews"), Galileans, Samaritans and Idumeans were all Israelites. Their main disagreement was over where God (Yahweh) was to be worshiped. Which temple was Yahweh's temple (or were they all)? A "Judean" was a Yahweh worshiper who insisted that the true temple of Yahweh was the temple in Judea (in Jerusalem). A "Samaritan" was a Yahweh worshiper who insisted that the true temple was in Samaria (on Mount Gerizim). Thus, in John's Gospel we read the disciples saying, "Rabbi, the Jews were just now trying to stone you, and are you going there again?" (Jn 11:8). Modern readers might be confused. The Jews tried to stone Jesus? Weren't the disciples also Jews? No. The disciples considered themselves and Jesus Galileans, not Judeans ("Jews"). Jesus' opponents, the Judeans ("Jews"), fretted over how Jesus viewed the Judean temple. To a Judean, it was quite believable to accuse a Galilean of wanting to destroy the temple in Jerusalem (Mt 27:40). After all, the Judeans had destroyed Yahweh's temple in Samaria. It's not surprising that while he is in the Judean temple, Jesus is accused of being a Samaritan (Jn 8:48). John's Gospel provides more insight into the ethnic dynamics of Jesus' day.

ministry (Judean and Galilean) than in the other Gospels.[7] Unlike in Luke, where Jesus makes one journey to Jerusalem (to condemn the profaned temple and to die), John's Jesus is a frequent visitor and speaker in the temple. In fact, there is no journey, no call to follow Jesus to Jerusalem to die. Unlike the Mosaic Jesus of Matthew speaking from the mountaintops, John's Jesus

---

[7]Richard Bauckham makes a compelling argument that John's Gospel is more, rather than less, chronologically accurate and historically reliable than the Synoptic Gospels; see Bauckham, *Jesus and the Eyewitnesses: The Gospels as Eyewitness Testimony* (Grand Rapids: Eerdmans, 2006).

comments little about the law (Torah). He says more about the temple, but none of it good (Jn 2:16). His Father's house isn't going to be in Jerusalem (Jn 14:2-3). Rather, Jesus is not of this world, and his kingdom is not of this world; the world neither understands nor receives him. He is returning to his Father. Where he is going, we can't follow (Jn 13:33). He will have to return to take us there (Jn 14:3).

John's Jesus will insist that it didn't matter if one was a Judean or a Samaritan; that is, it didn't matter which temple you preferred. He tells a Samaritan, "The hour is coming when you will worship the Father neither on this mountain [Gerizim] nor in Jerusalem" (Jn 4:21).

True worshipers of Yahweh would no longer be defined by geography: "The hour is coming, and is now here, when the true worshipers will worship the Father in spirit and truth, for the Father seeks such as these to worship him" (Jn 4:23). In fact, the kingdom of God becomes less about a king in Jerusalem and more about eternal life realized in the present.

Although the ideal disciples may be the unnamed ones, this Gospel has plenty to say about the Twelve. Jesus clearly is the one in control. His disciples often don't know what their Master is up to. On

SO WHAT?
Following John's Jesus

Later in Jesus' ministry there is a warrant out for his capture; he was nearly stoned in the Jerusalem temple; it was dangerous to be anywhere near Jerusalem. He and his disciples were hiding across the Jordan River. His disciples are not surprised when Jesus doesn't answer the plea to help a sick Lazarus. (Lazarus had already died, but the disciples didn't know that.) The disciples are stunned when Jesus later announces that they will travel to the outskirts of Jerusalem. Jesus could have quieted their fears by assuring them that they would not be arrested; all would be fine. He doesn't. Disciples are merely to follow Jesus. Jesus is the Master who doesn't tell his followers all that he's up to. He still doesn't. When we ask, "Where are you going?" his answer is still the one he gave the first disciples: "Come and see" (Jn 1:39). As in all the Gospels, when they see where he's going, they find the cross. It is Thomas who represents true discipleship: "Let us also go, that we may die with him" (Jn 11:16).

his last earthly night, John's Jesus announces, "I do not call you servants any longer, because the servant does not know what the master is doing" (Jn 15:15). This is a change to prepare them for the cross.

In all the Gospels Jesus heads to Jerusalem knowing his fate, accepting that his arrest and crucifixion were coming. That is, Jesus is in complete control. John's Jesus is doing the same and emphasizing it more. It is the hour of his glory. When he is "lifted up" (double meaning of crucifixion and exaltation), he draws all people to himself. The crucifixion in John is victorious. Jesus is slain when the Passover lambs are slain: "it was the Day of Preparation" (Jn 19:31). None of his bones were broken (Jn 19:36; cf. Ex 12:46; Num 9:12); he is the acceptable sacrifice. The Gospel is all about him. John's Jesus didn't travel about talking in parables about the kingdom of God; he talked about himself. He is life. Believe in him.

What If This Were Our Only Jesus?

If John's Jesus were the only one, we would have no birth stories: Jesus was there, with God, from the beginning. As with Mark, we wouldn't celebrate Christmas. Unlike in Mark, though, the humanity of Jesus is hard to see. We don't witness Jesus' baptism by John the Baptist. The Spirit doesn't propel Jesus anywhere. Jesus looks to see where his Father is working, and Jesus decides to join his Father's work (Jn 5:19). There is no temptation—how could he be tempted? God has come to dwell among us. He waits by the well in Samaria. We're told that he is tired, but John clearly notes that Jesus has a divine appointment to keep (Jn 4:4). Perhaps the most human moment in Jesus' life, in the garden of Gethsemane, is gone. John, depicting Jesus as God walking among us, uses little war imagery. Unlike Mark's Jesus, who is in combat with the devil, John's Jesus is not involved in casting out demons. It is easy to see the influence of John's Gospel on many of our Western churches today. We have a preexistent (Jn 1:1) and otherworldly (Jn 8:23) Jesus.

John's Gospel doesn't offer a view of Jesus that is incompatible with the Synoptics, but (although it is often overstated) John's Jesus does resonate some with Greek philosophical thought. As he did with the concept of *logos*, John reaches out to Greeks with the idea that this present world is a world of copies; the true reality belongs to the world above. Since Jesus is from above (Jn 8:23), it isn't surprising that he is the true light, the real bread, the true life, the way to the Father (and the way out of this world).

John's Gospel doesn't tell of some things that are important to us, such as the Sermon on the Mount, how to pray, or the breaking of the bread at the Last Supper. He expects his readers to know the Synoptic stories, such as Jesus' baptism and his calling of the disciples. John assumes that his readers know the details they need to make sense of the story. John writes not to retell the Synoptic story, but rather to comment on the story's meaning. John knows that his readers have already heard the Jesus story. For example, John mentions that many in Jerusalem believed in Jesus because of the "signs" that he had done (Jn 2:23), yet at that point John had only told of one miracle, and it happened in Galilee. He mentions the resurrection, clearly expecting his readers to know about it (Jn 2:22), even though the account won't be told in this Gospel until John 20. Likewise, John explains Judas is "a devil" because he will betray Jesus (Jn 6:70-71), yet that story isn't told until John 13. In John 6 John expects his readers to know that the bread at the Lord's Supper is Jesus' body, even though John won't relate that saying of Jesus at all. The case can be made that the Gospel also includes some stories to clarify lingering questions about the first temple clearing (Jn 2:21-22), the subordination of John the Baptist to Jesus (Jn 1:20-27; 3:28-30; 5:36; with the clincher: "John [the Baptist] performed no sign" [Jn 10:41]), the restoration of Peter (Jn 21:15-19), the relationship of Peter and the beloved disciple (Jn 21:20-22) and his death (Jn 21:23).

Since Jesus' kingdom is

SO WHAT?

"You Must Be Born Again" *(Jn 3:7 NIV)*

Most evangelicals use texts from John, such as John 3:7 (and perhaps most famously, Jn 3:16), for evangelism, but John's Jesus gives no Great Commission. He lays out no missionary agenda for his disciples. Rather than trying to bring in new converts, the disciples are to care for Jesus' sheep (Jn 21:15-17). Their focus is inward, to take care of each other. In John it is Jesus, the good shepherd, who calls new sheep (Jn 10:1-18).

"not from this world" (Jn 18:36), John's Jesus shows little interest in the concerns of this world, notably Roman rule, the poor, the marginalized and the

sick. By the pool in Jerusalem "lay many invalids—blind, lame, and paralyzed" (Jn 5:3), but Jesus heals only one, in order to reveal his glory. He never
talks about forgiving debt (Mt 6:12; 18:21-35; Lk 7:36-50; 16:1-13) or helping
the poor. Jesus' only comment about the poor in John's Gospel is that the
money for an extravagant gift was rightly spent on Jesus, because "You
always have the poor with you, but you do not always have me" (Jn 12:8).

Christians who read too much of John's Gospel and not enough of Matthew's
might talk about eternal life but not about caring for "one of the least of these"
(Mt 25:31-46). John's Jesus shows little interest in how one lives life on this side
of the tomb. The Christian life is about eternal life. Even his kingdom is not about this life, this world (Jn 18:36). He says "believe in me" and not "follow me." If there had been beatitudes, they would be describing life in heaven later. If this were our only Jesus, disciples wouldn't be taught to pray, "Thy kingdom come, on earth as it is in heaven." This Jesus talks about himself and not God's kingdom, and certainly not about a kingdom breaking into this life. This Jesus preaches not, "The kingdom of God has come near; repent" (Mk 1:15), but rather, "I am the resurrection and the life. Those who believe in me, even though they die, will live" (Jn 11:25).

We are often told that John's Gospel has a "realized eschatology." To purists, this

SO WHAT?
. . . .
Judgment Day

Once in John, Jesus mentions a final judgment day, when good deeds matter: "For the hour is coming when all who are in their graves will hear his voice and will come out—those who have done good, to the resurrection of life, and those who have done evil, to the resurrection of condemnation" (Jn 5:28-29). But this seems to be a passing comment. The overwhelming impression in John is that when we stand before God, all that matters is what we think about Jesus. "Those who believe in him are not condemned; but those who do not believe are condemned already, because they have not believed in the name of the only Son of God" (Jn 3:18). In John's Gospel judgment day isn't about the sifting of deeds; it's not about how the rich man treated Lazarus (Lk 16:20). Our judgment day happens when we accept or reject Jesus. Most evangelicals draw their judgment day scenario from John.

means that kingdom has already come (been "realized") in the ministry of Jesus. In effect, we shouldn't expect anything else, because it is already here. Most now read John along with the rest of the New Testament as offering a more mediating perspective: the kingdom is already here, and yet we still await the final consummation. In other words, the last days have arrived, and we are living in them; yet, it takes the rest of the New Testament to dig this out of John. If we had only John's Gospel, we wouldn't see eschatology as "realized" because we wouldn't have emphasized that there is an eschaton. There is no God on the throne at a future judgment day: "The Father judges no one but has given all judgment to the Son" (Jn 5:22). The Son judges, and he did so on the cross: "Now is the judgment of this world" (Jn 12:31). On the night of his arrest Jesus announces, "The ruler this world has been condemned" (Jn 16:11). Our hope is not in a second coming. The promise of Jesus in John 14 is fulfilled in John 20.

John's Gospel doesn't describe the watershed event when Jesus asked, "Who do you say that I am?" We would be wrong, however, to think that John's Jesus didn't care who we say he is. It is *the* question for this Jesus as well. In this Gospel it is solely about whether one accepts or rejects Jesus, the light that has come into the world (Jn 1:12; 3:19). What you believe about Jesus is your judgment day (Jn 3:18, 36; 8:24). Perhaps evangelicals love the Gospel of John so much because the only thing that matters is what one thinks about Jesus.

READ MORE ABOUT IT

Bauckham, Richard J. *The Testimony of the Beloved Disciple: Narrative, History, and Theology in the Gospel of John*. Grand Rapids: Baker Academic, 2007.

Blomberg, Craig L. *The Historical Reliability of John's Gospel: Issues and Commentary*. 2nd ed. Downers Grove, IL: InterVarsity Press, 2011.

Carson, D. A. *The Gospel According to John*. Pillar New Testament Commentary. Grand Rapids: Eerdmans, 1991.

Keener, Craig S. *The Gospel of John*. 2 vols. Peabody, MA: Hendrickson, 2003.

———. "John, Gospel of." In *Dictionary of Jesus and the Gospels*, edited by Joel B. Green, Jeannine K. Brown and Nicholas Perrin, pp. 419-36. 2nd ed. Downers Grove, IL: IVP Academic, 2013.

Yarbrough, Robert W. *1-3 John*. Baker Exegetical Commentary on the New Testament. Grand Rapids: Baker Academic, 2008.

Discussion Questions

1. In John's Gospel a lot of people say a lot of positive things about Jesus, such as that he is a teacher come from God (Jn 3:2). John's Jesus doesn't seem content with this. Likewise, our culture often says kind things about Jesus. What do you think constitutes an adequate profession of faith about Jesus today?

2. What does the miracle of turning water into wine point out about Jesus (Jn 2:1-12), since Jesus doesn't use the empty wine pots readily at hand but rather the jars used for Jewish ceremonial cleansing?

3. Jesus told his first disciples, "Come and see" (Jn 1:39). He later tells the crowd that he does what he sees his Father doing (Jn 5:19-20). What might John's Jesus say to your friends who are seeking "God's will" for their lives (cf. Jn 4:34)?

4. John's Jesus can seem otherworldly. He doesn't speak about matters of everyday life, such as Roman politics, poverty, demon possession or debt. Has a preferential fondness for John's Gospel negatively impacted the Western evangelical church? If so, how, and what should we do about it?

5

PAUL'S JESUS

W̱e used to call it "testimony time." Having grown up in Baptist
churches in the 1960s and 1970s, I saw this happen often. During
evening worship services the pastor would ask for members to stand and
share with the church "what Christ has done for you." And, one by one, a
half-dozen believers—men and women, youth and adults—would be inspired by the Spirit to speak spontaneously about the work of Christ. Their
testimony would take one of two tracks: either they would talk about how
Jesus died on the cross for their sins, or they would recount an event in their
lives when Christ's presence was especially evident. In other words, their
testimony focused on their personal experience of Christ—either retelling
the story of their conversion or talking about what Christ had done for them
recently. To the best of my memory, in all the years of countless testimonies,
no one ever mentioned a story from the Gospels. Evidently, when answering
the question "What has Christ done for you?" it never occurred to anyone
to talk about what Jesus did before the crucifixion—no parable, no miracle,
nothing about his remarkable life. The historical works and words of Jesus
don't seem to be relevant to our everyday lives. Indeed, when we give testimony in church to "what Christ has done for us," some might even say we
sound a lot like the apostle Paul.

WHO DOES PAUL SAY THAT I AM?

Paul writes about Jesus, but he rarely mentions the things that Jesus said and did.[1] On one occasion he mentions what happened "the night when [the Lord Jesus] was betrayed" (1 Cor 11:23-25). A couple of times he refers to something that Jesus taught (1 Cor 7:10; 9:14; perhaps also 1 Thess 4:15). Clearly, then, the apostle had some access to and interest in details of Jesus' life.[2] But, for the most part, Paul focused his attention on three days of Jesus' life, explaining the theological significance of the death, burial and resurrection of Christ. This is why Pauline terms such as "justification" and "reconciliation" and "sanctification"—words that appear rarely in the Gospels—have become to us nearly synonymous with the gospel. Yet we wonder, can you talk about the gospel without mentioning "justification"? Paul used all kinds of metaphors to make sense of the cross of Jesus Christ. It's not that the apostle tried to explain the event itself; he never describes what happened the day Jesus died. Rather, Paul spent a lot of time explaining what the death of Jesus meant. Why? Other than the fact that a Messiah dying a cursed death was inexplicable (who could make sense of such a senseless death?), why did Paul keep trying to explain the death and resurrection of Jesus? It's because he believed that the God of Israel was at work, doing something incredibly unique, in the cross of Jesus Christ.

Paul's view of Jesus turns on his interpretation of the cross. If Paul had remained convinced that Jesus was nothing more than a messianic pretender, and that his shameful death was God's final verdict—God's curse—on Jesus, then nothing else in the life of Jesus would have mattered to Paul. No miracle story, no insightful teaching, no inspiring sermon, no dedicated disciple, none of this changed Paul's mind about Jesus. Even though he probably never met the historical Jesus, it is evident that Paul had heard about him; he knew enough about Jesus and his followers to set out on a campaign to destroy the movement by persecuting persons who believed in Christ. Paul knew that his crusade against Jesus was righteous (Phil 3:6); his mind was made up. No theological argument could convince him otherwise. But what about the testimony of faithful Christians? We would like to think that Paul was ridden with guilt after witnessing the martyrdom of

---

[1]See David B. Capes, "Jesus Tradition in Paul," in *Encyclopedia of the Historical Jesus*, ed. Craig A. Evans (New York: Routledge, 2007), pp. 446-49.

[2]For echoes and allusions to Jesus' teaching in Paul's letters, see Seyoon Kim, "Jesus, Sayings of," in *Dictionary of Paul and His Letters*, ed. Gerald F. Hawthorne, Ralph P. Martin and Daniel G. Reid (Downers Grove, IL: InterVarsity Press, 1993), pp. 474-92.

Stephen. But Acts tells the opposite story: Stephen's courage (would Paul see it as delusion?) inspired Paul to try even harder to stamp out the Jesus movement (Acts 8:3; 9:1-2).

As usually happens in relationships, Paul's opinion about Jesus changed after he met him. Of course, this was no ordinary meeting. Paul called it "apocalyptic"—a revelation (Gal 1:12, 16). Acts records the dramatic event: Paul's encounter with the resurrected Messiah on the Damascus Road changed everything (Acts 9:3-19). It's hard to hold onto the idea that Jesus is cursed by God when the Lord Jesus confronts you personally in all his messianic glory (scholars refer to this event as a "Christophany," meaning "appearance of Christ"). It's also difficult to overestimate the significance of Paul's experience that day. In fact, the apostle won't let us. He talked about his experience of Christ all the time. In nearly every letter that he wrote, Paul doesn't start with a theological argument about the importance of Jesus Christ; rather, he almost always begins with his ongoing experience of Christ (or his converts' experience of Christ). That is significant. Theologians today assume that if we can understand Paul's theology, we will know everything that he thinks about Jesus. If we could simply make sense of Paul's ideas, crawl into his mind

SO WHAT?
. . . .
Paul's Letters Are Hard to Understand (2 Pet 3:16)

At first blush, Paul may seem simple. How complicated is the "Romans Road" (all have sinned, the wages of sin is death, Christ died for us, and we need to believe in our heart and confess with our mouth)? Yet, we are the ones simplifying complex topics. "Christ is the end of the law" (Rom 10:4). That's plain, we might think. But Paul still observes Torah (keeps the law). Paul argues that we are no longer under the law (1 Cor 9:20; Gal 3:23), but his converts see him keeping the law and urging other Jews to do so. When Gentiles try to keep the law, he tells them not to, but he bases his argument on the law. Paul is not fickle; he is complex. We must study his letters and not dumb them down. We must let Paul speak for himself instead of rushing to squeeze him into a grid that we have figured out ahead of time. Paul's letters are worth the work.

and sort out his mental processes as he read the Scriptures, we would understand Paul's Jesus.[3]

To be sure, Paul spilled much ink grounding his interpretation of Jesus in a thick, theological reading of the Scriptures. But, Paul's view of Jesus also depended on his experience of Christ. And that shouldn't surprise us. After all, Paul's "conversion experience" didn't begin with some kind of epiphany while studying Isaiah. He didn't read about the "suffering servant" one day and cry out, "Eureka! This explains the cross of Jesus Christ." Instead, Paul repented; he changed his mind about Jesus because of his encounter with the Lord—an experience that didn't stop with the Christophany on the road to Damascus (2 Cor 12:1-10).

No tabula rasa. On that fateful day on the road to Damascus Paul didn't come with a blank mental tablet upon which Christ inscribed the gospel. In fact, the way Paul describes the encounter reveals that he already knew what the Christophany meant. We tend to think that Paul went scrambling to make sense of what happened, puzzling over the inexplicable while sitting in the Arabian Desert. This is a common fiction applied to Paul (which says more about our Western sensibilities regarding self-discovery than about the apostle): we see Paul poring over the Scriptures in the wilderness, building his "new" theology from the ground up, having to answer the question "What happened to me?" before he could preach the gospel. Nowhere does Paul or Luke describe such a scenario. In fact, Acts tells us that "immediately [Paul] began to proclaim Jesus in the synagogues, saying, 'He is the Son of God'" (Acts 9:20). Furthermore, Paul writes about the Christophany as if he were prenatally prepared for it (Gal 1:15). He described his first encounter with Christ as a prophetic calling, like one of the prophets of old. Like Isaiah, Paul's vision of God's glory came with a commission as well as a prediction that Israel wouldn't listen (Is 6:1-13; Rom 10:16-21). Like Jeremiah, Paul was appointed by the word of the Lord to preach to the nations in order "to destroy and to overthrow, to build and to plant" (Jer 1:4-10; 1 Cor 3:6-10; 2 Cor 10:4-5). Paul saw all of it through the lens of his Jewish heritage; he understood what seeing a

---

[3]This is the approach taken by many Pauline scholars, such as N. T. Wright, whose massive explanation of Paul's theology comprises two volumes totaling over 1,600 pages: *Paul and the Faithfulness of God* (Minneapolis: Fortress, 2013).

resurrected Messiah meant because Paul was a Jewish man.[4]

Paul grew up hearing stories about seers receiving visions, prophets hearing oracles so that Israel would know what the Lord was about to do. For hundreds of years all of these stories, all of these prophecies had been building a set of expectations in the minds of the Jewish people. When all the promises come true, when the messianic age dawns on God's people, when the notorious Day of the Lord finally arrives, when God visits Israel there will be hell to pay for some and heavenly reward for others. So, the way Paul saw it, the Christophany was another sign that the long-awaited Day of the Lord was dawning on them: "the night is far gone, the day is near" (Rom 13:12). "The fullness of time had come" because "God sent his Son, born of a woman, born under the law" (Gal 4:4), and for Paul that meant that he had a front-row seat for the end of the world (1 Cor 10:11).

Many things were supposed to happen on the day of divine visitation, when God shows up and makes good on all the promises that he gave to Israel. We don't have space here to rehearse the catalog of Jewish eschatological (end-time) expectations, but the resurrection of the dead certainly was a major feature of the end-of-the-world scenario according to the Pharisees (2 Macc 7:9, 14; 12:44; *4 Ezra* 7.26-44, 88-101; *2 Bar.* 30:1; 50:2-4; Wis 3:1-10). Therefore, it must have made quite an impression on Paul the Pharisee that a no-longer-dead-but-very-much-alive Jesus appeared to him. More than that, Paul recognized that God conquered death—the ultimate enemy of all creation—through Christ's resurrection, thereby insuring Jesus' eternal kingship as Son of David, Son of God: "the gospel concerning his Son, who was descended from David according to the flesh and was declared to be Son of God with power according to the spirit of holiness by resurrection from the dead" (Rom 1:3-4). Although we don't know this for certain, it seems Paul worked backwards, from the resurrection to the cross, to make sense of what God accomplished through Christ. Since Christ was raised from the dead (something that only God can do), and death is the result of sin, then the cross must have reversed the curse of the law of sin and death (Rom 7:24–8:4; 1 Cor 15:16-18). Paul goes so far as to say that Christ's cursed death on the cross was necessary to remove the curse

---

[4]For an introduction to Paul and his world, see David B. Capes, Rodney Reeves and E. Randolph Richards, *Rediscovering Paul: An Introduction to His World, Letters and Theology* (Downers Grove, IL: IVP Academic, 2007).

that the law brings against Israel and all humankind (Gal 3:10-14) so that the blessings of God could be realized by all of Abraham's faith-born children, both Jews and Gentiles (Gal 3:15-29). Christ took away the curse by becoming cursed, and Christ defeated death by dying—the cross and the resurrection proved it.

Since Paul interpreted the death and resurrection of Christ as an end-of-the-world event, he believed that God was the one who did it. Therefore, it shouldn't surprise us that God is featured as the main subject of Paul's writings. For example, in Romans Paul refers explicitly to God the Father around 160 times and to the Lord Jesus Christ less than seventy times. And, even when he doesn't mention God (e.g., when describing "election" or "predestination"), Paul assumes that his converts know that he's writing about what God has done through Christ (e.g., "in hope we were saved" [Rom 8:24], what scholars call the "divine passive"). That is not to say, however, that Paul had a diminutive view of Christ, as if he were some kind of demigod or angel. In fact, Jesus' equality with God appears to be a given for Paul. Indeed, the apostle often applied to Christ Scripture that explicitly refers to Israel's Lord God (Phil 2:10-11, referring to Is 45:23). On most occasions when Paul refers to "the Lord," he is talking about Jesus Christ (1 Cor 8:6). The correlation is unmistakable. Paul's Jesus is God. Therefore, everything that God ever said or did, from Adam to Abraham to Moses to David to the prophets, finds meaning in Jesus. Paul's favorite titles for Jesus—"Lord," "Christ," "Son"—are loaded with the freight of Jewish expectations

SO WHAT?

My Own "Damascus Road" Experience

Like Paul, many of us often talk about our own personal encounter with Jesus. But few of us actually have had an experience like Paul's. Besides, do we see the same results in our lives that Paul saw in his? Can our own change be described that dramatically? Paul gave up all things for Christ (Phil 3:8). His perspective on everything changed. He put his resume in the rubbish bin. Singleness for the gospel became the preferred option. He found himself in unfamiliar countries for the sake of the gospel. How much are your priorities rearranged? For you, has "everything become new" (2 Cor 5:17)?

of God and the last day. In other words, Paul had the story of God and Israel buzzing in his head when he made sense of his encounter with Jesus on the Damascus Road. And, therefore, when he turned around and read the Scriptures (the Old Testament) in light of what he saw, he found Christ, as well as his own gospel experience, on every page (2 Cor 3:12–4:5).

So, everything changed for Paul because of the Christophany on the Damascus Road: his perspective, his identity, his mission, his purpose, even his theology (especially his view of Israel and the law). Paul saw Jesus differently, saw how God was at work in the world differently, and therefore saw himself differently too. "From now on, therefore, we regard no one from a human point of view; even though we once knew Christ from a human point of view, we know him no longer in that way. So if anyone is in Christ, there is a new creation: everything old has passed away; see, everything has become new!" (2 Cor 5:16-17).

This is very revealing. Just as Paul couldn't write about the work of Christ without referring to God, Paul couldn't talk about Christ without talking about himself. Whenever Paul explained the significance of God's work in Christ, he couldn't help but speak of his own significance: "All this is from God, who reconciled us to himself through Christ, and has given us the ministry of reconciliation" (2 Cor 5:18). To defend the gospel, his view of Jesus, was the same as defending his apostleship (Gal 1:6-12). And we can see why, because Paul believed that his authority as an apostle came from the Christophany (1 Cor 9:1; 15:1-11). The presumption behind the resurrected Christ's commission of Paul was that the apostle to the Gentiles would know the gospel from the start because he received it from God (Gal 1:12; Acts 9:15-22). And, to know Christ, to preach the gospel, was also to know suffering, to experience the cross—a life predicted by the resurrected Christ ("I myself will show him how much he must suffer for the sake of my name" [Acts 9:16]) and confirmed by Paul ("For his sake I have suffered the loss of all things" [Phil 3:8]). Paul's view of Christ was a reflection of himself.

Crucified with Christ. For Paul, the gospel is more than a message; it is a way of life. The death of Christ is more than a theological necessity: "Christ died for our sins in accordance with the scriptures" (1 Cor 15:3); the cross is a necessary experience: "I have been crucified with Christ" (Gal 2:19). In

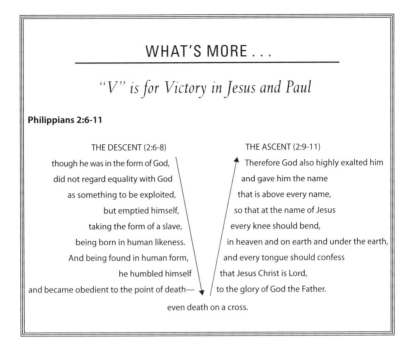

WHAT'S MORE . . .

"V" is for Victory in Jesus and Paul

Philippians 2:6-11

THE DESCENT (2:6-8)

though he was in the form of God,
did not regard equality with God
as something to be exploited,
but emptied himself,
taking the form of a slave,
being born in human likeness.
And being found in human form,
he humbled himself
and became obedient to the point of death—

THE ASCENT (2:9-11)

Therefore God also highly exalted him
and gave him the name
that is above every name,
so that at the name of Jesus
every knee should bend,
in heaven and on earth and under the earth,
and every tongue should confess
that Jesus Christ is Lord,
to the glory of God the Father.

even death on a cross.

other words, the gospel is not merely a proposition, a fact to know, a theological solution to the human condition. The gospel is a person: the Lord Jesus Christ. Therefore, knowing Jesus was inseparable from preaching the gospel message. Experiencing Christ was foundational to Paul's theological claims about Jesus. Paul knew Jesus Christ, not only through ongoing "revelations" (visions and oracles) but also through Christ's indwelling Spirit (another end-of-the-world sign). Paul believed that the actual Spirit of Christ/the Holy Spirit animated his body. And, through the Holy Spirit, Paul believed that he experienced the story of Jesus Christ, particularly his death, burial and resurrection. That is quite astounding. It's one thing to say, "I know a man because I've met him." It's quite something else to say, "I know a man because his Spirit is producing in me the story of his life." So, this is what Paul means when he says that he identifies with Christ. He believed that he knew what Jesus felt when he was crucified (even though Paul was never impaled on wood), because he bore on his body the "stigmata" of Jesus (Gal 6:17). He believed that he was buried with Christ (even though he was still alive), because he was baptized into a watery grave by Christ's family (Rom 6:4). He believed that he was already raised

with Christ (even though his body was falling apart), because he was re-
newed on the inside by Christ's Spirit every day (2 Cor 4:16-18). Participating
in the death, burial and resurrection of Jesus was the narrative of Paul's life
in Christ.[5]

This is why Paul can't talk about Christ without talking about himself.
Whatever happened to Christ, Paul believed would happen to him.
Therefore, Paul's daily experience of Christ continued to inform his inter-
pretation of Jesus. For example, when Paul encouraged his converts to
remain faithful to the Lord during his absence, he compared his imminent
return to Thessalonica to the parousia (return) of Christ (1 Thess 2:17–3:13).
When Paul was in a Roman prison awaiting trial, he interpreted what happened to Jesus through the looking glass of his own circumstances. Jesus
Christ emptied himself of divine privileges when he was executed by the
Romans (Phil 2:5-8). Paul did the same when he gave up his status to know
the crucified Christ in his sufferings (Phil 3:4-11). Furthermore, Paul
wanted his converts to have the "same mindset," to follow the "same example" (Phil 1:29–2:5; 3:15-17). As the Lord's chosen emissary, he identified
with Jesus so closely that to imitate Paul was the same as imitating Christ
(1 Cor 11:1).

All of this was by divine design, what Paul called "grace." To be "conformed to the image of [God's] Son" was the destiny of Paul and every
believer in Christ (Rom 8:29), because this is the way God overcomes the
world (Rom 8:31-39). God conquered sin and death through the cross and
resurrection of Christ. And, according to Paul, God continues to overcome
the world of sin and death through the Christ-shaped lives of those who
believe the gospel—the body of Christ. Paul knew that he couldn't do this
by himself. The story of Christ's life is much bigger than the apostle. So,
Paul experienced Christ in the church as well—a body of believers who
reign with Christ because heaven and earth overlap, the end of the world
has already happened (1 Cor 10:11; Eph 1:20–2:7). Indeed, by reflecting the
mirror image of Christ, the church was supposed to show what the end of
the world looks like now: God reigning over all creation through Christ-
shaped, cruciform lives (2 Cor 6:2-10). What a strange way to rule the world!

---

[5]See Rodney Reeves, *Spirituality According to Paul: Imitating the Apostle of Christ* (Downers Grove,
IL: IVP Academic, 2011).

Life comes through death, strength is found in weakness, wisdom is revealed by such foolishness, honor is claimed by boasting in the shameful cross of Christ. The sufferings of Christ produced resurrected lives (2 Cor 4:16–5:5). Why else would Paul live on the edge of danger, risking his life every day (1 Cor 15:30-32)? And, even though he discovered that most of his Jewish kinfolk refused to believe it, Paul thought that Israel shouldn't be surprised by his scandalous gospel, because it was predicted by the law and the prophets (Rom 3:21–4:25; 9:1–11:12).

> ## SO WHAT?
> . . . .
> *Following Paul's Jesus Is Downward Mobility*
>
> The way up is down. We talk a lot about leadership; Paul talked about servanthood. "Servant leader" is usually just tacking on the word "leader" so that we feel better about the servant part. Most of us don't mind being a servant until we are treated like one. The call to follow Christ isn't a call to be exalted but to be humbled. Following Christ landed Paul in jail, not on an award platform.

Israel's hero. Line up the major characters of the Old Testament—Adam, Abraham, Moses, David—and Paul would say that Jesus outdoes them all. Paul's Jesus is the visible image of the invisible God, creator and sustainer of all things (Col 1:15-20). Therefore, going back to the beginning of the story, Paul's Jesus was able to correct Adam's mistake; as the premier prototype of humanity, Christ restored the image of God (Rom 5:12-21; 1 Cor 15:20-28, 42-57). Abraham modeled resurrection faith, but Jesus is the resurrected Lord who made God's promises to Abraham come true (Rom 4:1-25; Gal 3:6–4:7). Moses gave the law, a "ministry of death, chiseled in letters on stone tablets," but Christ finished it, bringing the law to its appointed end, thereby establishing eternal life, providing true freedom, and inscribing divine glory "on tablets of human hearts" (2 Cor 3:7–4:18; Gal 3:19–4:11; 4:21–5:6, 13; Rom 7:1–8:23). Jesus launched David's kingdom, exalted to the right hand of God, reigning even now until he puts every enemy under his feet (1 Cor 15:24-28, 50-57; Phil 2:9-11; 3:20-21; Col 2:13-15; 3:1-4). Jesus was Israel's "superhero" because he finished what God started. Every reclamation project, every covenant, every promise God ever made was fulfilled in the Lord Jesus Christ. Israel didn't need to look anywhere else. Jesus embodied every hope for Paul, for his kinfolk, for his converts, and for all creation. It was just a matter of time for time to catch up with this glorious reality.

Since Paul's Jesus is already the Lord of all creation, Paul believed that Jesus is the Lord of time too. This is why, when Paul explained the mechanics of Christ's work, he never seemed to be troubled by the problem of time. Christ existed before time, and therefore he created all things—even time. So, God was at work in Christ before time began (1 Cor 2:6-9; Eph 1:4). Of course, there came a time—what Paul calls "the fullness of time" (Gal 4:4)— for God's Son to be born. But, Paul believed that Christ could and did appear on earth before his time (1 Cor 10:4). Christ could even bend time to God's purposes, making the Day of the Lord stretch out for days (Rom 13:11-12; 1 Thess 4:14–5:10; 2 Thess 2:1-3). In fact, according to Paul, the end of the world (resurrection) had already happened in time. So, Paul could speak of the resurrection of Christ in the past, present and future tenses. Indeed, Paul seemed to operate with what might be called "resurrection time." Because of the ongoing work of Christ, Paul believed that the present is constantly being redeemed by the future in light of the past: "everything old has passed away; see, everything has become new!" (2 Cor 5:17). That's why Paul constantly wrote "but now" as he tried to explain to his converts (especially the Gentiles) the significance of Christ and his work. Like yeast eventually leavening the entire lump of dough, the cross and resurrection of Christ was the apocalyptic reclamation of everything God had made, even to the ends of the earth. Therefore, all things begin and end in Jesus Christ (Col 1:16-17).

How Is This Jesus Different?

In the four Gospels Jesus anticipated that his disciples would carry on his work by remembering what he did and said. They were to make disciples by teaching their converts the works and words of Jesus. This is the dominant assumption in the Gospels when it comes to preserving the legacy of Jesus: because they knew him, those who followed him would be the ones to make disciples. But, on a few occasions Jesus intimated that his disciples would know him in a mystical way, either by his spiritual presence (Mt 18:20; 25:37-40; 28:20) or through the power of the Holy Spirit (Jn 14:16-20, 25-26;

15:26–16:7). What is suggestive in the Gospels is dominant in Paul's letters. That is, Paul seems to be the one to explain what Jesus meant when he said that his disciples would know him because they experienced his spiritual, empowering presence. And, as far as Paul is concerned, such a personal experience of Christ is available to all who believe, whether they knew the earthly Jesus or not. Indeed, Paul believed that knowing Christ through firsthand experience was no less important than gaining secondhand information about Jesus from James, Peter and John (Gal 1:11-12; 2:2-9). So, Paul was the perfect apostle to the Gentiles, for his converts could know Jesus just like Paul did. Regardless of background—whether Jew or Gentile, male or female, slave or free—to believe the gospel is to know Paul's Jesus, and to know Paul's Jesus is to experience the story of his life. This symbiotic relationship—both "Christ in us" and our "being in Christ" (what Paul called *koinōnia*, "fellowship" or "participation")—was Paul's major contribution to understanding Jesus.

Many of Paul's theological ideas about the Lord Jesus Christ overlap. For example, because Paul believed that "in Christ God was reconciling the world to himself, not counting their trespasses against them" (2 Cor 5:19),

---

WHAT'S MORE . . .

Kingdom Language

Jesus (in Palestine) talked a lot about the kingdom of God—there on the outskirts of the Roman Empire. John's Gospel (probably in Ephesus) preferred to talk about the kingdom as "eternal life." Paul's mission took him to the heart of the empire. The closer you get to Rome, the more politically loaded a word such as "kingdom" becomes. Not every reference in the New Testament has imperial overtones, not every New Testament action or saying had the Roman Empire in its sights, but Paul here may well be avoiding politically charged language. He preferred "life in the Spirit" to share the gospel message in a way that stayed on track without sidetracking the listeners into local politics.

it's sometimes difficult to distinguish who did what in the logistics of salvation. In other words, in the work of reconciliation—turning enemies into friends—is God at enmity with humanity and is Jesus the friend of all? Or, when Paul refers to "the Lord," is he always talking about Christ? To put it in theological terms, it seems like Paul's talk about God (theology) overlaps with his talk about Christ (Christology). The same thing happens when the apostle is writing about the church as the "body of Christ." For example, when he refers to being "baptized into Christ Jesus," is he speaking christologically (identifying with Christ) or ecclesiologically (identifying with the church)? Ask a child brought up in church, "Where is Jesus?" The child either will answer, "He's in here" (pointing to the heart), or will say, "He's in heaven" (pointing up to the sky). We have Paul to thank for that. Such overlapping makes it hard to draw clear lines of separation. Did the world come to an end in the death and resurrection of Jesus Christ? Yes or no? Paul wasn't the only one overlapping ideas. Did Jesus believe in the kingdom present or the kingdom come?

Scholars call this "dialectic," opposing ideas held together in tension. They have come up with a handy phrase to make sense of these competing temporal and cosmic realities in Paul's thought: "already but not yet." Paul can speak of something as already a reality but as not yet happened. Paul used the "already but not yet" dialectic to explain the work of Christ: the resurrection of the dead, the end of the world, the identity of Israel, the defeat of Satan, and victory over sin. These things have already happened in Christ for the believer. And yet, they won't be fully realized until Christ comes back. Thus, I can speak of already having victory over sin and death but still not yet have it fully realized. Or, to put it in cosmic terms, heaven has already invaded earth because Christ has been raised. And yet, creation still groans for God's glory, when he makes all things new. We see the creative genius of Paul whenever he explained the work of Christ, both what Jesus did and what he continues to do for believers and all creation.

Finally, Paul's interpretation of the cross is one of the apostle's greatest contributions to our understanding of Christ. According to Paul, the cross of Jesus is God's work done not only for us, but also to us and through us. Paul used terminology from the world of commerce, law, politics and religion to explain how Christ's death effects salvation. These metaphors—

justification, redemption, propitiation, reconciliation, atonement—sound like Christian terms to our ears. But, for the most part, these words didn't carry much theological freight until Paul used them to make sense of the mysterious work of Christ crucified. Sometimes we push these metaphors

WHAT'S MORE . . .

Paul's Rich Imagery for Salvation

For the apostle, the riches of salvation are too great to be described in a single word or phrase. He used not only the Scriptures but also expressions from everyday life to describe the work of Christ Jesus.

1. *Reconciliation* is a relational metaphor drawn from political and religious life; Paul used it to describe how every person is separated from God and at odds with each other. According to Paul, Jesus did all that was necessary so that we can enjoy restored, healthy relationships with God and others (see 2 Cor 5:17-21).

2. *Redemption* is a common word of commerce, frequently used in Paul's Bible to describe God's liberation of the Hebrews from slavery in Egypt. Paul assumed that everyone is enslaved to spiritual powers, sin and death. On the cross Jesus purchased our freedom from sin's power and other dark powers that would destroy us (Rom 3:21-26).

3. *Justification* is a metaphor drawn from court. At its root the word indicates putting a person in a right and proper relationship (in this case with God). Some see this more as a declaration that we are in the right (despite our wrongdoings); others understand justification as God transforming us until we are "right."

4. *Adoption* is a metaphor drawn from family life; it implies a prior state of isolation or familylessness. According to Paul, Christ believers are adopted into God's family because Jesus is God's Son (Gal 4:4-6).

too far, trying to work out the logistics of how God made believers righteous through the cross. But, we can't blame Paul for that. Most of the time Paul used these metaphors as illustrative explanations—more suggestive than definitive. For example, every time we work through Paul's argument in Romans 3, students want to know how Christ's "sacrifice of atonement by his blood" is "effective through faith" (Rom 3:25). But, Paul doesn't tell us how. He simply claims that it is. We may want to know the inner workings of the mechanics of salvation, but Paul had more interest in teaching his converts what difference the cross makes in the everyday life of the believer—what we like to call the "so what?" factor. This, more than anything else, is what makes Paul's interpretation of Jesus different. So, it makes perfect sense that Paul would write letters and not a literary Gospel (as Luke did). And yet, behind every letter is the Gospel story of Paul's Jesus.

WHAT IF THIS WERE OUR ONLY JESUS?

We wouldn't know much about the flesh-and-blood Jesus if we relied exclusively upon Paul's letters. In fact, it's easy to get the impression from Paul (and other New Testament letter writers) that knowing Jesus requires very little biography—what Jesus taught, how he lived. Rather, we act as if all we need to know about Jesus is that God sent him to die for our sins and raised him from the dead so that one day he would come back to take us home. Seemingly inspired by Paul, we might be tempted to reduce Jesus to a theological idea, a necessary sacrifice for us. Then the gospel and the "Roman Road" would be the same thing. In fact, the only thing that Paul would be good for is to give us the ABCs of how to

SO WHAT?

I'm "Saved." Now What?

Many people suppose that Paul's primary concern was about evangelism and "the by-and-by." So, the Christian life is reduced to "getting saved and going to heaven." Well, what should we do after we are finally convinced that we are "saved"? What do we do now, before the by-and-by? Some think that we make sure that our friends are saved; that's how our faith is lived out at work. We talk to our co-workers about being saved. But this is a misreading of Paul. He actually doesn't talk about evangelism much. Nowhere does Paul encourage his converts to "go and share their faith." Instead, he spends most of his time teaching the church how to be the body of Christ.

get saved.[6] Furthermore, we would hold up Paul as the model of what a dramatic conversion should look like. All of us would need to tell the story of a striking encounter with God, a precise moment when we "saw the light." Every Christian must have a personal "Damascus Road experience." And, since Paul never forgot his Damascus Road, neither should you. In fact, if you can't remember yours, some argue, maybe you aren't saved. But this is where we have completely misread Paul. Paul didn't expect his converts to experience the Christophany, because not everyone is called to be the apostle to the Gentiles. Remember, Paul interpreted his initial encounter with Christ as a prophetic calling. To put it bluntly, Paul had a "Jewish" experience on the Damascus Road, not a "Christian" one. So, if we actually followed Paul's example, testimony about our "Damascus Road experience" would be not about how we "got saved" but rather about how God called us to a certain ministry.

If Paul's Jesus were our only Jesus, we would talk a lot more about the return of Christ. We would encourage our young people not to marry, since the time is short. But for those who couldn't control their sexual desires, we would encourage marriage only if it benefited the church. Since Paul wrote little about social justice, we would count on God sorting out the problems of the world on the Day of the Lord. In the meantime, we wouldn't try to win the culture wars, since God is the one who judges "outsiders." Rather, we would devote all of our energies to taking care of our own business, building up the body of Christ, trying to show unbelievers what the end of the world is supposed to look like now—a people marked by faith, hope, love. Paul's Jesus is concerned that we cast off (like old clothing) vices such as anger, wrath, malice, slander and abusive language (Col 3:8) and put on virtues such as compassion, kindness, humility, meekness, and patience (Col 3:12). Even though Paul was very involved in church planting and wanted others to support his efforts, he didn't encourage his converts to start new congregations. So, we wouldn't try to overwhelm the world by planting a multitude of house churches. Rather, we would encourage "the church" within each city to be obedient to Christ.

Indeed, one of the ways we would learn about Paul's Jesus would be to study carefully the church. Paul's Jesus inhabits Christians as the Spirit of

---

[6]What Scot McKnight calls pejoratively the "soterian gospel"; see McKnight, *The King Jesus Gospel: The Original Good News Revisited* (Grand Rapids: Zondervan, 2011), pp. 28-44.

God inhabits the temple. We are the "body of Christ." Therefore, mutual concern among church members would be viewed the same as taking care of Christ. We might be organized more like the Amish, where the communities look after their members. There would be less focus on outsiders and more care for our own. We would constantly monitor the health of the body. We would worry a lot about church and how we are doing it. Are we are observing the Lord's Supper correctly? Are wives talking too much? Are husbands loving their wives sacrificially? And what about spiritual gifts? Are members using them properly or just showing off? Do slaves complain too much? Are owners too harsh—wait, slaves? Lawsuits wouldn't sully the church's reputation, hanging out our dirty laundry for all to see. We would be harder on our church leaders. We might have questionnaires for prospective elders (who would have to be older than fifty). We would want to know things such as "Is your wife good at hospitality? Do you like to argue? How many glasses of wine do you drink per day? Are you a good teacher?" We would have no trouble with the double standard that leaders must be held to higher moral code. We would never allow young pastors to lead our churches. In fact, a handsome man, young and oozing charisma, would be a bad sign for us, disqualifying him from consideration.

That's what is striking to most of us. Paul seems to be obsessed with things that we think really don't matter. We may appreciate that Paul emphasized having a personal relationship with Jesus through everyday experiences of Christ's spiritual presence. But to us, Paul seems to put too much weight on the collective identity of the church, talking as if it were just as crucial to the witness of Christ. In fact, the only way to make sense of Paul's Jesus and our life in him is to rely upon our reading together the Scriptures—the real-life, Jewish, flesh-and-blood story of God's dealing with Israel and the world. Therefore, the life, death, burial and resurrection of Christ had to make sense "according to the Scriptures" because Paul's Jesus was the man who fleshed out the story of Israel's hope that one day God would "tear open the heavens and come down" (Is 64:1). That's why, for Paul, the Old Testament functioned as his literary Gospel.

So, imagine what we would do if we didn't have Matthew, Mark, Luke or John. How would we know Jesus and make sense of our experience of Christ? We probably would follow Paul's example, poring over the Old Testament to see the story of Jesus and our life together in Christ on every page. Paul would remind us that we are part of a bigger story. A recent conversation with a student reveals our myopia. Having just heard a lecture on Galatians 3, trying to follow the implications of Paul's argument, a student raised his hand.

Student: Why does Paul spend so much time talking about Abraham? Who cares? As long as you believe in Jesus, that's all that matters.

Me: But Jesus was a Jew. Doesn't that make any difference to you?

Student: Well, yeah. I guess he had to be *something* because he was human.

Me: So his ethnicity is irrelevant?

Student: No, not for him. But, it really doesn't matter to me.

Me: But what about the promises God made to Abraham?

Student: I get that. It was really important to Paul. But he was Jewish too. Why should it matter to me?

Me: The Galatians were Gentile converts; Paul acted like it should matter to them. (*Pause*) Did you attend vacation Bible school when you were a child?

Student: Yes (*looking a little confused*).

Me: Didn't you sing the song? "Father Abraham, had many sons, many sons had father Abraham." Everybody sing: "I am one of them, *and so are you*. So, let's just praise the Lord . . . right arm, left arm. . . ."

Student (*after the class has quieted down*): Yeah. I never really understood why we sang that song.

Telling the story of our conversion experience wouldn't be enough. For Paul's Jesus, it is essential that we are children of Abraham. Sorting out how we participate in the grand narrative of God's reclamation of all things through Christ Jesus—being conformed to the death, burial and resurrection of Christ—would compel us to share our common experience, our fellowship in Christ, the story of our lives. Then we might appreciate why Paul's advice to his converts was grounded in the rich, theological soil of Israel's story. Paul's Jesus is good news; he is the fulfillment of every promise that God made to Abraham and his children. The Day of the Lord has come; the crucified Christ is raised from the dead. To know Paul's Jesus is to experience the power of his resurrection and the fellowship of his sufferings as his body. To share the gospel is to offer the sacrifice of our lives as the revelation of Christ. Then we would imitate Paul, perhaps even telling stories from the Old Testament, as we give our testimony to what Christ has done for us.

READ MORE ABOUT IT

Barclay, John M. G. "Jesus and Paul." In *Dictionary of Paul and His Letters*, edited by Gerald F. Hawthorne, Ralph P. Martin and Daniel G. Reid, pp. 492-503. Downers Grove, IL: InterVarsity Press, 1993.
Capes, David B., Rodney Reeves and E. Randolph Richards. *Rediscovering Paul: An Introduction to His World, Letters and Theology*. Downers Grove, IL: IVP Academic, 2007.
Fee, Gordon D. *Pauline Christology: An Exegetical-Theological Study*. Peabody, MA: Hendrickson, 2007.
Gorman, Michael J. *Cruciformity: Paul's Narrative Spirituality of the Cross*. Grand Rapids: Eerdmans, 2001.
Reeves, Rodney. *Spirituality According to Paul: Imitating the Apostle of Christ*. Downers Grove, IL: IVP Academic, 2011.
Witherington, Ben, III. "Christology." In *Dictionary of Paul and His Letters*, edited by Gerald F. Hawthorne, Ralph P. Martin and Daniel G. Reid, pp. 100-115. Downers Grove, IL: InterVarsity Press, 1993.

DISCUSSION QUESTIONS

1. Why did the Christophany have such a profound impact on Paul?

2. How could Paul encourage his converts to imitate him as he imitated Christ when he never met the historical Jesus? Are we in the same position as Paul? Should we encourage others to imitate us as we imitate Christ? Why or why not?

3. What was Paul's major contribution to the gospel?

4. Which was more important to Paul: the cross or the resurrection of Christ?

5. If we were to accept Paul's view of Christ as our own, how would it change our church's priorities?

6

THE PRIESTLY JESUS

Religion and politics are not supposed to mix—in polite company, that is. "The separation of church and state" is a mantra as American as apple pie. Many of us don't have priests, and most of us don't want a king. We handle both of those things ourselves. We do our own praying and we vote for our leaders. So when we read in the Bible about priest-kings—powerful individuals in whom religious and political authority is concentrated—we see it as a sweet but antiquated idea. Consider Psalm 110, a key passage for the book of Hebrews: the Lord God directs the king (Messiah) to take his place at God's right hand until his enemies can be subdued. Then God pledges an oath that must happen; it is not negotiable. You are going to get a priest-king whether you want one or not.

This book called "To the Hebrews" is addressed to Christians who knew well the Old Testament and sacrificial system. They had likely attended the temple and/or paid the temple tax. Regardless, they knew what temples were for. They were facing opposition and challenges severe enough to stop some in their tracks and to send them packing back to their ancestral faith, one protected by Roman law. The author of Hebrews—let's call him "the Preacher," for the letter was likely a sermon before it was a letter—is urging them not to abandon the priest-king whom God has installed. So he moves back through the tradition to show that in every way Jesus is better than, more than, and greater than any shadow of salvation that they have known before.

WHO DOES THE PREACHER SAY THAT I AM?

Jesus, the Great High Priest. The major innovation in Hebrews is this: the preacher's Jesus is the exalted Christ, the great, heavenly high priest who has finally provided an effective sacrifice for sin (Heb 7:27; 9:11-12, 26-28). This theme is developed in the midsection of the letter, but there is a hint of it in the poetic opening as the Preacher describes the work of Jesus: "When he had made purification for sins, he sat down at the right hand of the Majesty on high" (Heb 1:3 [cf. Heb 9:14, 26-28]). Making purification for sins is, of course, the chief task of the temple priests (Heb 5:1-4; 9:1-10), and the Preacher offers a priestly interpretation of the sacrifice and death of Jesus. But much is made of the fact that when Jesus entered the world, he was not yet ready for the task—an idea that strikes many modern readers as odd, if not slightly heretical.

Although Jesus was God's Son, co-creator and sustainer of the world, the embodiment of divine Wisdom, he still lacked what was needed to take on all his high priestly duties. What made him "right for the job" was something that could happen only on earth. The priestly Jesus had to enter our broken, fallen world, take on feeble flesh like ours, be tempted in every manner as we are, and then suffer at the hands of cruel executioners. According to Hebrews, Jesus was the pioneer of salvation precisely because what he suffered made him the perfect high priest (Heb 2:10; 5:9; 9:9; 12:23). Even though he was already God's Son, he had to learn obedience through suffering (Heb 5:8). Like the rest of the children of Abraham (Heb 2:17), he was tested in every way so that he could sympathize with humanity's weaknesses (Heb 4:15). He was tempted, but he never fell into sin. It is here that the language of incarnation intersects with Jesus' move toward priestly perfection.

The Preacher says (Heb 5:7), "In the days of his flesh, Jesus offered up prayers and supplications, with loud cries and tears, to the one who was able to save him from death, and he was heard because of his reverent submission." The phrase "the days of his flesh" suggests the incarnation, but it also underscores how prone Jesus was to the vicissitudes and weaknesses faced by every person (cf. 2 Macc 11:6). Many relate this passage to Jesus' prayer in the garden of Gethsemane (Mt 26:36-46; Mk 14:32-42; Lk 22:39-46), but it need not be any more than the recognition that Jesus lived a priestly life as well as died a priestly death. If Jesus ever lives to be an advocate for humanity, those intercessions did not begin when he sat down at the right hand of God in heaven; they began during his time "in the flesh." Suffering, then, is what made Jesus fit for the job as a priest, not just the suffering that he experienced as he crossed the threshold of death, but all the sufferings and hardships that he endured because of his human flesh.

WHAT'S MORE . . .

What Is a Priest?

If Hebrews makes so much of Jesus as the Great High Priest, perhaps it is important to stop here and ask, "What is a priest? What does a priest do?" The answers may well have been clear to the preacher's first audience, but may not be to ours today. Simply put, a priest is a mediator between God and humankind.

A priest communicates God's love and blessings to us

God
↓
priest
↓
people

God
↑
priest
↑
people

A priest carries our concerns up to God

In Jesus' day the main duties of priests were carried out in the sacred precincts of the Jerusalem temple. They had daily duties as well as special ones during sacred times such as Sabbaths and festivals, especially the Day of Atonement. When God gave the law to Israel at Sinai, he directed the tribe of Levi to serve as priests among the people. He set up a system of repentance, restitution and sacrifices that would help to deal with the guilt and some of the consequences of sin. But, as the author of Hebrews tells it, neither the law nor the actions of the priests were effective in dealing with the injury that sin continued to exact against God's good creation. Sin had to be dealt a final, lethal blow. So the priestly Jesus comes into the world to establish a different kind of priesthood (see the textbox "What Is a Priest?"), for no priest from the world of copies and shadows could completely eradicate sin and its ill effects. Salvation would come—after all, God had promised a new covenant (Jer 31:31-34)—but it could come only from above, where realities and patterns reside.

The Preacher is convinced that what is most real, what is most true, is the unseen. So he spends valuable time contrasting the heavenly realities with the earthly shadows. Of all New Testament books, none uses a more explicit Platonic ideal. In other words, what is true and real exists in the heavenly world; this earthly realm has only copies. The Preacher, citing Exodus 25:40, says, "They [Levitical priests] offer worship in a sanctuary that is a sketch and shadow of the heavenly one; for Moses, when he was about to erect the tent, was warned, 'See that you make everything according to the pattern that was shown you on the mountain'" (Heb 8:5). According to tradition, when Moses ascended Mount Sinai, he peered into heaven to behold the true tabernacle and all its furnishings; it was to serve as a pattern for the artisans below to copy as they assembled the earthly tent.

Put another way, what appears real and true to the naked eye is, in fact, fleeting and flimsy, lacking in true substance. The temple in Jerusalem was considered the holiest place on earth. It seemed real enough, with its massive stone construction, constant flurry of activities and daily sacrifices. But the Preacher declares that as real as the temple appeared to be, it was merely a copy or shadow of another place, the heavenly temple. Whatever took place in the shadowy temple below provided temporary relief from the problems that plagued God's people, but it could not effect the permanent change that people needed and longed for. This is where the priestly Jesus, the Great High Priest, comes in.

After he made purification for sins (the crucifixion), he passed through the heavens (the ascension) on his way to take his place at God's right hand (Heb 4:14-15). Whereas many high priests have lived and died down below, there is only one true high priest, who has been appointed by God (Heb 5:5;

cf. Ps 2:7). The priestly Jesus has already entered in the holiest place to minister in the sanctuary and true tent erected by the Lord himself. Earthly sacrifice with the blood of goats and bulls is but a shadow of what goes on in the heavenly temple. The law that established this worship could not make anything perfect; it too was only a shadow of the good things to come. Therefore, the priestly Jesus has a more excellent ministry, is mediator of a better covenant, and offers better promises (Heb 8:6).

The contrast could not be starker. Down below, many priests offer sacrifices every day first for their own sins and then for the sins of others; the priestly Jesus, however, offers himself "once for all" for the sins of others (Heb 7:27). Because he was sinless, Jesus had no need to sacrifice for his own sins before offering an atoning sacrifice on behalf of others. Likewise, because he had been made perfect through his sufferings, the priestly Jesus had no need to sacrifice himself over and over again; his sacrifice was a once-for-all event that changed everything.

In his ascension Jesus entered the celestial temple with his own blood, for the heavenly temple needed a better sacrifice than what the blood of bulls and goats could provide (Heb 9:11-12, 23). The blood of Christ shed on the cross was destined to accomplish more than all the earthly sacrifices combined. So the priestly Jesus entered into heaven, into God's immediate presence, on our behalf once for all with himself as the sacrifice (Heb 9:24-26). So the Preacher's Jesus becomes the mediator of a new covenant fulfilling the words of the prophet Jeremiah (Jer 31:31-34). All of this was God's will through and through. Christ made a single sacrifice for sin, and then he sat down at God's right hand, waiting for his enemies to bow down and become his footstool (Heb 10:12-13). With a single offering Jesus perfected for all time those who come in faith. In language thick with temple imagery, the Preacher affirms,

> Therefore, my friends, since we have confidence to enter the sanctuary by the blood of Jesus, by the new and living way that he opened for us through the curtain (that is, through his flesh), and since we have a great priest over the house of God, let us approach with a true heart in full assurance of faith, with our hearts sprinkled clean from an evil conscience and our bodies washed with pure water. (Heb 10:19-22)

For the Preacher, the flesh and blood of Jesus, the true humanity of God's Son that has been shaped in the crucible of suffering, has become the means by which all men and women of faith now approach God. But there is more: through Jesus, who sits enthroned next to God, the faithful now offer a new kind of sacrifice, the sacrifice of praise, the fruit of lips that confess his name (Heb 13:15). The priestly Jesus has become the one "through whom" God is approached in worship and prayer.

Other New Testament writers dabbled in sacrificial imagery in order to express something of Jesus' transcendent significance (e.g., Mk 10:45; Rom 3:21-26), but the author of Hebrews does more to develop Jesus' priestly role than any other. In part, this has to do with a mysterious account found in Genesis and a rather minor figure who may not have been so minor after all.

How could a messiah be a priest? The priestly Jesus of Hebrews gains even greater status by virtue of his association with the mysterious figure Melchizedek. At strategic places in his letter (Heb 5:6; 7:17, 21) the Preacher applies to Christ the words of Psalm 110:4: "The LORD has sworn and will not change his mind, 'You are a priest forever, according to the order of Melchizedek.'" Melchizedek is one of the most interesting and enigmatic figures in the

SO WHAT?

The Pattern for the Earthly Temple

Modern people tend to look down on the Levitical system, with its bloody animal sacrifices and heavily decorated priests. We think that we have "moved on" to a more civilized faith by leaving behind all that talk of blood and guts. But we must remember that this wasn't an institution that the Hebrews invented in the hope that somehow God would like it; it was God's idea from the beginning. The earthly temple was built according to the celestial temple. God had Moses and the people of Israel set it up for a purpose. He designed the tent, its furnishings and the priestly garb. It wasn't something that the ancient Hebrews conjured up and God decided to tolerate for a while. When we talk about Jesus dying for our sins, we need to remember that this is Jewish, sacrificial language. Indeed, the priestly Jesus serves as a corrective to the anti-Semitism common among some evangelicals.

Hebrew Bible. We hear of him briefly as Abraham is returning from battle
(Gen 14:17-20). In the King's Valley, Melchizedek and the king of Sodom go
out to meet the victorious Abraham, offering him bread and wine, blessing
him, and collecting "a tithe" from the spoils of battle. The name "Melchizedek"
means "king of righteousness," and he is king over "Salem" (an early name

---

WHAT'S MORE . . .

Jesus the Great High Priest

Central to Hebrews is the contrast between the high priesthood of Jesus
and Levitical priesthood. Here are the main contours of that contrast:

Jesus the Great High Priest	Levitical Priests
From the tribe of Judah (Heb 7:13-14)	From the sons of Levi (Heb 7:11)
According to the order of Melchizedek (Heb 7:11, 15, 17)	According to the order of Aaron (Heb 7:11)
Became a priest by virtue of his resurrection (Heb 7:16)	Became priests by their physical descent (Heb 7:16)
Brought a better hope (Heb 7:19) and a better covenant (Heb 7:22)	Law made nothing perfect (Heb 7:18-19)
Made a priest with an oath (Heb 7:20-21)	Made priests without an oath (Heb 7:20)
Unique priest (God's Son), with a permanent priesthood, forever lives to make intercession (Heb 7:24-25)	Many priests required because death ended their service (Heb 7:23)
One-time sacrifice of the sinless one for the sins of all (Heb 7:26-27)	Daily sacrifices for their own sins and then for the sins of others (Heb 7:26-27)

---

for the city that would become Jerusalem), from the Hebrew root for "peace"
(*šlm*). These names and their associations offered the Preacher a rich opportunity to make connections with Jesus. If Melchizedek was the king of
righteousness and king of peace, how much more so is Jesus!

Melchizedek shows up only one more time in the Hebrew Bible, in Psalm
110, a psalm that seems to have functioned as a coronation psalm for Davidic
kings. The essential message of the psalm is this: when God installs his king

upon the throne in Jerusalem, he promises to defeat his enemies and establish him as an eternal priest in accordance with the order of Melchizedek. Although the promise could be applied to any Davidic king, the Preacher thought it especially appropriate as a way of underscoring the honor and significance of Jesus the Messiah, David's son.

What, then, should we make of Melchizedek as he steps out of the fog of history, disappearing only to return once in the psalms? Interestingly, he brought bread and wine to Abraham, the same elements Jesus later broke and gave to his disciples with the words of institution: "Take, eat; this is my body. . . . Take, drink; this is the blood of the new covenant." More significant to the Preacher is the fact that Abraham, the father of all Jews, paid a tithe to Melchizedek and received his blessing. Hundreds of years later God established an earthly priesthood through one branch of Abraham's family, the sons of Levi (the son of Jacob/Israel). He commanded the Levites to collect a tithe (10 percent) from the children of Abraham to demonstrate their fidelity to the covenant promises. But these latter-day priests belonged to an order that had already paid tithes to Melchizedek.

Although it is foreign to those of us born in Western, individualistic societies, ancient people had a more corporate understanding of personality. Accordingly, all the children of Abraham, including the Levites, were located in Abraham by virtue of their heritage. They were "the seed of Abraham," and so they were (in a real sense) present in him the day he received Melchizedek's blessing and offered him a portion of the spoils (Heb 7:4-10). By virtue of their ancestry, when Abraham was blessed, all future Levites were blessed in him. When Abraham paid a tithe, all future Levites (who were inside Abraham) paid a tithe to Melchizedek (and his order who were inside of him). By this "corporate" understanding, the one who blesses is greater than the one blessed, and the one who received tithes is greater than one who paid them. Therefore, Melchizedek (and Jesus, who belongs to his order) is ranked higher than all those priests who served in the temple in Jerusalem. Now, there is nothing to suggest that Jesus is related to Melchizedek by his physical ancestry. Melchizedek's own mysterious origins work against that (Heb 7:3). But the priestly Jesus is placed in Melchizedek's order by God's decree: "The LORD has sworn and will not change his mind, 'You are a priest forever, according to the order of Melchizedek.'" God's decree trumps physical descent. This meant, among other things, that if any Jewish Christians were tempted to cover their sins and guilt by appeal to the priests in Jerusalem, they should recognize that the priestly Jesus, like Melchizedek before him, occupies a higher rank and has provided a greater redemption. When Jesus takes away sin and guilt through his sacrifice, they are taken away for good.

For the Preacher, the mysterious figure of Melchizedek, king of righteousness and peace, was a precursor to the Prince of Peace. In his brief appearances in Genesis and Psalms Melchizedek opened a window into the mysterious plan of God to redeem the world. In Melchizedek we have an eternal priest who represents a higher order of priest-kings that ends with the priestly Jesus. There will never be another because he is the final, full, definitive revelation of God. There will never be another because his single sacrifice—once for all—is sufficient to cover the sins of the world. There will never be another because from his exalted place at God's right hand he rules the world with justice and exercises perfectly an eternal priesthood that perfects the imperfect, completes the incomplete, and orders the disordered.

Jesus, the Son of God. Throughout the sermon-turned-letter Jesus is referred to as "the Son," a title with both messianic and transcendent significance in other

---

SO WHAT?
. . . .
Pedigree Matters

Even though many Americans downplay the concept of ancestry, heritage and pedigree, most people in the world today consider it very important. Rather than asking the Scriptures to reflect our modern American values and reading Hebrews against our cultural expectations, we need first to understand the cultural ideals that they reflect. After all, there is something to family and how you are brought up. We know that DNA matters, not just in matters of health, but also in the kind of persons we become. We accept predestination as a biological reality. "The reason I look and act like my father is because I am his son." So too, the Jewish people accepted the fact that God predestined certain individuals for royalty (tribe of Judah) and others to serve him as priests (the Levites). So, the question was "How could a 'son of David' be a priest of God?"

New Testament books. Much of the argument for the letter turns on the conviction that as God's Son, Jesus' status is exalted far above any of God's earlier messengers. Prophets may have spoken for God in the past, but in the last days God has spoken finally through his Son (Heb 1:1-2). Angels may have mediated God's covenant to Israel, but God has never invited them to sit at his right hand or called them "Son" (Heb 1:3-14). Moses may have been faithful to God—he led the Hebrew slaves from bondage, gave them God's law at Mount Sinai, and shepherded them through the desert—but Christ is faithful over God's house as a "Son" (Heb 3:1-6). What Jesus accomplished as God's Son is more than, better than, greater than that of all previous messengers. This is because the priestly Jesus is the heir of all things, co-creator and sustainer of the world (Heb 1:2-3).

In the hymnic opening to the letter the language of divine Wisdom is clearly associated with Jesus. As we noted earlier, Paul's Jesus and John's Jesus have already been connected with Wisdom. When the Preacher identifies Jesus as co-creator, sustainer, the reflection of God's glory, the exact imprint of God's being, he is explicitly linking God's unique Son with Wisdom (see, e.g., Prov 8:21-31; Wis 9:9; Sir 24:8; Bar 3:9–4:4). This means that Jesus existed before his earthly sojourn, participated in the world's creation, and embodies divine Wisdom. Closely related to this is the incarnation, a theological claim that the Preacher takes in new and important directions. For example, when God "brings the firstborn into the world," he directs all the angels to worship him (Heb 1:6). The Preacher quotes Psalm 8:4-6, a psalm celebrating God's creation and care of humanity, and associates it with the priestly Jesus, who for a little while was made lower than the angels (Heb 2:5-9). In another bit of exegetical play he places Psalm 40:6-8 (LXX) on the lips of the priestly Jesus when he "came into the world" with "a body you [God] have prepared for me" (Heb 10:5). Indeed, the incarnation is acknowledged early and often in this letter to Hebrew Christians and expressed through very earthy language about Jesus' body, flesh and blood.

The suffering, death and resurrection/exaltation of Jesus play key roles in Hebrews. The Preacher elaborates on these crucial events in a series of playful yet involved scriptural exegeses. Psalm 110:1, in particular, is a passage that many Christian writers found to be important in describing

Jesus' enthronement to the right hand of God (cf. Acts 2:34; Eph 1:20; Col 3:1). More than any other book, Hebrews explores this psalm and works out the implications of other aspects of it (e.g., Ps 110:4). Unlike some other New Testament books, Hebrews has only passing reference to the parousia (Heb 9:28). The Preacher's focus, it seems, is on the past and present work of Christ.

How Is This Jesus Different?

We are accustomed to thinking of Jesus of Nazareth in Galilee. He is at home on the road, moving from village to village teaching in the synagogues, a Jesus who proclaims the reign of God and heals the sick to manifest heaven's will. In the Gospels Jesus eats fish besides the lake and sets out in a boat for the eastern shore. The priestly Jesus is most at home in the heavenly temple. He is not so much *from* this world as *for* this world. Nowhere else do we have Jesus described in such a priestly role. Other New Testament writers portray him as prophet, Lord and Messiah, but never as priest. John's Jesus was often at odds with the temple priests and denounces what the institution had become under the control of the reigning religious authorities. But in a fashion that would make Plato proud, the Preacher emphasizes not the temple below but the real temple above. The priestly Jesus is in reality a heavenly Jesus.

The main reason that the priestly Jesus had to come in the flesh was to offer himself as the perfect sacrifice. So in many ways the historical details of Jesus' life are not important. What he actually said and did may be the subject of another sermon, but not this one. Here is a Jesus who is always the same—yesterday, today and forever. His authentic voice is heard primarily through the Greek version of the Old Testament, not in parables or pronouncement sayings. He both preexisted his earthly, fleshly sojourn as a co-creator with God and postexisted it, exalted to the right hand of God, where he lives forever to make intercession on behalf of the faithful. It may have been important that Melchizedek actually lived in history, but we know little about his life. Melchizedek becomes important for the Preacher and his audience because of what Scripture says about him. Likewise, it is important that Jesus lived in history, but Hebrews says little about his life. The priestly Jesus is important primarily because of what Psalm 110 says about him. As Melchizedek shows up, in flesh, at a particular time to do a particular thing, so also does Jesus. He must be here on this earth, living a sinless life, suffering, and becoming a sacrifice so that he can do the important thing of offering the true sacrifice in heaven, in the true temple.

What If This Were Our Only Jesus?

If the priestly Jesus were the only Jesus, we'd talk about salvation more in terms of perfection, purification and completion. In the closing verses of Hebrews the Preachers says it well: "Now may the God of peace, who brought back from the dead our Lord Jesus, the great shepherd of the sheep, by the blood of the eternal covenant, make you complete in everything good so that you may do his will, working among us that which is pleasing in his sight, through Jesus Christ, to whom be the glory forever and ever. Amen" (Heb 13:20-21). Whereas the first covenant failed to bring about the perfection necessary for humans to have a right relationship with God (Heb 7:11, 19; 9:9), Jesus achieved it by suffering in real flesh to become the final, perfect, unblemished sacrifice. The salvation that he brings therefore makes perfect all who embrace him in faith.

Since the Preacher apparently was fond of Plato's worldview, we would read Plato and perhaps even see him as "a Christian before Christ." Therefore, we'd grow to appreciate Philo of Alexandria (ca. 20 B.C.–A.D 50), who attempted a synthesis of his Jewish faith with Greek philosophy in ways that are still with us today. We would read Plato or Philo not as Scripture but perhaps alongside Scripture devotionally, much the way many Christians today read C. S. Lewis, A. W. Tozer and Thomas à Kempis.

Our focus, then, would be on a better country, the city to come, the heavenly Jerusalem (Heb 11:14-16; 13:14). We would agree with many evangelicals who view salvation primarily as escape from this world of shadows to the world above: "For here we have no lasting city, but we are looking for the city that is to come" (Heb 13:14). The created order below has been shaken and spoiled; it will not endure. But the heavenly cannot be shaken or spoiled; it will endure forever. Therefore, we would talk exclusively about the importance of going to the spiritual place called "heaven" when we die. In the meantime, we would look for Christ to appear a second time to save us (Heb 9:27-28), eagerly waiting in faith as our spiritual ancestors did (Heb 11).

Given the importance of Psalm 110 in Hebrews and the perpetual call to remember Jesus seated at the right hand of God, Ascension Sunday would carry more weight on the church calendar than Easter does. Although references to the resurrection are not absent (e.g., Heb 13:20), they are eclipsed by the Preacher's constant refrain drawn from the psalm.

Since Jesus dominated the priestly landscape so completely and perfected the office, churches wouldn't refer to their ministers as "priests." To call another person a "priest" or to establish a priesthood would seem irrelevant at best if not downright sacrilegious. As a result, Martin Luther would have never made "the priesthood of every believer" a central tenet of the Protestant Reformation. I don't carry my own needs and prayers to God; I have a mediator.

The Old Testament would be foundational to Christian theology and practice, just as it was to the unknown author of Hebrews. But since the Preacher quotes exclusively

---

SO WHAT?

Jesus Is Better Than . . .

The priestly Jesus allows us to affirm that truth can be found in other traditions. Asserting that Jesus is better doesn't require us to denigrate other belief systems. Pointing out all the things wrong with another's beliefs isn't necessary. Last summer, when I worked with ancestor worshipers on an island in the South Pacific, I didn't need to denounce their old beliefs. I started with the opening of Hebrews: "Long ago God spoke to our ancestors in many and various ways by the prophets, but in these last days he has spoken to us by a Son, whom he appointed heir of all things, through whom he also created the worlds" (Heb 1:1-2). I spoke about how Jesus is better.

---

from the Septuagint (the Greek translation of the Hebrew Bible), we probably would insist on a translation of the Greek version rather than the Hebrew version. That may mean that we'd have a few more books in our Bible, books such as 1–2 Maccabees, Wisdom of Solomon and Sirach, to name a few. Likewise, to follow the example laid down in this letter, we'd be listening for Jesus himself to speak to us through the Scriptures. Although Isaiah is the one prophesying in Isaiah 8:17-18, the Preacher assumes that he is listening to Jesus talking (Heb 2:13). Similarly, Psalm 40 may be a Davidic psalm, but the Preacher hears the voice of the priestly Jesus coming through loud and clear (Heb 10:5-6). With Hebrews as our guide, we may well read the Greek Old Testament listening for the authentic voice of Jesus.

Finally, if the priestly Jesus were the only Jesus we knew, we would sing songs praising Jesus as much for being our high priest as our atoning sacrifice. Next to the familiar pictures of the crucifixion of Jesus, stained-glass windows would feature Abraham bending his knee to Melchizedek. We would have passion plays that re-created Jesus entering the heavenly tabernacle, wearing the priestly vestments and offering himself as the eternal sacrifice. Then, as he sat down at the right hand of God, we would sing hymns of enthronement about our king, the priest of Melchizedek: King of Kings, Lord of Lords, and Priest of Priests. And with our songs of praise, we would see all of it as a shadow of things to come, a glimpse into the heavenly world, joining a worship service already in progress. Drawing near to the heavenly mountain, we would worship Jesus the priest-king with longing anticipation and reverential fear, having no doubts that our God is a consuming fire who inhabits the praises of his people.

Read More About It

Attridge, Harold W. "Hebrews." In *The Oxford Encyclopedia of Books of the Bible*, edited by Michael D. Coogan, pp. 361-67. Oxford: Oxford University Press, 2011.

Guthrie, George H. *Hebrews.* NIV Application Commentary. Grand Rapids: Zondervan, 1998.

Johnson, Luke Timothy. *Hebrews: A Commentary.* New Testament Library. Louisville, KY: Westminster John Knox, 2006.

Lane, William L. "Hebrews." In *Dictionary of the Later New Testament and Its Developments*, edited by Ralph P. Martin and Peter H. Davids, pp. 443-58. Downers Grove, IL: InterVarsity Press, 1997.

Discussion Questions

1. What do priests do? When have you been a priest for another person? When has someone else been a priest for you? How does this relate to the finished work of Christ?

2. What role have the incarnation, resurrection and ascension played in making Jesus the Great High Priest?

3. If Jesus' sacrifice is "once for all," what sort of sacrifice today are his followers called to make?

4. Hebrews elevates the priestly and sacrificial role of Jesus. Can you think of other New Testament passages where the writers celebrate Jesus' sacrifice?

5. If the letter to the Hebrews were all we had, what would we know about Jesus? What would we not know? What difference would it make?

7

The Jesus of Exiles

Are we living in the end times? How many times can Christians get psyched over that? Modern-day prophets were announcing Jesus' return in the year 2000. They supposed that God likes round numbers (and uses the same calendar that we use). The turning of the calendar to 2000 (which we nicknamed Y2K) didn't turn out to be such a big deal, and, obviously, Jesus didn't come back. A generation ago Hal Lindsey was warning us that Jesus was coming back in 1984. I wondered if I should go to college. After all, if the Lord was returning in the 1980s, what's the point? When we get close to 2030, I suspect that Christian preachers will start announcing the Lord's return (two thousand years after his resurrection). Whenever preachers announce that the Lord is returning and then Jesus doesn't, the ridiculing starts. Nonbelievers have an easy target, when they complain: "Where is the Lord? I thought he was returning." This isn't a modern problem. Christians in the time of Peter were wrestling with the same issue. They too were being ridiculed: "In the last days scoffers will come, scoffing and indulging their own lusts and saying, 'Where is the promise of his coming? For ever since our ancestors died, all things continue as they were from the beginning of creation!'" (2 Pet 3:3-4). Peter's church, in essence, asked more pointedly, "If the promised Messiah has come, why are we still suffering? Where is his kingdom now? He's not much of a king if he can't protect his subjects from suffering." Peter chides them for being surprised at suffering: "Beloved, do not be surprised at the fiery ordeal that is taking place among you to test you, as though something strange were happening to you" (1 Pet 4:12). In fact, Peter will suggest that we walk in Jesus' steps and join in his suffering as the path of atonement: "But rejoice insofar as you are sharing Christ's sufferings, so that you may also be glad and shout for joy when his glory is revealed" (1 Pet 4:13).

In this chapter we will look at the "leftovers" of the New Testament—though they don't deserve to be treated as such. These are usually referred to as the General Epistles. Traditionally, these letters were grouped as "catholic," meaning "universal"; that is, they were not addressed to a specific church. It is commonly thought now, however, that these letters were sent to specific congregations to address specific issues. If so, do we have reason to group together James, 1–2 Peter and Jude as sharing a similar perspective on Jesus? We think that these letters present Jesus from a Palestinian Jewish viewpoint.

In the centuries before Jesus many Israelites believed that they were still living in exile, not yet experiencing the promised restoration. In their thinking, the return of some Israelites to Palestine under Cyrus and the Persians was not the fulfillment of the promises of God to Jeremiah and Ezekiel, because they were still a conquered people, living under foreign rule. Large groups of Israelites still lived in Babylonia and Egypt. In Jesus' day many considered the temple in Jerusalem "Herod's Temple" and not the one the Messiah would build. Government was still in the hands of Gentiles (first the Persians, now the Romans). They contended that God's promised restoration had not yet come. Many Christians, both Jewish Christians and some of the new Gentile Christians, adopted this same viewpoint, seeing themselves as still living in exile. Jeremiah wrote to encourage God's people in exile during his day, and Peter re-preached this message to his flock.[1]

In 1 Peter God's people are told that they are "God's elect, exiles scattered throughout the provinces" (1 Pet 1:1 NIV). Even though the Gentiles were "once not a people" (1 Pet 2:10), they are now part of God's Israel, "a chosen race, a royal priesthood, a holy nation, God's own people" (1 Pet 2:9). Yet, since the exile wasn't over, they are to live as "aliens and exiles" (1 Pet 2:11) in this world.

---

[1]See the fuller discussion in E. Randolph Richards, "The General Epistles and Hebrews: In Exile but on the Brink of Restoration," in *The Story of Israel: A Biblical Theology*, by C. Marvin Pate et al. (Downers Grove, IL: InterVarsity Press, 2004), pp. 240-45.

Although in exile many of the Christians expected their exile would soon be over. King Jesus would return. His restoration (heaven) was to happen in Palestine (Jerusalem), and the end was near (1 Pet 4:7). Therefore, Christians were to settle down and make their homes during the exile (planting vineyards, as Jeremiah had encouraged), but they were not to become complacent. They were in an exile that was soon ending; therefore, Christians

---

WHAT'S MORE . . .

1 Peter's Re-preaching of Jeremiah's Message to the Exiles

God has a word for his people in exile.	Jer 29:1-3	1 Pet 1:1-2
God is using a foreign empire to mold his people.	Jer 29:4	1 Pet 1:3–2:10
God's people should submit to this empire and live in peace.	Jer 29:5-7	1 Pet 2:11–4:11
God has a plan for his people.	Jer 29:10-14	1 Pet 4:12
God tells his people to expect suffering, judgment, restoration.	Jer 29:15-23 Jer 29:24-32 Jer 30:1–31:20	1 Pet 4:12-16 1 Pet 4:17–5:9 1 Pet 5:10
God tells his people to live in Babylon as aliens.	Jer 31:21-26	1 Pet 5:12-14

---

were to live as sojourners. These letters then address that challenge. So, James and 1 Peter are encouraging their congregations how to live wisely in the interim, while Jude and 2 Peter are focused more specifically upon a problem with some false teachers: "Certain intruders have stolen in among you, people who long ago were designated for this condemnation as ungodly, who pervert the grace of our God into licentiousness and deny our only Master and Lord, Jesus Christ" (Jude 4), and these false teachers "promise them freedom, but they themselves are slaves of corruption" (2 Pet 2:19).

What, then, do these letters tell us about Jesus? Well, he seems to get little attention from James and Jude even though they were brothers of Jesus. Both call him "Lord" and not "brother." James mentions Jesus only twice in

108 verses, while his brother Jude mentions him six times in just twenty-five verses. In the letters of Peter, James and Jude, Jesus' teachings are not quoted either. Paul and John refer to what Jesus said, but these letters do not. Since we know some of Jesus' teachings from other sources (like the Gospels), we know that some of the things taught by James or Peter are actually teachings of Jesus. For example, Peter tells his readers that if they suffer for doing what is good, they are blessed (1 Pet 3:14), echoing Jesus' saying from the Sermon on the Mount (Mt 5:10), but Peter doesn't say he is quoting Jesus. He also repeats Jesus' teaching when he instructs, "If you are reviled for the name of Christ, you are blessed" (1 Pet 4:14), from "Blessed are you when people revile you . . . on my account" (Mt 5:11). Likewise, Peter cautions leaders not to lord their authority over their flocks (1 Pet 5:1-3), as Jesus cautioned (Mt 20:25-26). James also echoes a Jesus saying from the Sermon on the Mount (Mt 5:36-37), advising his readers to let their "yes" be "yes" (Jas 5:12).

WHO DOES JAMES SAY THAT I AM?

This is a bare-bones Jesus. James refers to "the Lord Jesus Christ" twice. If it weren't for these two verses (Jas 1:1; 2:1), there would be nothing uniquely Christian in the letter.

James is a Jewish wisdom letter. Like Proverbs, James talks about God a lot, referring to him as "the Lord and Father" (Jas 3:9). Anyone who lacks wisdom should ask God (Jas 1:5), because wisdom comes from God (Jas 1:8). God gives the crown of life (Jas 1:12); in fact, it is God who is the giver of all gifts (Jas 1:17). The righteousness that we pursue is God's righteousness. The religion that we practice is done before God (Jas 1:27) and focuses on the marginalized, whom God has chosen (Jas

---

SO WHAT?
. . . .
What Makes a Letter or Art "Christian"?

Is James a Christian letter if he mentions Jesus only twice? "Of course, it is," we would insist. Yet, we commonly critique Christian artists if their film or song doesn't mention Jesus repeatedly and prominently. The Christian gospel isn't just biography about Jesus; it is also about how his followers should live. The entire New Testament is gospel.

2:5). We believe that God is one (Jas 2:19), although James implies that this faith is inadequate if not accompanied by righteous deeds, such as were shown by Abraham, who believed God and was called "the friend of God" (Jas 2:23). We ought not to practice unrighteous deeds, such as cursing others who are made in God's image (Jas 3:9). We need to choose whose friend we are: the world's or God's (Jas 4:4). So, James admonishes us to submit to God and draw near to him (Jas 4:7-8). In the meantime, we should learn from the suffering of the prophets, who spoke in God's name (Jas 5:10) and from the endurance of Job, who saw God's purpose (Jas 5:11), and we should pray for God's help, as Elijah, a fellow human being, did and yet saw great things (Jas 5:17).

So, does James talk only about God and say nothing about who Jesus is? No, his references are few but powerful. Jesus is "the Lord Jesus" (Jas 1:1; 2:1). It is certainly Jesus' name that is the "excellent name that was invoked over you" (Jas 2:7). James stands in the Christian tradition of citing Old Testament passages that referred to Yahweh and applying them to Jesus (or "lord," *kyrios*).[2] For example, James talks about the coming of the Lord (Jas 5:7-8), but it is unclear if the Lord is God or Jesus. There is a conceptual overlap. It is fair to say that in James there seems to be an underdeveloped Christology and an undefined blending of the roles of God and Christ. James is not alone in this. In 2 Timothy we see another example: "In the presence of God and of Christ Jesus, who is to judge the living and the dead, and in view of his appearing and his kingdom . . ." (2 Tim 4:1) and "From now on there is reserved for me the crown of righteousness, which the Lord, the righteous judge, will give me on that day" (2 Tim 4:8). It is not readily apparent in 2 Timothy who is the judge, who is appearing, and whose kingdom it is. Likewise in James, we see the coming of the Lord (Jas 5:7-8) and Judge (Jas 5:9), in whose name we anoint for healing (Jas 5:14). Since James talks mostly about God, we might

---

[2]Note, for example, the Shepherd of Hermas: "Under the shade of this willow had assembled all those who were called by the name of the Lord" (Herm. *Sim.* 8.1.1); "They whose branches were found withered and moth-eaten are the apostates and traitors of the Church, who have blasphemed the Lord in their sins, and have, moreover, been ashamed of the name of the Lord by which they were called" (Herm. *Sim.* 8.6.4); "No one shall enter into the kingdom of God unless he receive His holy name . . . a man cannot otherwise enter into the kingdom of God than by the name of His beloved Son" (Herm. *Sim.* 9.12.4-5). See David B. Capes, *Old Testament Yahweh Texts in Paul's Christology*, Wissenschaftliche Untersuchungen zum Neuen Testament 2/47 (Tübingen: Mohr Siebeck, 1992).

assume the returning judge is God; yet, is that whose name they should invoke for healing?

James's teaching becomes a mirror in which we can see a reflection of Jesus. This Jesus resembles Matthew's, preaching about life in God's Kingdom. Our "yes" should be "yes" (Jas 5:12). We should be keeping the law (Jas 2:10). In fact, we should be good, Torah-obedient Jews who believe in the Lord Jesus Christ and who await the return of God to make things right. As with Luke's Jesus, the villains are often wealthy. James also warns us to be wary of riches, which deceive. The rich trust in their wealth for protection from the disasters of life. Yet wealth doesn't last; it rots and rusts (Jas 5:3). The poor are likewise warned against trusting in wealth. They chase wealth by seeking the favor of wealthy patrons (Jas 2:1-7). Repeating the warning of Proverbs, "Do not boast about tomorrow, for you do not know what a day may bring" (Prov 27:1), James uses a common Jewish image[3] of our lives as a mist, lasting only at the Lord's discretion, to denounce the wealthy who make plans to travel and conduct commerce (Jas 4:13-15). Wealth evaporates, and patrons can't be trusted.[4] Our trust should be in God alone, demonstrating that faith through works. "What good is it, my brothers and sisters, if you say you have faith but do not have works? Can faith save you?" (Jas 2:14). "So faith without works is also dead" (Jas 2:26).

Who Does Peter Say That I Am?

Peter is sympathetic to folks like us: "Although you have not seen him, you love him; and even though you do not see him now, you believe in him and rejoice with an indescribable and glorious joy" (1 Pet 1:8). We have indescribable joy over the salvation of our souls, in spite of suffering trials. In

---

[3] See, for example, Job 7:7, 9; Ps 39:5; Sir 11:18-19; Wis 2:1-4; 15:8; 2 Esd 4:24.

[4] A more careful reading reveals that James is upset with wealthy persons who pursue wealth by unethical practices such as dishonestly withholding wages from their workers. Likely, these are the same villains portrayed in many parables of Matthew's Jesus: landowners who abuse their tenants. Such condemnation stands in the Old Testament tradition, condemning those who "oppress" the poor, portraying them as the wealthy and powerful. James 2:6 (and elsewhere only Acts 10:38) uses the Greek verb *katadynasteuō*, which the Septuagint uses for the wealthy exploiting the poor: Jeremiah 7:6; 22:3; Ezekiel 18:7, 12, 16; 22:7, 29; Amos 4:1; 8:4; Habakkuk 1:4; Zechariah 7:10; Malachi 3:5 (see Peter H. Davids, *James*, New International Biblical Commentary [Peabody, MA: Hendrickson, 1989], pp. 112-13). Therefore, James admonishes the wealthy to treat employees honestly, for their cries reach the ears of the Lord of hosts (Jas 5:4), who is returning to judge (5:7-9).

fact, Peter (like James) argues that suffering for Jesus has positive effects, refining our faith like gold in a furnace (1 Pet 1:7) and producing virtuous fruit in our lives (Jas 1:2-4); so, we should endure suffering with joy. Peter's message isn't gloomy, though, because our suffering will be short-lived due to the Lord's imminent return (1 Pet 4:7; cf. Jas 5:8).

But, what does Peter actually tell us about Jesus? Unlike James, Peter mentions Jesus frequently. Peter is the "apostle of Jesus Christ" (1 Pet 1:1; 2 Pet 1:1). His first letter opens by identifying his recipients in a trinitarian way, as "chosen and destined by God the Father and sanctified by the Spirit to be obedient to Jesus Christ" (1 Pet 1:2). Jesus' resurrection is our imperishable inheritance (1 Pet 1:2-4) protected by the very power of God. By the precious blood of Christ we were ransomed from our futile ways that we inherited from our ancestors (1 Pet 1:17-19). Yet, Peter knows that this is not readily evident now in this age of suffering, and so he notes that it is faith in our salvation that will be revealed in the last days (1 Pet 1:5), which is soon (1 Pet 4:7; 2 Pet 3:3). In fact, the return of Jesus is emphasized much more than his resurrection (1 Pet 1:7, 13). Like God's people of old, we will suffer. We should expect nothing less, for our King himself suffered, and so shall we.

SO WHAT?

What Is Christian Suffering?

It is easier to describe what it is not:

1. It is not experiencing inconveniences amidst affluence. When your cell phone loses reception or your flight is delayed, this is not Christian suffering.

2. It is not losing the American "culture war." When a plaque bearing the Ten Commandments in your local courthouse is taken down, this is not Christian suffering. Nor is it when your "Christian" representative loses an election.

3. It is not the common trials of human existence. Getting sick, experiencing the death of a loved one, losing a job—these are suffering, but such are common to humankind, and so they are not Christian suffering.

So what is Christian suffering? Perhaps it would be best to ask our Christian sisters and brothers in parts of Asia, the Middle East and other parts of the world. They suffer violence for the sake of the gospel.

In spite of keeping their communities above reproach, Christians should expect the fiery ordeal of suffering for faithfulness as they await God's restoration: "And after you have suffered for a little while, the God of all grace, who has called you to his eternal glory in Christ, will himself restore, support, strengthen, and establish you" (1 Pet 5:10).

Although Peter says little of Jesus' earthly ministry, he adds an intriguing episode not found in the Gospels: "For Christ also suffered for sins once for all, the righteous for the unrighteous, in order to bring you to God. He was put to death in the flesh, but made alive in the spirit, in which also he went and made a proclamation to the spirits in prison, who in former times did not obey, when God waited patiently in the days of Noah, during the building of the ark" (1 Pet 3:18-20). Much ink has been spilled trying to explain this difficult reference. Most of Peter's hearers knew the Genesis 6 story of Noah as it was retold and elaborated in *1 Enoch*, where supernatural sons of God have offspring with the daughters of men, giving rise to demonic forces. Whether Peter is referring to Jesus preaching victory over fallen angels locked in prison or victory over demonic forces is unclear. Some Christian traditions use these cryptic verses to suggest that Jesus descended into hell to preach (offer salvation) to the dead; however, this view is more difficult to defend, since the New Testament elsewhere doesn't use "spirits" to refer to the dead. Regardless, Peter provides quite a colorful addition to the Jesus story.

Who Does Jude Say That I Am?

Jude's letter may seem brief to us, but it was of a typical length for a letter of his time. We might conclude that Jude says a lot about who Jesus is, because in his twenty-five verses Jude mentions Jesus six times. Three references tell us a little more than merely the title "Lord." Jude addresses his letter "To those who are called, who are beloved in God the Father and kept safe for [or "by"] Jesus Christ" (Jude 1). From this address we may infer either that God the Father keeps us safe for the benefit of Jesus or that Jesus keeps us safe. Jude refers once to Jesus as "Master and Lord" (Jude 4) instead of just "Lord." In the third reference Jude encourages his readers to "keep yourselves in the love of God; look forward to the mercy of our Lord Jesus Christ that leads to eternal life" (Jude 21). More literally, that verse says "the mercy of our Lord Jesus Christ to eternal life." Modern translators are assuming (drawing from other parts of the New Testament) that Jesus is the agent bringing us to eternal life. This certainly is likely (in light of the rest of the New Testament) but is more than Jude actually says.

In reality, Jude tells us almost nothing about Jesus. Unlike most of the New Testament (and modern Christianity), Jude tells us as much about the Spirit as he does about Jesus. It is those without the Spirit who are causing divisions and troubles in Jude's church (Jude 19). The solution is for Jude's people to build each other up and to pray in the Holy Spirit (Jude 20). Yet, as we might expect from a letter of twenty-five verses, Jude tells us little about either one. In fairness, the brief letter of Jude is addressing the matter of false teachers disrupting his church, and so we must not place wide expectations on it.

HOW IS THIS JESUS DIFFERENT?

These letters are mostly about what we do rather than what Jesus did. They talk about Christian living, not Christ's life. The story of Jesus is assumed. Peter mentions walking in Jesus' steps (1 Pet 2:21), but he doesn't tell us what those were. How is this Jesus different? He is the major assumption. There are reflections back to Jesus, but these letters assume that we already know about him. He is in the background. The help for daily living is Jewish wisdom, not abiding in John's

SO WHAT?

False Teaching Can Be Found Inside the Church

For Jude and 2 Peter, the greater problem perhaps wasn't persecutors on the outside, but rather the respected teacher on the inside. Amputation was the cure for this gangrene. "Go along to get along" and "tolerance" are American values that can lead us to allow false teaching. We must know what we believe. We need to know the great doctrines of the church that have been true for two thousand years and not put up with false teaching. Beware of the celebrity teacher who comes up with new doctrine. We stand on the shoulders of great saints. New is not always better.

Jesus. The metaphor is Israel in exile, not Paul's "body of Christ" or Luke's "following Jesus to the cross." So when James is offering help to his congregations, he offers wisdom. As Christians, we need to make wise decisions. There is no contrast of saved and lost, but one of wise and foolish Christians. Peter encourages virtue. Our character is formed by suffering—ours, not Christ's. Christ's suffering is emphasized more as an example (1 Pet 2:21), although he does use some atonement language (1 Pet 2:24; 3:18).

In James, Jude and Peter our faith in God, seen clearly in our good works to our neighbors in need, will make us friends of God. There is no talk about salvation from the kingdom of darkness or deliverance from evil, other than passing comments such as "Set all your hope on the grace that Jesus Christ will bring you when he is revealed" (1 Pet 1:13). There is no clear description of the gift of eternal life through Jesus Christ. Peter alludes to a sacrificial redemption, "You were ransomed from the futile ways inherited from your ancestors . . . with the precious blood of Christ, like that of a lamb without defect or blemish" (1 Pet 1:18-19), but we would really need other parts of the New Testament to make sense of this. Likewise, when Peter says, "You have been born anew, not of perishable but of imperishable seed, through the living and enduring word of God" (1 Pet 1:23), we can see "new birth" and Jesus as the Word of God, but we would need John's Gospel to do so.

Jude's church members should build each other up, "pray[ing] in the Holy Spirit" (Jude 20), to overcome the divisions troubling the church. Like James and Peter, the believers are to keep themselves in the love of God (Jude 21), saving others by snatching them from the fire (Jude 23).

What If This Were Our Only Jesus?

Clearly, Jesus is important; he is the Lord. More than that, James, Peter and Jude are saturated in Jesus; their teachings are rooted and grounded in those of Jesus. Are we to resist the prowling devil (Jas 4:7; 1 Pet 5:8-9) because Luke's Jesus prayed for Peter when the devil wanted to sift the disciples like wheat (Lk 22:32)? The Sermon on the Mount, teachings of Matthew's Jesus, shows up in the teachings of Peter and James (if we knew to look for it). James admonishes us, "Do not swear, either by heaven or by earth or by any other oath, but let your 'Yes' be yes and your 'No' be no, so that you may not fall under condemnation" (Jas 5:12). Thus, we have the essence of Jesus' teachings on oaths, but we would not have known that it was from Jesus. Peter tells us that even if we suffer for doing good, we are blessed (1 Pet

3:14)—a teaching that we learn from Matthew's Jesus (Mt 5:10). James asserts that God is a generous giver, probably reflecting Jesus' teaching: "If you then, who are evil, know how to give good gifts to your children, how much more will your Father in heaven give good things to those who ask him!" (Mt 7:11). In regard to leadership, Peter instructs his elders, "Do not lord it over those in your charge" (1 Pet 5:3). This teaching clearly goes back to the Jesus of the Synoptics (Mt 20:25; Mk 10:42; Lk 22:25) and is reflected in Paul (2 Cor 1:24). In fact, Peter doesn't tell us that his image of ministry as a shepherd arose from John's Jesus, when he restored Peter (Jn 21:15-17). Without the rest of the New Testament, we would not know that these apostolic teachings were actually dominical teachings. Jesus' voice is here, but we wouldn't know it, because we are hearing only the echoes of his voice.

What else would we know about Jesus? We would know that he suffered, and likely for doing good (since we are to imitate him). We certainly would know that he was raised from the dead and seated on the right hand of God (1 Pet 3:22), and that this would be revealed to everyone at the end, which was near. Nonetheless, if this were our only Jesus, we would know few facts about him and little teaching from him. We would know nothing of Mary or Joseph or even the other apostles. In fact, we would know that there were apostles, but we would only know two by name (Peter and Paul). Evidently, apostles were to write letters, since Peter and Paul both did (2 Pet 3:15-16). We would also know that Jesus had at least three slaves (Peter, James and Jude), and that the last two were brothers, but we wouldn't know or even suspect that they were also brothers of Jesus. Jude refers to Jesus as "Master" (Jude 4), but we would likely assume that he meant it in the ordinary sense of a slave's master. We would likely assume that these three were actual slaves of Jesus rather than slaves in the figurative sense that we know from other parts of the New Testament.

We would celebrate Easter, but we wouldn't know when to do it, and we wouldn't know any details about it. We wouldn't know details about the crucifixion or burial. We wouldn't know about Jesus' trials or even who killed him; we would have a passing reference to his "wounds" (1 Pet 2:24). When we read in Roman or Jewish sources that Jesus was a condemned criminal, we would wonder why and might dispute it as slander.

We would have a very Jewish and messianic Jesus, but we would not have a divine one, unless we put very serious weight on 2 Peter 1:1. This verse can be translated "through the righteousness of our God and Savior Jesus Christ," where both "God" and "Savior" refer to Jesus. This is likely the preferred translation,[5] rather than "through the righteousness of our God and of the Savior Jesus Christ," another possible option. However, if the Jesus of exiles were our only Jesus, it is unlikely that we would make such an incredible claim about him based upon one disputed translation in a letter address.[6]

WHAT'S MORE . . .

A Looser Canon

If this were our only Jesus, we might also have a different view of Scripture and canon. James tells us that the Scriptures say that God "yearns jealously for the spirit that he has made to dwell in us" (Jas 4:5), but this verse isn't found in our Old Testament, nor is the saying that James encourages us to use: "If the Lord wishes, we will live and do this or that" (Jas 4:15). Jude refers to several sayings and stories that are not found in the Old Testament. From other sources we know these actually come from *1 Enoch* and an apocryphal story of the burial of Moses (Jude 9) that probably came from the (now lost) ending to the *Testament of Moses*. Peter refers to Tartarus (*tartaraō*), the Greek place of the dead (2 Pet 2:4), a term not used by Christians elsewhere. Peter describes Noah as a preacher of righteousness (2 Pet 2:5), an image from Jewish tradition but not from Genesis. Because two of the three writers (Peter and Jude) use imagery from *1 Enoch*, we might be tempted to assume early Christians considered *1 Enoch* to be inspired. Peter refers to "the true proverb" and quotes Proverbs 26:11 and then another saying that appears to be an ancient Mediterranean proverb (2 Pet 2:22), which is not part of our canon. We might ask what this Jesus might look like, but we would also wonder what our Bible would look like.

---

[5]Following the Granville Sharp Rule; see Daniel B. Wallace, *Greek Grammar Beyond the Basics: An Exegetical Syntax of the New Testament* (Grand Rapids: Zondervan, 1996), pp. 272, 276-77, 290.
[6]Likewise, the very persuasive argument that the New Testament applies Old Testament passages of Yahweh to Jesus probably would not have been made if the Jesus of exiles were our only Jesus. Yahweh Christology comes from the pattern across a wide spectrum of New Testament authors and passages. In a similar vein, we would not even consider the variant reading of "Jesus" (instead of "Lord") in Jude 5. Only from 1 Corinthians 10 are we aware of a Christian tradition of placing Jesus in the exodus.

Our understanding of the divinity of Jesus is built upon multiple deeds and sayings by and about Jesus from other parts of the New Testament. Peter's comment is only one very small part of a large argument. If this were our only Jesus, would we pray to him, sing songs about him, or worship him?

Although our knowledge of Jesus would be slim, we would know plenty about how to act as believers. We would watch our words, especially our teaching, but our teaching would be largely about what we do, not what we believe (orthopraxy rather than orthodoxy). We would talk more about living (now) like Jesus. What would our churches do if James's were our only Jesus? We would likely emphasize three cardinal sins: a shallow faith (one without works), loose tongues (false teaching) and insensitive wealth (oppressing the poor). We would take care of the poor and the widows (Jas 1:27; 2:1-7, 14-17), knowing salvation comes from faith *and* works (Jas 2:14-26). We would have no teaching from Paul to balance this out. The emphasis would be on sanctification rather than justification, on the now rather than the later.

Our churches would emphasize our actions, not Christ's (1 Pet 1:14). We would stress resisting the devil, making wise decisions, enduring temptation and resisting sin (without referring to the power of the indwelling Spirit) in order to receive our crown of life (Jas 1:12). In order to be holy we would cleanse our hands and purify our hearts by obeying the truth (Jas 4:8; 1 Pet 1:15, 22). Our righteousness should be like Abraham's—a faith justified by works (Jas 2:22-23). Entry into the eternal kingdom of our Lord and Savior Jesus Christ (2 Pet 1:3-11) requires God's grace, since "His divine power has given us everything needed for life and godliness" (2 Pet 1:3). But it would also take our own moral efforts to complete our faith before the coming of Christ (2 Pet 1:5, 10), perhaps even "hastening the coming of the day of God" (2 Pet 3:12).

Our evangelism would look different. "Predestination" wouldn't likely be a part of our vocabulary. Christians might take virtuous living more seriously, worrying that worldly living could cause the loss of salvation. Without Paul's assurance that "the one who began a good work among you will bring it to completion by the day of Jesus Christ" (Phil 1:6), we would likely read Peter's warning more gravely: "For if, after they have escaped the defilements of the world through the knowledge of our Lord and Savior Jesus Christ, they are again entangled in them and overpowered, the last state has become worse for them than the first. For it would have been better for them never to have known the way of righteousness than, after knowing it, to turn back from the holy commandment that was passed on to them" (2 Pet 2:20-21). Christians could forsake knowing Jesus and be worse off at the end than they were at the beginning. We would not speak of the faithful as being predestined but only the unfaithful: "They stumble because they disobey the word, as they were destined to do" (1 Pet 2:8).

What would our preaching sound like? The Jesus of exiles appeals particularly to the disenfranchised. You who feel that you don't belong, don't despair. You are part of God's people, the true Israel. You are a building block, being assembled with others to make a new temple for God. "Come to him, a living stone, though rejected by mortals yet chosen and precious in God's sight, and like living stones, let yourselves be built into a spiritual house" (1 Pet 2:4-5). The call is not to invite Jesus into your heart, but rather to hear the Jesus of exiles call you to come and join his community. "But you are a chosen race, a royal priesthood, a holy nation, God's own people, in order that you may proclaim the mighty acts of him who called you out of darkness into his marvelous light. Once you were not a people, but now you are God's people" (1 Pet 2:9-10).

Our sermons would sound more like Proverbs. Preachers would emphasize wisdom, making wise decisions. They would emphasize deeds, actions. There would be less talk of theology and more practical advice. We would talk less about heaven and more about living holy lives now as we await our restoration. This present heaven and earth will be purified by fire and made new (2 Pet 3:10-12), so we ought to be "leading lives of holiness and godliness" (2 Pet 3:11), striving to make wise decisions now, climbing the ladder of virtue: "You must make every effort to support your faith with goodness, and goodness with knowledge, and knowledge with self-control, and self-control with endurance, and endurance with godliness, and godliness with mutual affection, and mutual affection with love" (2 Pet 1:5-7).

If this were our only Jesus, modern preachers wouldn't say, "Our freedom in America was bought with the price of spilt blood" (confusing the language of Jesus' sacrificed blood with the blood of American soldiers). In the gospel of the Jesus of exiles there would be no "freedom fighters." We are called to submit to, not fight, authority. We are to endure suffering, not eradicate it. While we await God to reveal our new community (1 Pet 4:13), we must live in our current surroundings as foreigners, endure suffering, entrust ourselves to the faithful Creator and do good (1 Pet 4:19). Just as the Jesus of exiles experienced suffering, so will we. We are told, "My brothers and sisters, whenever you face trials of any kind, consider it nothing but joy" (Jas 1:2). We would expect to suffer for our faith, enduring it "because you know that the testing of your faith produces endurance" (Jas 1:3).

As Jesus' suffering led to divine vindication, so will ours. All the foolish talk about a "health and wealth gospel" would be gone. In fact, our gospel would be anti-wealth (Jas 1:11). While our church today calls rich members "blessed," if James's were our only Jesus, we would say, "Come now, you rich people, weep and wail for the miseries that are coming to you. Your riches have rotted, and your clothes are moth-eaten. Your gold and silver have rusted, and their rust will be evidence against you, and it will eat your flesh like fire. You have laid up treasure for the last days" (Jas 5:1-3). American Christians are encouraged to save for retirement, plan for the future, set goals. If this were our only Jesus, we would speak more about living for today, not hoarding for tomorrow. "Yet you do not even know what tomorrow will bring. What is your life? For you are a mist that appears for a little while and then vanishes. Instead you ought to say, 'If the Lord wishes, we will live and do this or that'" (Jas 4:14-15). If James's were our only Jesus, procrastination might not even be considered a fault.

Although James, Jude and Peter describe God as the judge, Peter's Jesus will encourage us to await his revealing to vindicate us from our present suffering. So, when King Jesus appears, restoring us from our exile of suffering, and he asks, "Who do you say that I am?" we will answer, as James or Jude or Peter, "the Sovereign Lord, by whose name we are called."

Read More About It

Bauckham, Richard J. *Jude and the Relatives of Jesus in the Early Church.* Edinburgh: T & T Clark, 1990.

———. "2 Peter." In *Dictionary of the Later New Testament and Its Developments,* edited by Ralph P. Martin and Peter H. Davids, pp. 923-27. Downers Grove, IL: InterVarsity Press, 1997.

Davids, Peter H. *James*. New International Biblical Commentary. Peabody, MA: Hendrickson, 1989.

Jobes, Karen H. *1 Peter*. Baker Exegetical Commentary on the New Testament. Grand Rapids: Baker Academic, 2005.

Moo, Douglas J. *The Letter of James*. Pillar New Testament Commentary. Grand Rapids: Eerdmans, 2000.

Webb, Robert L. "Jude." In *Dictionary of the Later New Testament and Its Developments*, edited by Ralph P. Martin and Peter H. Davids, pp. 611-21. Downers Grove, IL: InterVarsity Press, 1997.

Discussion Questions

1. You may have encountered Christians who have undergone genuine suffering for the gospel. What can you say to them in light of Peter's exhortations?

2. Christians today emphasize professing faith in Christ. How might James's Jesus help us to live daily?

3. Jude and 2 Peter caution us about the celebrity teacher who espouses new and novel (but false) doctrines. If this happened in your local church, how should you respond?

4. Peter reminds us to pursue virtue, yet pursuing virtue is seldom discussed in many churches today. Why?

5. How might your local church be different if it emphasized more the Jesus of exiles?

8

THE APOCALYPTIC JESUS

If Jesus were a character in a political cartoon, what would he look like? That question may seem a little odd because most of what has been written about Jesus (whether in the Bible or outside the Bible) is set before the reader as "the real Jesus." This is what he said. This is where he lived. This is what he did. Therefore, this is what he means. These writers try to make Jesus come alive, giving a human face to his ancient voice so that readers would know him, admire him, follow him, perhaps even worship him. We all seem to be looking for a recognizable Jesus, a human one—even larger than life—one that matches our mental images of him with the power of his personality. He must be charming, endearing, witty, smart, passionate, gentle, warm and downright embraceable. In other words, we want a likeable Jesus, a familiar Jesus, a take-him-home-for-dinner-to-meet-your-parents Jesus. Everyone should be able to relate to the real, flesh-and-blood Jesus because, after all, he is one of us. That's why the seer's view of Jesus in Revelation is so shocking, so disturbing, so disorienting. In this "revelation of Jesus Christ" (Rev 1:1) Jesus doesn't appear to be human at all. Instead, John sees a heavenly man with eyes of fire and a sword-like tongue—a terrifying figure who is not pleased with the church. He sees a seven-eyed-seven-horned lamb that looks like it came from a graphic novel—a silent creature that stoically unleashes devastation on earth. This is not the Jesus we have come to know and love. Rather, John's vision of Jesus seems like a nightmare, and many of us would rather look away and pretend as if the apocalyptic Jesus never existed.

Who Does the Seer Say That I Am?

The Apocalypse (another name for the book of Revelation) is a strange world. So, it shouldn't surprise us to find a strange Jesus there. It's not that he's completely unrecognizable; there is something familiar about him because of the imagery that we derive from the Gospels and Epistles. In fact, Revelation counts on the ability of the seer (and readers) to identify Jesus, as he always appears without introduction. It's left up to us to infer that Jesus is the lamb, the rider on the white horse, and the fearsome figure who dictates the letter at the beginning of the Apocalypse. Some have suggested that he is the first of the four horsemen, the grim reaper of the grain harvest, and perhaps even the mighty angel with the little scroll. Who can tell? Indeed, the apocalyptic Jesus doesn't self-identify until the very end (Rev 22:16). Revelation relies upon those who have "eyes to see" Jesus and "ears to hear" what he commands.

Throughout the Apocalypse it's also difficult to tell when Jesus is talking. Publishers of red-letter editions of the New Testament have the impossible task of trying to guess which words are the words of Christ. Did Jesus command the seer to write (Rev 1:11)? Is he the unidentified voice from heaven (Rev 10:4, 8; 11:12)? Should the seven beatitudes appear in red letters (Rev 1:3; 14:13; 16:15; 19:9; 20:6; 22:7, 14)? What makes it more intriguing is that neither the lamb nor the rider on the white horse says anything. In other words, except for the remarks to John and the letters at the beginning (Rev 1:17–3:22) and personal greetings at the end (Rev 22:12-16), the apocalyptic Jesus appears silent throughout the unfolding drama of the book. Indeed, the lamb never speaks, and the warrior "King of kings" talks only with his sword at the final battle. It's easy to see that the apocalyptic Jesus is defined more by what he does than by what he says. Therefore, in the "revelation of Jesus Christ" (Rev 1:1)—not just a revelation *from* Jesus Christ, but a revelation *about* Jesus Christ—it's the actions of Jesus the author, the sacrificial lamb, and the warrior that dominate the Apocalypse.

Jesus the dictator of a letter. John the seer and Paul the apostle have much in common. Both experienced postascension Christophanies. Both wrote letters to churches. Both ministered to congregations in the same region of Asia Minor, especially Ephesus. Both referred to Jesus as a lamb

(Rev 5:6; 1 Cor 5:7), a letter writer (Rev 2:1; 2 Cor 3:3) and a conquering king (Rev 19:16; 1 Tim 6:15). Both emphasized the imminent second coming of Christ (Rev 22:20; 1 Thess 4:16), warned of a satanic messenger of great deception (Rev 12:18–13:10; 2 Thess 2:3-10), and expected suffering for the righteous (Rev 7:14; Phil 1:29). Both described the spiritual war in heaven between God and evil powers (Rev 12:1-12; Col 2:13-15). Both showed little interest in the earthly Jesus. And yet, for all their similarities, even a casual reader notices significant differences. For example, where Paul was reticent to give a description of what he saw during his visions of Jesus (2 Cor 12:2-4), John tells it all. When Paul wrote a letter, he claimed that Jesus was "speaking in me" (2 Cor 13:3) as he gave his advice, even though he made distinctions between his opinions and Jesus' commands (1 Cor 7:10-12). John, however, left no doubts about the authority of his words; he was merely Jesus' stenographer, writing down verbatim what Jesus said. For Paul, the realization that "the end is near" meant that there was still time for unbelievers to turn to God (Rom 11:25). For John, "the end is near" meant that time has run out, and no one can repent (Rev 22:10-11). Paul included apocalyptic imagery in his letters; John has a letter embedded in the Apocalypse.

It's that feature—a letter within Revelation—that makes us wonder. Why would the apocalyptic Jesus dictate a letter to John to give to the "angels" of the seven churches? Why not do what he did before, like he did with Paul—inspire John to write a circular letter to the Ephesians—especially if the seer is to be identified with the author of the Johannine letters? In other words, if Jesus had followed the customary pattern of inspiration, shouldn't the "letter to the seven churches" appear in our canon as 4 John, separated from the rest of the Apocalypse? Well, there are two obvious implications. First, the embedded letter must be very important to the overall message of Revelation; the entire Apocalypse (even the letter to the seven churches) was to be read by all the churches (Rev 1:3; 22:18-19). Second, the fact that the apocalyptic Jesus must speak "directly" to the seven churches—readers get to see Jesus dictate the letter, hearing his voice in his words—may indicate the need of John's community to see the absent-yet-present work of Jesus. In other words, the seven churches not only needed to hear a word from the Lord, but also they needed to see Jesus. In fact, audition and vision are intricately related in the Apocalypse so that "those who have ears to hear" are enabled to see the King and his kingdom.[1]

In the first-century Greco-Roman world powerful rulers had to send messages to their regents all the time. Letter traffic bridged the center of power to the farthest reaches of their dominion. So, when Jesus appears as the Daniel-like Ancient of Days (Dan 7:9-14), holding the cosmos in his right hand, it isn't surprising that such a powerful ruler would send a message to his co-regents. As seven lampstands in heaven (the menorah?), the seven churches are regnant with the splendor of Jesus' reign (Rev 1:12-13, 20). But the situation on earth—the farthest reaches of Jesus' kingdom—was far less illuminating. Even though they reigned with Christ in heaven, the seven churches were having a hard time extending his kingdom on earth. Some were experiencing persecution (Smyrna and Philadelphia). Some were harboring false teachers (Pergamum and Thyatira). Others had lost their first love (Ephesus), were dead in their complacency (Sardis), or had decided to serve mammon rather than God (Laodicea). The presence of Jesus' kingdom was barely visible on earth. This is why the King dictated the letter: it was the last warning, from his lips to their ears. His regents needed to get their act together because he was coming soon to take matters into his own hands.

The dire tone of the letter matches the scary image of its author. Imagine how confusing it would have been otherwise. The Christophany of the first chapter of Revelation doesn't match the familiar figure of the resurrected Lord we see in the Gospels—a kind man who makes breakfast, gently scolds Peter, and demurely shows his scars. Rather, this terrifying Lord is so angry that fire shoots from his eyes; his piercing gaze sees everything. "I know your works. . . . I know your affliction. . . . I know where you are living" (Rev 2:2, 9, 13). Because of his sharp tongue, his words cut like a knife. "Repent. . . . If not, I will come to you and remove your lampstand. . . . I will come to you soon and make war. . . . I will come like a thief" (Rev 2:5, 16; 3:3). This Christ looks and sounds more like the fearsome, ominous God of the Old Testament than the love-your-neighbor, friend-of-sinners, compassionate-miracle-worker of the New Testament.

---

[1]See David A. deSilva, *Seeing Things John's Way: The Rhetoric of the Book of Revelation* (Louisville, KY: Westminster John Knox, 2009), pp. 285-97.

It's no wonder the seer fell at Jesus' feet like a dead man (Rev 1:17). The apocalyptic Jesus scared the living daylights out of him. And, it's quite apparent that the Christophany was supposed to have the same effect on the seven churches, which is why Jesus talked directly to them. And yet, these dire warnings and harsh threats were not dished out as retribution. Rather, because Jesus knew them so well—the unique challenges facing each church—the letter was meant to encourage believers to be faithful "witnesses," a "kingdom of priests" serving God until Christ returns (Rev 1:6; 5:10). The fact that the apocalyptic Jesus disciplined them proved that he loved them (Rev 3:19). His desire to come as a welcomed friend (not a vindictive tyrant), sharing the rewards of his Father's throne, should have inspired the churches to have ears to hear what the Spirit was saying (Rev 3:20-22) and eyes to see what lay ahead (Rev 4:1).

Behold the lamb. To hear the word is to envision the kingdom. The seer counted on this to be true for those who heard the Apocalypse because the same thing happened to him: hearing led to seeing. He heard the voice

SO WHAT?

Jesus Versus God?

Sometimes we cast the God of the Old Testament as if he were the antithesis of Jesus. He was stern; Jesus is kind. He was a punisher; Jesus forgives. He was full of wrath; Jesus is love. We begin to sound like an ancient heretic, Marcion, who threw out the Old Testament and carved up the New Testament. Although we are dismissive of Marcion's radical moves, often we neglect select parts of the Hebrew Scriptures in order to rehabilitate God's reputation as a "warrior." We can even imagine that Jesus was trying to help out God's image—like a PR makeover. In truth, the face of the apocalyptic Jesus is the face of God— the God whom Israel knew and loved, the God who rescued the Hebrew slaves from humiliating servitude. We picture this fearsome God of the Old Testament as if he is unlovable and unloving; yet, he was the one who began the plan of saving humankind. Besides, Jesus was known to get angry at times, and he talks about hell more than anyone else in the New Testament (Paul never mentions it at all). So, when we look at the apocalyptic Jesus, perhaps we are permitted to see what Moses could not: the very face of God.

like a trumpet then he saw Jesus in the middle of the seven lampstands. He heard, "Come up here, and I will show you what must take place after this" (Rev 4:1). Then he saw the timeless worship of God in his throne room. The same pattern is repeated ten times throughout Revelation (Rev 1:10-12; 4:1-2; 5:5-6; 7:4, 9; 9:13-16; 14:13-16; 16:15-16; 17:1-6; 19:9, 17-18; 21:9-14). The seer hears one thing before he sees something else. Hearing and seeing are ironically linked in the Apocalypse, giving the unmistakable impression that one cannot make sense of what is seen until one hears. In fact, it takes an insider, one who understands the irony, to see why hearing is seeing and how seeing is believing. This is particularly evident when John hears that the one who is worthy to open the sealed scroll is "the Lion of the tribe of Judah," but then turns to see "a Lamb standing as if it had been slaughtered" (Rev 5:5-6). To outsiders, there's no way a fierce lion would be mistaken for a vulnerable lamb. But to insiders, those who have ears to hear and eyes to see, the correlation makes perfect sense. Jesus' sacrifice is both the reason and the way God's kingdom comes to earth.[2]

John's vision of God's throne (Rev 4:2–5:14) describes it in images like

WHAT'S MORE . . .

Ancient Thrones

Ancient kings sat on elaborate thrones, chairs made of expensive wood, embedded with jewels and embossed with gold. Seated on a throne having armrests that looked like a leopard's head and chair legs that resembled lion claws, the enthroned king appeared as the ruler of all creation; even his hands resting on the arms of the chair gave the appearance that he was petting the heads of these wild cats. Carved in the back of the chair was a family scene with official symbols of the kingdom, often depicting the royal family as heirs to the throne.

[2]Loren L. Johns, *The Lamb Christology of the Apocalypse of John: An Investigation into Its Origins and Rhetorical Force*, Wissenschaftliche Untersuchungen zum Neuen Testament 2/167 (Tübingen: Mohr Siebeck, 2003), pp. 158-205.

those of many other ancient thrones. It is encased with precious gems, surrounded by wild beasts, inscribed with family symbols and a picture of the heir to the throne.

At first the sacrificial lamb appears "in the midst of the throne" as a static symbol, as if he were a picture carved in the back of the chair. Then, all of the sudden, the lamb moves out from the midst of the throne and takes the scroll out of God's hand. The dramatic revelation of the one "who is worthy to open the sealed scroll" sets the rest of the Apocalypse in motion. The lamb will effect God's will on earth because he is worthy of worship, power, wealth, wisdom, might, honor, glory and blessing—every royal privilege—because he was slaughtered, having ransomed the people of God (Rev 5:9-14). The apocalyptic Jesus reigns in heaven because he has established a kingdom of priests, purchased by his blood, to serve God on earth. Indeed, "they will reign on earth" because they offer themselves as a living sacrifice just like Christ. They will follow the lamb "wherever he goes"—even to death—for this is the way the Apocalyptic Jesus rules the world (Rev 14:1-5).

The work of Christ is pictured as an accomplished fact, an irreversible force, especially when it comes to the meaning of his death. The lamb is already slaughtered. His blood has already "ransomed for God saints from every tribe and language and people and nation" (Rev 5:9). Except for one possible inference (Rev 11:13), the purchasing power of the atonement is over. No one "gets saved" during the Apocalypse. Indeed, Jesus' death as an atoning work is muted in John's revelation. Instead, the blood of the lamb works like laundry detergent for faithful witnesses, making the garments of the martyrs white (Rev 7:14). Christ's sacrifice is the weapon of warfare that empowers the faithful on earth to defeat Satan (the "accuser" [Rev 12:10]), having "conquered him by the blood of the Lamb and by the word of their testimony" (Rev 12:11). Sealed as first fruits to be sacrificed to God, the faithful follow the lamb as undefiled, blameless, unimpeachable witnesses—mirror images of Christ (Rev 14:2-5). In other words, in the Apocalypse the death of Christ benefits the saved, not the lost. Christ's sacrifice is more than a gift to receive; his death is a model to imitate. The martyrs are destined to die like the apocalyptic Jesus did because they reign with him on earth. Their blood is mingled together with the blood of all the saints and prophets of times past (Rev 16:6; 17:6 [perhaps even Christ?]).

Echoing the Eucharist, their bloody sacrifice will therefore work like wine: purifying the earth, placating the wrath of God, and making the kings of the earth drunk with power, sealing the day of God's judgment against them (Rev 14:17–15:1; 17:1-6; 18:2-3). Only the faithful are sober enough to see the Day of the Lord coming.

Hail the conquering hero. It's hard to tell what kind of lamb Jesus is supposed to be in Revelation. Is he a Passover lamb? Exodus imagery appears throughout the Apocalypse; the plagues that are poured out like bowls mimic the ten plagues of Egypt and are introduced by the song of Moses and the lamb (Rev 15:1–16:21). Could he be identified as the lamb of daily sacrifice (Ex 29:38), or the sacrifice required for purification (Lev 12:6; 14:10), or even the sacrificial lamb that is required to redeem every firstborn male (Ex 13:13)? Since the lamb also has horns,

---

SO WHAT?
. . . .

The Final Battle

God is at war, but the final battle is won by Jesus through his sacrifice. Our blood may be spilled, not on the battlefield but as martyrs, mingling our sacrifice with other believers around the world and through the ages. Even now, believers are giving their lives as a faithful witness for the kingdom. This is how we wage war: not by killing our enemies but by dying for them.

---

some think that the sacrificial model is eclipsed by the forceful, ram-tough imagery of a ruler who would lead Israel in battle against the enemies of God as featured in Jewish apocalyptic literature (*1 En.* 89.45). Of course, there are several features of the apocalyptic lamb that defy even Jewish identification. For example, this lamb appears as an über-ram, having seven horns and seven eyes. This lamb unleashes the devastating plagues of the sealed scroll. This lamb is a shepherd of celibates (Rev 7:17; 14:4). This lamb marries a pure bride (Rev 19:7-9). These different "revelations" of the lamb force readers to hold together competing images in order to make sense of the work of the lamb. Does he die for his enemies or kill them? Does he promote celibacy or marriage? Is he a sacrificial lamb or a battering ram?

The Apocalypse is a story of warfare: Christ versus Satan, good versus evil, the armies of heaven versus the kings of the earth. This is what's supposed to happen at the end of the world, when justice finally comes to earth. So, when the lamb triggers the final conflict by unleashing weapons of mass destruction on earth, it seems as though the kingdom of God comes through violence, which automatically raises this question: has God given up on the plan to rule the world through the sacrifice of Christ? Is this why the lamb looks more like a ram, the "lion of Judah" ready to devour his enemies? That is to say, has God lost patience and decided to "kick butt" because of what his enemies did to his Son, finally goaded into action by the faithful martyrs who have cried out for eternity, "Sovereign Lord, holy and true, how long will it be before you judge and avenge our blood on the inhabitants of the earth?" (Rev 6:10). Does Revelation picture the end of the world as the time when God finally gets his hands dirty with the messy bloodshed of war? Not necessarily.

Notice first what started it all. What moved the lamb to take hold of the scroll and break its seals? It was worship. When the lamb is worshiped as God, then the will of God (the opened scroll) comes to earth. Indeed, worship is an act of warfare against the fallen powers of this world. When God is worshiped, the kingdom comes. Second, God doesn't wage war alone; these battles are fought by heavenly and earthly adversaries who are staking their claim of dominion over the whole earth—not only territory on the earth, but also above and underneath the earth. Angels fight fallen powers in the air, and the fallout of their warfare crashes into earth. Satan, the accuser, is thrown down to earth because he is kicked out of heaven by Michael "and his angels" (Rev 12:7-12). Satan wreaks havoc on earth because he has nowhere else to go; his evil charade of power on earth confirms his defeat. This is why earthly plagues are celebrated with "hallelujahs" in heaven: the worse things get, the surer the sign of God's just rule coming to earth. So when human forces clash on earth—the faithful witnesses of the lamb versus the kings of the earth—there must be heavenly consequences. Martyrs are celebrated as victorious even though they are "overcome" by evil adversaries on earth (Rev 13:7; 20:4). Followers of the lamb look like they lost the war on earth, slaughtered for their testimony of Jesus. However, they enter heaven's praise as conquering soldiers because they have waged warfare just like their leader, the victorious Lamb of God. But does this mean that the injustice of shedding innocent blood will last forever? Will the killing ever end? Will evil ever be spent? When will the war be over? And, how will it end? Who will stop the madness?

There eventually comes a time when the apocalyptic Jesus must confront all enemies, both demonic and human, and bring an end to all the injustice on earth. It is the last battle, often called "Armageddon." And yet, even this notorious final conflict has a strange, unexpected ending. We often hear that Armageddon will be the war to end all wars—one, last, bloody battle—but a careful reading of the Apocalypse shows that there is no war at the end of the world. To be sure, when the apocalyptic Jesus appears at the end to do battle with the kings of the earth, he comes as "the man on the white horse." He rides with the armies of heaven, ready to "tread the wine press of the fury of the wrath of God" (Rev 19:15). He will vanquish every foe; he will be the "King of kings and the Lord of lords" (Rev 19:16). And, how does he do it? With mighty weapons of war? Heavenly atomic bombs? Irrepressible armored tanks? Super stealth fighter-jets? No, he kills his enemies with his words. With the same sharp tongue that he used to correct his church, Jesus wields his sword (the only weapon he needs!) to overcome all enemies: the kings of the earth, the demonic beasts, even Satan himself. In the words of Martin Luther, "One little word shall fell him." The end comes when God says, "It is finished" (Rev 16:17; 21:6). Like a judge who is righteous and true, the apocalyptic Jesus will issue the final verdict on all evil, sending the enemies of God to the eternal, fiery prison that we call "hell." Jesus is a lion who rules like a lamb; he's a heavenly warrior who fights like a judge. Like a king who is the Alpha and Omega, Jesus the first word will have the last word when heaven invades the earth. And, once heaven and earth are one, this lamb shall reign as the temple and lamp of God—a temple that welcomes the "kings of the earth" who once opposed him and is a light that shines for all nations (Rev 21:22-26).

How Is This Jesus Different?

The Revelation of John looks like a photographic negative of the Gospels and Acts. When Jesus performed miracles on earth, it seemed as though the glorious work of heaven had come for a little while. The kingdom of God invading earth pushed back the darkness of evil and suffering; Christ defeated the enemies of God through his death and resurrection. Not surprisingly, therefore, when the apostles continued the work of Jesus Christ on earth through signs and wonders, they offered heavenly praise when they were persecuted (Acts 5:40-41). Instead of crying out, "How long, O Lord?" these faithful witnesses prayed, "Grant to your servants to speak your word with all boldness" (Acts 4:29). In other words, in the Gospels and Acts we see "from below," from an earthly perspective, the story of God's kingdom coming to earth. Rather than conducting one massive cosmic battle of the forces of good versus evil, Jesus casts out demons one person at a time. Instead of executing a swift harvest by the blade of a sharp sickle, Jesus advances the kingdom slowly, like yeast leavening the dough. As heaven comes to earth, we get brief glimpses of glory, visions of what happens when we pray, "Thy kingdom come; thy will be done." The Gospels and Acts teach us that good things can happen in spite of a fallen world.

In the Revelation of John, however, we see the same story from a different perspective. With the seer's feet firmly planted on the ground, he takes temporary flight to the heavenlies and sees the work of Christ on earth "from above." From a heavenly point of view, we join the seer in witnessing the terrestrial world refined by the fiery presence of God's celestial throne. It's as if earth is temporarily caught up into the holiness of heaven. Indeed, as earth is elevated to heaven's purpose, we get glimpses of purification, visions of what happens when we pray, "Come, Lord Jesus!" The Apocalypse teaches us that bad things happen in spite of a heavenly invasion. Therefore, it is ironic that when Acts tells the story of the church's witness on earth, we have a somewhat optimistic, open-ended account of the kingdom of God advancing to the ends of the earth, despite persecution, because the gospel is an invitation for unbelievers. The Apocalypse, on the other hand, tells a dark, rather fatalistic tale of the world reluctantly, yet inevitably, giving into the irrepressible reign of God coming from heaven because the gospel is a sealed scroll of judgment against unbelievers. We have a hopeful story of Acts on earth and a gloomy tale of Revelation from heaven—same story, different perspective.

The same is true when it comes to the revelation of Jesus Christ in the Gospels and the Apocalypse: same person, different perspective. On earth Jesus was a compassionate savior; in heaven he is an impartial judge. When he walked on earth, he was known as "the mercy man," a friend of sinners and the enemy of priests; as he reigns in heaven, he is worshiped as "the warrior lamb," a ruler of priests and the enemy of the unrighteous. He spoke often of the kingdom of God coming to earth, according to the Gospels; he never says a word as the reign of God comes to earth, according to Revelation. On earth he was loved; in heaven he is feared. As the Gospels tell the story, Jesus was destined to die on earth; as Revelation finishes the story, the apocalyptic Jesus is destined to rule the earth. On earth he was the sacrificial lamb; in heaven he is the lionized lamb. In the Gospels Jesus challenged his disciples to carry a cross to Jerusalem; in Revelation Jesus assumes that his disciples are ready to die because of the New Jerusalem. The Jesus of the Gospels is the one we *want* to follow; the Jesus of Revelation is the one we *must* follow. On earth we get glimpses of his deity; in heaven we can barely see his humanity. In all of the New Testament you can't find a more different Jesus than the Jesus of the Revelation of John.

What If This Were Our Only Jesus?

Even though he appears as a lamb in the Revelation of John, the apocalyptic Jesus isn't a very cuddly character. In fact, this Jesus isn't the man we want to see in the pictures we hang on the walls of church buildings. The portrait of the lightly tanned, gently handsome man, the cheerful teacher with children playing at his feet, even the wiry figure impaled on a cross—none of these familiar icons appear in the Apocalypse. If all we had were Revelation to inspire us, our paintings of Christ would be so gruesome, so scary, that no one would dare to place them in our sanctuaries, especially in the halls of our children's buildings. Can you imagine? The average visitor would think that we were decorating for a haunted house, not a house for worship. If we re-created what John saw, we might cause everyone to faint from the sight of this awful man. Indeed, when John sees the end of the world, the apocalyptic Jesus is not very endearing at all. So, none of us would be tempted to think of him as our "best friend." We wouldn't develop any warm, fuzzy feelings for the apocalyptic Jesus. Rather, the only thing we would be compelled to do is fall on our faces in fear and awe, hoping that his frightful gaze didn't fall on us.

Think of how difficult it would be to evangelize unbelievers. No one could "sell" this Jesus, making him desirable, no matter how intensive the training. How could any of us rehab his apocalyptic image? Who would believe in a bizarre character that looks like he came straight out of a graphic novel, the seven-eyed, seven-horned lamb? Who would "fall in love" with a sharp-tongued, fiery-eyed Jesus? Even more telling, how could any of us convince others to "follow the Lamb wherever he goes" (Rev 14:4), especially since that would mean imminent death? "The slaughtered lamb wants *you* to die!"—hardly the slogan that would result in an evangelism explosion. The only part that might be halfway appealing is "the man on the white horse" who comes at the end with his cavalry to save the day. In fact, that's the only redeemable image of Jesus in the Apocalypse. We all want a hero who wins the battle by killing his enemies— that is, as long as Christ's enemies are not any of our family or friends. And, that's when even the warrior Christ is no longer appealing. Truthfully, if all we had were the

SO WHAT?
. . . .

*Familiarity
Can Breed Contempt*

We can become so familiar with Jesus that it can lead to casualness and even contempt, patting him on the back like an old buddy. When we make Jesus so approachable, there is no wonder, awe or fear. Aslan the lion, the Christ figure in C. S. Lewis's *The Chronicles of Narnia*, is feared as well as loved. When we lose fear, we become too relaxed, drop titles, and, before you know it, lose respect.

I remember watching the 1956 film version of the classic musical *The King and I*, starring Yul Brynner as the king. All adults fall to the ground face down in fear and respect whenever the king enters the throne room. In one scene, his youngest son enters and runs to his father the king, weaving among the prostrate adults to sit at his dad's feet. Children need to feel free to run up to Jesus, but the apocalyptic Jesus reminds us that mature Christians need to rediscover that he is King, and there is a time to fall on our faces and worship.

apocalyptic Jesus, few of us would want to follow him. Besides, would we even know how? With only the seven beatitudes and the enigmatic warnings to the seven churches to guide us, what else would we do except grit our teeth and hold on to the end until it all hits the apocalyptic fan?

Yet, the warrior Christ is not the final image of Jesus in the last book of the New Testament. Rather, the Apocalypse ends with a story of paradise, a lamb that enlightens the city of God and nourishes the faithful with streams of crystal-clear water that flow from the throne of God (Rev 21:22–22:5). And, the silent lamb finally speaks up. Jesus seemingly sheds his apocalyptic costume and speaks directly to the church, like he did at the first, with re-assuring words: "I am coming soon to reward the faithful" (cf. Rev 11:18; 22:12). An urban paradise of golden streets attended by a vast, lush green space is held out at the end to inspire followers to pray, "Come, Lord Jesus!" (Rev 22:20),[3] which exposes the assumptions behind the vision of the scary image of Jesus and the prospect of inevitable persecution for following the lamb. Revelation was written for believers already committed to Christ. An apoc-alyptic Jesus would persuade no one to believe and follow. Who would listen? Who can see it? Indeed, this Jesus speaks to those who have eyes to see and ears to hear, and he wants to know one thing: will you follow the lamb to the end?

READ MORE ABOUT IT

Beasley-Murray, G. R. "Revelation, Book of." In *Dictionary of the Later New Testament and Its Developments*, edited by Ralph P. Martin and Peter H. Davids, pp. 1025-38. Downers Grove, IL: InterVarsity Press, 1997.

Hurtado, Larry W. "Christology." In *Dictionary of the Later New Testament and Its Developments*, edited by Ralph P. Martin and Peter H. Davids, pp. 176-77. Downers Grove, IL: InterVarsity Press, 1997.

Johns, Loren L. *The Lamb Christology of the Apocalypse of John: An Investigation into Its Origins and Rhetorical Force*. Wissenschaftliche Untersuchungen zum Neuen Testament 2/167. Tübingen: Mohr Siebeck, 2003.

Keener, Craig S. "Lamb." In *Dictionary of the Later New Testament and Its Developments*, edited by Ralph P. Martin and Peter H. Davids, pp. 641-42. Downers Grove, IL: InterVarsity Press, 1997.

Witherington, Ben, III. *Revelation*. New Cambridge Bible Commentary. Cambridge: Cambridge University Press, 2003.

---

[3]Compare Paul's Aramaic prayer, *marana tha* ("Our Lord, come!") in 1 Corinthians 16:22.

DISCUSSION QUESTIONS

1. Why do many people tend to ignore the picture of Jesus in Revelation? Is the fear of Christ a good attitude for Christians to adopt?

2. If Christ were to send a letter to our churches today, what would he say? Would the content be different from the letter to the seven churches?

3. How does the apocalyptic Jesus reign as the Lamb of God? How are Christians supposed to follow his example?

4. Revelation is filled with images of warfare. Why?

5. If Revelation were the only portrait of Jesus we had, how would our methods of evangelism and services of worship change?

PART II

Introduction

Jesus Outside the Bible

We have looked at lots of pictures of Jesus from the New Testament. We rediscovered that Mark's Jesus encourages us to spend less time talking and more time actually doing things that bring in the kingdom. Mark's Jesus reminds us that we are at war. When we rediscover Luke's Jesus, we have eyes that notice those standing on the margins of our society. Reading the entire New Testament helps us to rediscover the stories of Jesus that our society has glossed over or sidelined as intolerant, unacceptable or out-of-date. We rediscover Jesus leading us to actions and themes that we have ignored.

Nonetheless, the New Testament writers weren't the only ones talking about Jesus. When Jesus originally asked, "Who do people say that I am?" he wasn't merely concerned with the opinions of his followers. Throughout the ages people have sought to understand who Jesus is. Clearly, we privilege the Scriptures, but it would be the height of arrogance to assume that we have cornered the market, that we have exhausted all possible interpretations, that we have extracted all possible insights. We can learn from what others, even outsiders, have said about Jesus. On occasion, they may provide a perspective that we have overlooked or even suppressed as we have read our canon of Scripture. Other times, it will help us to clarify exactly what we believe when we have to differentiate our understanding of Jesus from theirs. We will see in one group that they appear to get God right but Jesus wrong. Another seems to get Jesus right and God wrong. Does that matter?

We think it does. Nonetheless, drawing out those implications may help us to rediscover Jesus.

Obviously, groups through the ages have been saying who they think Jesus is. We cannot discuss all of them. We have chosen those that we believe most impact us in the modern West. These are the ones who have colored our image of Jesus. For this reason, we will discuss the Muslim 'Isa (Jesus), the Mormon Jesus, the Jesus of Western scholarship, but not the Jesus of Tibetan Buddhism. This is not to argue that one picture of Jesus is more important (or more accurate) than another, but some have impacted us more directly. For example, you might begin reading the chapter on the cinematic Jesus wondering why this image of him matters to you, but we are confident you will see how much we have been influenced by this image, for the Jesus we see portrayed in film finds his way into the pious prayers of many churchgoers.

In part one we looked at the biblical pictures of Jesus. We finished each chapter by asking how that particular image, for example the Jesus of Hebrews, should influence us to consider a fuller picture of Jesus. How can we have more of James's Jesus or Luke's Jesus in our understanding? How can Jude help us rediscover Jesus? In part two we again will be asking how an image of Jesus has influenced us. Those outside our faith have described Jesus as a righteous angel or a true prophet. Is that how we see Jesus? How might that image help us to rediscover Jesus, seeing him through their eyes?

Nonetheless, there may also be aspects in my image of Jesus that I have picked up from other sources that I need to expunge in favor of a more biblical picture. In my church we tend to sing songs that invite us to cozy up to Jesus like a best friend. Yet, the apocalyptic Jesus reminds us that our Savior isn't just the "lover of my soul," the sweet man holding lambs or sitting with children in his lap. He is a scary figure who inspires reverential silence. What kind of Jesus are our praise songs leading us to worship? One popular song suggests that we will run up to Jesus for a bear hug when we reach heaven, but the apocalyptic Jesus compels us to fall to the ground in fear and awe. When I pray for Jesus to rescue me, am I envisioning Luke's Jesus or America's Superman Jesus? Which Jesus am I really following? Considering the various manifestations of Jesus outside the Bible may help us see the difference.

9

THE GNOSTIC JESUS

Is it possible that we have missed the real Jesus? Have the New Testament Gospels, the apostles and the church fathers suppressed the truth about him in order to foist upon the unknowing public a series of lies and falsehoods? Did powerful popes and church councils hide central facts about the real Jesus in order to secure their positions of power and wealth? Well, if you listen to conspiracy theorists and read some of the more sensational books about lost Christianities and secret Gospels, you might get that impression.

Consider, for example, the hype surrounding the National Geographic Society's publication of the *Gospel of Judas*.[1] A scholar who worked on the project describes it as "one of the greatest discoveries of this century."[2] Inside the dust jacket of the book, here is how the editors describe it:

> Here was a gospel that had not been seen since the early days of Christianity, . . . a gospel told from the perspective of Judas Iscariot, history's ultimate traitor. And far from being a villain, the Judas that emerges in its pages is a hero. . . . Judas Iscariot is presented as a role model for all those who wish to be disciples of Jesus and is the one apostle who truly understands Jesus.

Many will believe the claims made in the book simply because they are sanctioned by the National Geographic Society, one of America's most trusted institutions.

[1] *The Gospel of Judas: From Codex Tchacos*, ed. Rudolphe Kasser, Marvin Meyer and Gregor Wurst (Washington, DC: National Geographic Society, 2006).
[2] Rudolphe Kasser, quoted in Herbert Krosney, *The Lost Gospel: The Quest for the Gospel of Judas Iscariot* (Washington, DC: National Geographic Society, 2006), p. 8.

But we should see through the hype. This is a fragment of a fourth-century document; it is not "early." The *Gospel of Judas* may be written as if it were told from Judas's perspective, but there is no evidence that the historical Judas had anything to do with it, or that it offers any reliable information regarding what really happened to Jesus. In addition, top scholars are not as certain as the book's editors as to whether Judas is a hero in the story or a demon. What it does represent is an additional Gnostic portrait of Jesus current in the second to fourth centuries.

Who Do Gnostics Say That I Am?

Let's consider a few of the many Gnostic texts available and what they have to say about Jesus.

The Gospel of Peter. When Serapion (d. 211), bishop of Antioch, visited the church at Rhossus, he heard them reading publicly from a document called the *Gospel of Peter*. Initially, he felt that there was no harm in it and granted them permission to keep using it. After studying it, however, he withdrew his permission because it appeared favorable to the Docetic Gnostics (Eusebius, *Hist. eccl.* 6.12).

Only a part of the *Gospel of Peter* is known to have survived until now. It contains the trial, death, burial and resurrection of Jesus, but it tells these events in a profoundly different way from the canonical Gospels. In particular, it contains a fierce anti-Jewish sentiment. It begins with the Jews and Herod, king of the Jews, refusing to wash their hands of the Lord's death. Pilate seems an impotent bystander as Herod, in collaboration with the Jews, orders the Lord's execution. Ironically, after his death the Jews, elders and priests realize the evil they have done, lament and cry out in anticipation of Jerusalem's destruction (*Gos. Pet.* 25).

The name "Jesus" never appears in the extant text; he is called "Lord," "Son of God," "Savior" and "King of Israel." When the Lord is crucified between two evildoers, the text reports that "he was silent, as if he had no pain" (*Gos. Pet.* 10).[3] Given the excruciating nature of death by crucifixion, this is a remarkable claim, encouraging the reader to assume that Jesus didn't have a real body.

---

[3] All quotations of the *Gospel of Peter* are from Bart D. Ehrman and Zlatko Pleše, *The Apocryphal Gospels: Texts and Translations* (Oxford: Oxford University Press, 2011).

WHAT'S MORE . . .

What Is Gnosticism?

1. "Gnosticism" is a modern umbrella term used to describe several complex religious-philosophical movements that flourished in the second through the fourth centuries A.D. Outsiders referred to adherents as "Gnostics" (*gnostikoi,* "knowers"), but they referred to themselves as "the elect," "Christians," "the enlightened," "the offspring of Seth," "the spiritual ones" (*pneumatikoi*) and in other ways.

2. Gnosticism is not a single movement; it took on various forms based primarily upon the movements' leaders or their theological concepts.

3. Gnostics distinguished between the true God, considered to be utterly transcendent and unknowable, and the creator God. This ultimate, the true God ushered in wave after wave of other beings (emanations); each emanation was less pure and unknowable, finally reaching an emanation—a god—who could be known but who was not particularly pure or holy. This lower, inferior god is usually identified with the creator God of Genesis.

4. Gnostics distinguished strictly between matter (evil) and spirit (good), considering this present material world as evil.

5. Humans have the misfortune of being a good spirit trapped in a material body. The spirit belongs ultimately to the sublime, spiritual realm.

6. The problem isn't sin, but rather that humans have forgotten their true selves. Now this malady can be defined as ignorance (they do not know their true origin and destiny) or forgetfulness (they have forgotten who they are).

7. Salvation consists of imparting secret knowledge to the humans and awakening them from their slumber.

8. To accomplish this salvation, the true God sends a redeemer from the Pleroma (the grouping of emanations) to bring this knowledge.

9. Since matter is evil, some Gnostics claimed that Christ only appeared to be human; he was in fact divine. This belief is known as Docetism, from the Greek word *dokeō* ("to seem, appear"). Likewise, the tendency arose in some circles to consider the sufferings of the earthly Christ as more apparent than real.

Prior to his death, the Lord cried out from the cross: "My power, O power, you have left me behind!" (*Gos. Pet.* 19). This variation on the cry of dereliction (cf. Mt 27:46; Mk 15:34) is expressed as a statement rather than a question. What is this power that leaves him? Is it the Christ-spirit that leaves behind the body of the man Jesus? Furthermore, after the Lord said this, he was "taken up." Since the body still hung on the cross, what part of the Lord is "taken up" to heaven? The divine spirit? Perhaps. Yet the body of the Lord continues to have power, for when they pull the nails from his hands and lay him on the ground, the earth quakes.

Perhaps the most memorable episode in the *Gospel of Peter* is the resurrection (*Gos. Pet.* 34-42). Jewish leaders prevailed on Pilate to seal the crypt with soldiers for three days in order to prevent disciples from coming to steal the body (cf. Mt 27:62-66). Despite this, a crowd gathered to see what would happen next. A great voice from heaven pierced the night sky, and two bright men descended to the tomb's entrance. The stone sealing the tomb rolled back on its own, and the two men went inside. Moments later three men emerged from the tomb, two supporting the other, followed by the cross. The men are described in cosmic terms. The heads of the two reached from the ground up to the sky, but the head of the other, apparently the risen Lord, went up beyond the skies. A voice from the heavens asked, "Have you preached to those who are asleep?" The cross, not the man, answered, "Yes."

When Mary Magdalene and the other women came to the tomb, they found a handsome young man dressed in bright clothing sitting in the tomb. He told them the one who was crucified has risen. He showed them the place where they laid the corpse, but it was empty. His last words to the women are provocative: "For he has risen and left for the place from which he was sent" (*Gos. Pet.* 56).

After reading what remains of the *Gospel of Peter*, we can see why the bishop urged the church at Rhossus not to use it. The talking cross usually gets our attention, but the bishop likely objected also to the additions that are friendly to Docetic interpretations: its anti-Jewishness, the absence of reference to the man Jesus, the lack of pain in crucifixion, the power that leaves him on the cross, the Lord "taken up" even as his body hangs on the cross, the extraordinary account of the Lord's resurrected body described in cosmic proportions, and the claim that the Son has gone back to the place from which he was sent.

WHAT'S MORE . . .

Nag Hammadi

Until 1945 most of the information that we had on Gnostics came from church leaders such as Irenaeus of Lyon (A.D. 130-200), Hippolytus of Rome (A.D. 170-236) and Tertullian of Carthage (A.D. 160-225). These leaders defended the true faith against false teaching and exposed "heretics." Since they regarded Gnostic doctrines as false, they focused much of their critique on Gnostic leaders such as Valentinus, Basilides and Cerinthus. So what they write is tinged with their own apologetic interests. But critics don't always get it wrong; much of what they say is consistent with archeological discoveries made in the twentieth century.

With the unearthing of the Nag Hammadi library in Upper Egypt in 1945, our knowledge of Gnostic movements grew exponentially. The papyrus codices found yielded about forty treatises, most of which were previously unknown. All of the treatises were written in Coptic and date from the third to the fifth centuries A.D. Most of the documents have Gnostic tendencies and at least a thin veneer of Christian content. As a result of the discovery of the Nag Hammadi library, we had for the first time complete documents written by and for Gnostic communities, not just fragments or carefully chosen excerpts.

The Gospel of Thomas. This book is the best known of the Nag Hammadi writings.[4] It is a collection of sayings (supposedly) from Jesus. These sayings, called "logia," are numbered for reference. While some scholars argue that the sayings are equal in authority and reliability to the New Testament

---

[4]When the Coptic version of the *Gospel of Thomas* was first read and studied, experts realized that these sayings were familiar. Roughly fifty years earlier three Greek papyri were unearthed in Oxyrhynchus (also in Upper Egypt). When published, they offered the world a first look at a number of previously unknown sayings of Jesus (P.Oxy. 1.654, 655). Unlike the Greek version, the Coptic *Gospel of Thomas* was not fragmentary; it contained a prologue plus 114 sayings, about half of which resemble sayings appearing in the canonical Gospels. Not all scholars are convinced that the *Gospel of Thomas* is Gnostic, since it lacks reference to Gnostic cosmology. However, a majority of scholars continue to see it as influenced by Gnostic teaching.

Gospels, most scholars think that the document reveals more about an esoteric Christian community in Syria or Egypt in the second-third centuries
than it does about the historical Jesus.

The image of Jesus that emerges from reading the *Gospel of Thomas* is
different from what we find in the New Testament. The difference is evident
in the prologue and first saying: "These are the secret sayings which the
living Jesus spoke and which Didymos Judas Thomas wrote down. (1) And
he said, 'Whoever finds the interpretation of these sayings will not experience death.'"[5] This sets the tone for the rest of the book. Throughout, Jesus
is presented as imparting knowledge to his closest disciples in the form of
secret sayings. These are not sermons for the masses but knowledge for a
few contained in esoteric mysteries (*Gos. Thom.* 62). As the one who records
these sayings, Thomas is given prominence. Salvation is promised to any
who seek and find the correct interpretation of these sayings. In contrast to
the New Testament, salvation in the *Gospel of Thomas* has nothing to do
with an atoning death or Jesus' victory in the resurrection; it is about
grasping the true meaning behind hidden sayings. Noticeably absent are
miracles, a travel narrative or a public ministry. In this document we have
closely held, tightly controlled bits of wisdom and knowledge supposedly
imparted by the "living Jesus."

To those in the know, the material world is like a dead body (*Gos. Thom.*
56). Jesus marvels how this great wealth (the spirit) has been able to make
its home in such material poverty (*Gos. Thom.* 29). But at least some people
are "the elect of the living father"; they are children of the light and have
ultimately come from the realm of light (*Gos. Thom.* 50). Even so, when
Jesus takes his place in the world and appears to them in flesh, they are in-
toxicated and blind (*Gos. Thom.* 28). The kingdom, Jesus said, is inside of
you (disciples) and outside of you. When you come to know yourselves, you
will be known and come to realize that you are "the sons of the living father."
But if you do not know yourselves, you will dwell in poverty for you are that
poverty (*Gos. Thom.* 3). Knowledge of one's true origin and nature liberates
a person from the material poverty of the world.

Although Jesus' origin and role do not figure prominently in these logia,

---

[5]All quotations of the *Gospel of Thomas* are from *The Nag Hammadi Library in English*, ed. James M.
Robinson (San Francisco: Harper & Row, 1988).

there are a few that are instructive. Here is a logion slightly similar to Matthew 16:15-20 (also Mk 8:29-30; Lk 9:20-21):

> Jesus said to his disciples, "Compare me to someone and tell me whom I am like."
> Simon Peter said to him, "You are like a righteous angel."
> Matthew said to him, "You are like a wise philosopher."
> Thomas said to him, "Master, my mouth is wholly incapable of saying whom you are like."
> Jesus said, "I am not your (sg.) master. Because you (sg.) have drunk, you (sg.) have become intoxicated from the bubbling spring which I measured out." (*Gos. Thom.* 13)

Thomas alone was enlightened. Afterward Jesus takes Thomas aside privately and instructs him further. When other disciples ask him what Jesus said, he responds, "If I tell you one of the things which he told me, you will pick up stones and throw them at me; a fire will come out of the stones and burn you up" (*Gos. Thom.* 13). Thomas appears to have it right; he understands Jesus best. Yet Thomas admits that his mouth is incapable of expressing whom Jesus is like. This inexpressibility signifies a high view of Jesus and associates him closely with the transcendent, unknowable God. Apparently, there are levels of secret knowledge. Even among the elite disciples some things must remain hidden, at least for now.

In another logion Jesus said, "It is I who am the light which is above them all. It is I who am the all. From me did the all come forth, and unto me did the all extend. Split a piece of wood, and I am there. Lift up the stone, and you will find me there" (*Gos. Thom.* 77). Jesus cryptically refers to himself as "the light which is above them all." He is the source of "the all." Ultimately, "the all" extends to him. These statements parallel New Testament language linking Jesus with creation (Jn 1:1-3; 1 Cor 8:6; Col 1:15-20). Furthermore, the saying appears to ascribe to Jesus a kind of omnipresence. Regardless of where you go or what you do, you will find the Gnostic Jesus there.

Finally, in another logion Jesus said to Salome: "I am he who exists from the undivided. I was given some of the things of my father" (*Gos. Thom.* 61). The esoteric language in this logion speaks of Jesus' preexistence, prior to creation. Although he does not specify what "things" the father shared with him, the statement links Jesus more closely to the father than any other living being.

The Second Treatise of the Great Seth. Though not as well known, the *Second Treatise of the Great Seth* provides a more comprehensive Gnostic worldview. The tractate contains a revelation spoken by Christ to Gnostic believers. It encourages them to stand against the ignorance in the apostolic church, which proclaims "a doctrine of a dead man" (*Treat. Seth* 60.22).

The drama begins with Christ's commission by the heavenly assembly to descend from the house of the Father of Truth to the creation below of the inglorious god of this world (*Treat. Seth* 50.1-25). As Christ comes down, he alters his shape, changes his form, and assumes the likeness of the Archons (spiritual powers) in order to avoid detection (*Treat. Seth* 56.20–57.10). Had they known that he was descending to the earth, they would have tried to corrupt him, for all souls descending from above are corrupted before they enter the earthly realm; the journey from spiritual to earthly realms is extremely hazardous. But Christ escapes detection and therefore escapes corruption.

Christ takes up residence in Jesus' "bodily dwelling" after casting out the soul already in residence. Disturbed, the Archons hastily crucify Jesus thinking that they can foil the Father's plan. But what they do not know is that the new soul of Jesus cannot die because it has not been corrupted in its descent from the assembly. Christ says, "I did not die in reality but in appearance" (*Treat. Seth* 55.18-19). In fact, the death that they devised for the Savior comes back on their heads. The tortures that they inflicted actually happen to another.

But in doing these things, they condemn themselves.

> Yes, they saw me; they punished me. It was another, their father, who drank the gall and the vinegar; it was not I. They struck me with the reed; it was another, Simon [of Cyrene], who bore the cross on his shoulder. It[6] was another upon whom they placed the crown of thorns. But I was rejoicing in the height over all the wealth of the archons and the offspring of their error, of their empty glory. And I was laughing at their ignorance. (*Treat. Seth* 56.4-19)

At Jesus' death the Christ-spirit is released in an event of cosmic proportions. The earth trembles and the souls of the dead are released to ascend and unite with the world above.[7]

---

[6]Contra the translation of Bullard and Gibbons in *The Nag Hamadi Library*.
[7]See April D. DeConick, *The Thirteenth Apostle: What the Gospel of Judas Really Says* (London: Continuum, 2007), pp. 127-30.

WHAT'S MORE . . .

An Early Form of Gnosticism

Beloved, do not believe every spirit, but test the spirits to see whether they are from God; for many false prophets have gone out into the world. By this you know the Spirit of God: every spirit that confesses that Jesus Christ has come in the flesh is from God, and every spirit that does not confess Jesus is not from God. And this is the spirit of the antichrist, of which you have heard that it is coming; and now it is already in the world. (1 Jn 4:1-3)

Scholars debate exactly how early Gnostic tendencies can be traced. Some think that they predate Christianity. Others argue that they arose simultaneously with Christianity. In this passage the elder John unambiguously decries any kind of "Christian" confession that denies that Jesus Christ has come in the flesh (cf. 2 Jn 7). Apparently, there are Christian groups that are denying the full humanity of Jesus; John believes that this teaching is threatening his church. It is so serious that he calls it "the spirit of antichrist."

The Gospel of Mary. This document is a fragmentary second-century Gnostic text written originally in Greek. In the first part the risen Savior speaks with his disciples before his departure. Asked by Peter about the nature of sin, the Savior says that sin is not a moral failure but rather the unwise mixture of the material and spiritual. The second part relates a special revelation given to Mary Magdalene by the Savior. Mary tells the male disciples about a vision and conversation that she had with Jesus. Though fragmentary, at least part of it has to do with the ascension of the soul through four powers on its way "to the rest of the time, of the season, of the aeon, in silence" (*Gos. Mary* 17.5-7). The very fact that the Savior disclosed such important information to Mary causes discord between Peter and Andrew. But Levi steps forward: the rest of the disciples must not reject her because apparently the Lord "loved her more than us" (*Gos. Mary* 18.14-15).

The Gospel of Truth. In this second-century Gnostic text Jesus is the revealer and teacher, the Savior who effects the redemption of those ignorant of the Father (*Gos. Truth* 16.38–17.3). If oblivion results from not knowing the Father, knowledge of the Father ultimately annihilates oblivion. So it is that Jesus Christ comes "in fleshly form" to enlighten those in the darkness of oblivion (*Gos. Truth* 18.13-18; 31.5-12). The Trinity consists of "the Father . . . the Mother, [and] Jesus of infinite sweetness" (*Gos. Truth* 24.7-8); but "Mother" here is likely a reference to the Holy Spirit, not Mary the mother of Jesus. There are interesting features to this text.

WHAT'S MORE . . .

Other Gnostic Accounts

We have only touched on a few of the Gnostic accounts of Jesus. There are many more, which portray Jesus in various ways, some more orthodox than others. Here is an incomplete list with approximate dating (all dates A.D.):

2nd Century	2nd–3rd Centuries	3rd Century	3rd–4th Centuries
Gospel of Thomas	Apocalypse of Peter	Second Treatise of the Great Seth	Tripartite Tractate
Sophia of Jesus Christ	Apocryphon of James	Hypostasis of the Archons	
Pistis Sophia	Apocryphon of John		
Gospel of Truth	Gospel of Philip		
Gospel of Judas	Gospel of the Egyptians		
Gospel of Peter			
Gospel of Mary			
Eugnostos the Blessed			
Dialogue of the Savior			
Melchizedek			

First, the death of Jesus is not defined in Docetic terms. No substitute dies in Jesus' place. No Spirit leaves the body escaping death.

> For this reason Jesus appeared; he put on that book; he was nailed to a tree; he published the edict of the Father on the cross. O such great teaching! He draws himself down to death though life eternal clothes him. Having stripped himself of the perishable rags, he put on imperishability, which no one can possibly take from him. (*Gos. Truth* 20.23-34 [cf. *Gos. Truth* 18.21-27])

Clearly, whatever the death of the body means, it cannot touch the essential nature of Jesus. Death involves stripping off the perishable and putting on the imperishable. Second, the death of Jesus disseminates knowledge of the Father and brings life to many, but there is no attempt to say how: "For this reason the merciful one, the faithful one, Jesus, was patient in accepting sufferings until he took that book, since he knows that his death is life for many" (*Gos. Truth* 20.10-14). Third, there is extensive reflection on the name of Father and the Son: "Now the name of the Father is the Son. It is he who first gave a name to the one who came forth from him, who was himself, and he begot him as a son" (*Gos. Truth* 38.7-10). Jesus bears the name of the Father (*Gos. Truth* 38.7–40.23).

HOW IS THIS JESUS DIFFERENT?

The Gnostic Jesus is quite different from the Jesus we meet in the Gospels and rest of the New Testament. If we look beyond the hype in conspiracy novels and dubious claims made on cable television channels, we realize that the Gnostic Jesus is not truly human in any meaningful sense.

> ## SO WHAT?
> *Americans Love a Conspiracy*
>
> Notice how often modern Gnostic views start by assuming that the "church" is involved in a conspiracy to hide the "real truth" and this new view is now going to expose it. Those with the secret knowledge can unlock the "code" and find the real Jesus. The automatic presumption is that the real Jesus will be found somewhere outside the New Testament.

But it would be incorrect to think that there is a single Gnostic perspective on Jesus; rather, we ought to think of a variety of Gnostic perspectives as our brief survey demonstrated.

The story of the Gnostic Jesus begins in the Pleroma when the divine assembly decides to send him down to the earth. The Jesus figure descends from on high, changing form and one way or another taking on flesh. He comes into the world as a revealer to the pneumatics, those who are spiritual. His essential form is spiritual, though he must take on flesh in order to dwell below temporarily. Still, he takes on flesh like an actor takes on a costume. In some Gnostic texts he inhabits the body of another. There is no true intermingling of divine and human natures. There is no incarnation. God has not become a human being.

Since salvation consists of recognizing one's true self, origin and destiny, the Gnostic Jesus is not a reconciler of humankind to God. He reunites the Gnostic with his or her true self. He helps the spiritual ascend back into the perfect realm of light and leave behind (without regret) the fallen material order. He comes to address human ignorance and forgetfulness; the threat is so immense that Jesus himself requires awakening before he can help others (*Soph. Jes. Chr.* 107.14-15). The Savior's work on earth consisted primarily of revealing the knowledge (*gnōsis*) of salvation. The focus of his ministry is not the masses, but instead special, elite disciples, only a few of whom seem to understand Jesus.

WHAT IF THIS WERE OUR ONLY JESUS?

If Gnostic Christianity had prevailed and the Gnostic Jesus reigned supreme, we would have never marveled at the mystery of the Trinity, for heaven would be popu-

---

SO WHAT?
. . . .

Why Does It Matter If Jesus Became Fully Human?

Most Christians today would agree with the Christian doctrine that Jesus was fully human, but then they interpret his life in ways that sound Docetic. Was Jesus really thirsty, or was it a ruse so that he could talk to the woman by the well in Samaria? Was he really frustrated with the disciples, or was he only pretending in order to teach them a lesson? Did he really need to ask in order to find out who touched the hem of his garment for healing? Was he really tempted by Satan, or was he merely going through the motions? Was he asleep in the boat because he was exhausted, or was he playing possum?

lated with many gods of different ranks. We'd sing hymns to an utterly un-knowable God and look down on the inferior creator God of Genesis. We would look at the world around us as evil. We'd have no phrases such as "creation care" or "ecological concern." Taking care of the planet would make no more sense than painting a building slated for demolition. Salvation is escape from this world, since the material order is by nature corrupt and destined to decay. For us, the bad news isn't sin or moral decay, but rather that we had fallen asleep and forgotten who we are; the good news is that the true God had sent a redeemer to impart the right knowledge and liberate us from this material prison. As a result, our favorite hymns would be songs like "I'll Fly Away."

As Gnostics, we would not be comfortable in our own skin, so we would deny Christ his. Since the Gnostic Jesus was divine and not human, we'd have theological debates about whether he left footprints when he walked on the sand. There would be no Christmas, no celebration of God made flesh, because flesh is inherently evil.

SO WHAT?

Are We Unintentional Gnostics?

We might be Gnosticizing if

- we find ourselves talking about heaven as an escape from this world, especially if we don't need a resurrection of our bodies;

- we think that a happy marriage (or other successful Christian goal) is achieved by attending a special seminar and learning the "secrets";

- we think that taking care of this world (ecology) is a waste of time because it is going to hell in a hand basket anyway;

- we think that the goal is to know about Jesus rather than follow him;

- we spend all of our time in the New Testament, ignoring the Old Testament.

We might make more of Jesus' baptism than we do today, for that was the day when the Christ-spirit came upon the man Jesus. Instead of being somber at the foot of the cross, we might laugh that the spiritual powers had been so duped that they crucified the wrong man. "Good Friday" was be-cause God had pulled a good one on his enemies. The "passion of Christ" was a ruse. We wouldn't ponder the pain of the crucifixion, for there had been none. We would not celebrate the Lord's Supper (Eucharist, Holy Com-

WHAT'S MORE . . .

Other Christianities

Gnostics were not the only sects to produce Gospels and accounts of Jesus' life. There are texts and traditions written and used by other Christianities in the first to the fourth centuries A.D. Before we leave this chapter, let's consider a few of the better-known examples.

With the ancient world filled with stories of the births and adventures of semi-divine beings such as Hercules and Apollonius of Tyana, it is little wonder that early Christians wanted to know more about Jesus. So, "infancy Gospels" were conceived and legends were born to answer fundamental questions such as these: Where did Jesus come from? Who were Jesus' parents? Did Jesus possess power and wisdom even as a child? The two most famous accounts are the *Protevangelium of James* and the *Infancy Gospel of Thomas*. In the New Testament Jesus' parents serve an important but subsidiary role. The infancy Gospels are dedicated to raising their profile. The *Protevangelium of James*, for example, is actually about the nativity of Mary and her remarkable life before she was chosen to give birth to Jesus. While there is some overlap with New Testament accounts, there are details added about her parents (Joachim and Anna), her upbringing in the temple, her betrothal to Joseph and her virginal birth. The *Infancy Gospel of Thomas* focuses on the

munion), for the body and blood had never been sacrificed for many.

Today more women would be involved in church governance, although some writings suggest that they would have to act like men. We'd ask them to refrain from having children; after all, a child only causes another good spirit to be trapped in a physical (evil) body. Likely, Christians would advocate single life over marriage or at least encourage celibate marriages. We would be sorrowful when parents brought home a newborn baby. Abortion would be a good thing, saving a spirit from the misery of physical captivity. We would be the first and most vocal advocates for euthanasia. We'd celebrate funerals because death releases us from this evil world and sends us back to the glorious realms from where we came.

Since the Gnostic Jesus was more revealer than healer, we would build miraculous deeds performed by Jesus between ages five and twelve. Initially, Jesus used his powers to curse and cause injury to others. But after being warned by villagers to control little Jesus or move, Joseph takes Jesus aside and trains him to use his power for good rather than harm. Apparently, this was a popular account among many Christians, as scholars have discovered numerous copies of it in various languages.

After the fall of Jerusalem (A.D. 70) Jewish Christianities flourished in places such as Pella until the fourth century A.D. The dominant sects were the Ebionites, Nazoreans and Elkasaites. They produced the *Gospel of the Nazoreans*, the *Gospel of the Hebrews* and the *Gospel of the Ebionites*. Though most of their *Gospels* are lost, fragments of them are contained in the writings of church leaders such as Eusebius, Jerome, Epiphanius, Clement of Alexandria and Origen. Jewish Christianities typically held to a low Christology, that is, they denied the deity of Jesus and thought that God adopted the man Jesus as his Son. Other features included esteem for the Jerusalem church and the family of Jesus, an apocalyptic orientation, a staunch anti-Paulinism, and an affirmation that Christians must continue to observe Jewish law.

The Jesus of these other Christianities eventually was rejected by what became orthodox Christianity. Over time these movements died off, and the literature that they produced was no longer copied and transmitted to the next generation. That is why the historical record about them is so fragmentary.

universities but not hospitals. Medicine is a bad thing; it just keeps us alive longer in this inglorious world. In Sunday school we'd ponder esoteric sayings, wondering who had the right interpretation, for only correct understanding leads to eternal life. Instead of being Catholics, Presbyterians and Baptists, we'd belong to the Ophite, Sethian or Valentinian sects. We would not preach against sin, for that is not really our problem. We'd tell fewer stories from the Bible—probably none from the Old Testament—and we would preach propositional sermons. Had we followed the example of some early Gnostics, we would be rabidly anti-Jewish and would applaud the Holocaust as perhaps divine retribution. We'd proclaim that our relationships fail because we don't *know* the "Five Secrets to a Successful Marriage." We'd declare that we have debt because we don't *know* the "Seven Steps to Christian Financial Freedom."

We may constantly worry whether we had accumulated the right knowledge, whether we said the right words in a prayer.

The Gnostic Jesus is fashionable today not just in popular press but also in church practice. We may be tempted to view the Gnostic Jesus as a blip on the radar screen of church history, a Jesus who "appears" in a few brief documents that were thrown away; however, the philosophy behind these Gnostic texts often finds its way into churches today. Even though the Gnostic Jesus was popular then in limited circles, he seems nearly universally popular today. Not just because he headlines a major National Geographic project or is the subject of conspiracy novels and movies.

The orthodox church eventually rejected the Gnostic Jesus, shutting the front door in the fourth century but forgetting to lock the back door. The lure of Gnosticism remains fresh. Want to start "something new"? Begin by critiquing the established church, suggesting that it's completely wrong. Claim to have esoteric experiences or special revelations (insights) from God. Offer to let others in on the "secrets" that you learned and that no one else has realized. Promise that these insights will make their lives everything they want them to be. Do you see how seductive Gnosticism can be for a leader? It makes us feel special. We know things that no one else does. The more people who follow us, the more it seems we are right. Gnosticism didn't die in the fourth century. Indeed, we will see that many of the pictures of Jesus outside the Bible have Gnostic tendencies.

READ MORE ABOUT IT

Franzmann, Majella. *Jesus in the Nag Hammadi Writings*. London: T&T Clark, 1996.

Koester, Helmut. *Ancient Christian Gospels: Their History and Development*. Philadelphia: Trinity Press International, 1990.

Perkins, Pheme. *Gnosticism and the New Testament*. Minneapolis: Fortress, 1993.

Robinson, James M., ed. *The Nag Hammadi Library in English*. San Francisco: HarperSanFrancisco, 1988.

Scholer, David M. "Gnosis, Gnosticism." In *Dictionary of the Later New Testament and Its Developments*, edited by Ralph P. Martin and Peter H. Davids, pp. 400-412. Downers Grove, IL: InterVarsity Press, 1997.

Yamauchi, Edwin M. *Pre-Christian Gnosticism: A Survey of the Proposed Evidences*. 2nd ed. Grand Rapids: Baker Books, 1983.

DISCUSSION QUESTIONS

1. Why do you think Gnostic Christianities and these other Christianities eventually failed?

2. Why do you think Gnostics had concluded that the material world is inherently evil?

3. What is it about the Gospel of John that caused Gnostics to favor it?

4. What do we lose if we give up on a truly human Jesus?

5. What aspects of Gnosticism are still with us today?

10

THE MUSLIM JESUS

A few years ago I was in London to present a paper at a conference at the University of London. The title of the conference was "The Muslim World in Transition." On the second morning of the conference I had breakfast with some of the speakers and attendees. Over coffee, cereal and pastries, the conversation proceeded slowly in bits of broken English. One of the young men from Turkey made a provocative statement: "We [Muslims] believe in Jesus just like you Christians." I thought carefully about what he said before I answered. I responded, "Well, what you say is true, but it is also not true. Muslims do believe in Jesus, but what you believe and how you assess his significance ends up being very different from what Christians believe." We then pressed deeper into the question. He talked about what Muslims believe. I talked about what Christians believe. Several others wandered in and joined the conversation. We listened to one another and spoke frankly from the heart. The conversation did not end in agreement, but it did end in clarity. Muslims have a high view of Jesus as a prophet of God, but Christians believe that Jesus is much more than a prophet.

WHO DO MUSLIMS SAY THAT I AM?

When Muhammad died at the age of sixty-three (A.D. 632), he left behind three things. First, he left behind a movement that has spread throughout the world. Second, he left behind the Qur'an. After his initial call and vision, Muhammad continued to receive visions and revelations. These were recorded in the Qur'an (Arabic for "recite"). The Qur'an consists of 114 chapters, or Suras, organized generally according to length, longest to shortest. As we will see, Jesus figures prominently in many Qur'anic passages. Third, Muhammad left behind his Sunna ("way" or "path"). Muhammad's life was considered so special that his followers were urged to study it carefully and follow his ways. To do so, the stories of Muhammad's deeds and sayings were written down and collected into the Hadith ("tradition"). The Hadith becomes the basis of Muslim practice, habits, customs and laws. The traditions codified in the Hadith are regarded as authoritative, but not as authoritative as the Qur'an. The Qur'an is considered the very words of God to Muhammad.

How Muslims view Jesus begins with Muhammad and is set primarily in the Qur'an. Later Muslim traditions about Jesus build upon what the Qur'an says about him first. As we will see, the *Gospel of Barnabas* presents a picture of Jesus similar to what we read about in the Qur'an. Many Muslims consider the *Gospel of Barnabas* to be the true gospel of Jesus, suppressed for centuries by powerful popes and church leaders. However, since the earliest manuscript is from the sixteenth century A.D. and written in Italian, many scholars and educated Muslims consider it a pious fiction created by a zealous convert.

So how and what did Muhammad know about Jesus? Christian groups had immigrated to the peninsula where Muhammad lived in order to avoid persecution by the Byzantine authorities. These Christians seemed to hold versions of Christianity rejected by the mainstream church. In order to maintain the purity of the faith, the Orthodox Church branded them heretics and pushed them away. We don't know what they believed, what stories they told or what Scripture they read. According to Muslim tradition, Muhammad was illiterate, so it is unlikely that he had much exposure to the Christian Scriptures. Still, the prophet of Islam does seem aware of certain claims made about Jesus by Christians, orthodox and otherwise, and episodes in some of the canonical and noncanonical Gospels. What is clear is that Christianity in Muhammad's day was deeply divided over doctrines, particularly doctrines dealing with the Trinity and the nature of Christ. This may account for why the Muslim Jesus is radically different than the Christian Jesus in several of these key matters.

Jesus the prophet. Throughout the Qur'an and Muslim tradition Jesus is portrayed as one in a long line of prophets sent by God. In order to be a true Muslim, one must believe in God, his messenger (Muhammad), his Scriptures, his angels, his messengers (the other prophets) and the "last day." Since

---

WHAT'S MORE . . .

The Bible Has Been Corrupted

According to the Qur'an, three Scriptures were revealed prior to Muhammad: the Torah to Moses; the Psalms to David; the Gospel to Jesus. For this reason, Jews and Christians are called "People of the Book" (Qur'an 2:105; 3:64). They seem to have special status with Islam because Muslims are told to believe the previous Scriptures in addition to the Qur'an.

> You who believe, believe in God and His Messenger and in the Scripture He sent down to His Messenger, as well as what He sent down before. Anyone who does not believe in God, His angels, His Scriptures, His messengers, and the Last Day has gone far, far astray. (Qur'an 4:136 [cf. Qur'an 5:66, 68])

So Muslims are urged to believe in these Scriptures. Yet there are Qur'anic passages that can be interpreted to say that the earlier Scriptures have been corrupted.

> So can you [believers] hope that such people will believe you, when some of them used to hear the words of God and then deliberately twist them, even when they understood them? (Qur'an 2:75)

> Some Jews distort the meaning of [revealed] words . . . twisting it abusively with their tongues so as to disparage religion. . . . God has spurned them for their defiance; they believe very little. (Qur'an 4:46)

Muslims, then, have an ambiguous relationship with the Torah and the Gospels. On the one hand, they are instructed to believe in these Scriptures; on the other hand, they think that these Scriptures may have been distorted by Jews and Christians who have swerved wide of the faith. Muhammad's revelation in the Qur'an comes to clarify and rehabilitate those earlier Scriptures.

Jesus is a prophet, in order to be a Muslim, one must "believe" in Jesus. Generally, the lists of prophets are not given in any particular order. For example:

> We[1] have sent revelation to you [Prophet] as We did to Noah and the prophets after him, to Abraham, Ishmael, Isaac, Jacob, and the Tribes, to Jesus, Job, Jonah, Aaron, and Solomon—to David We gave the book [of Psalms]—to other messengers We have already mentioned to you, and also to some We have not. To Moses God spoke directly. (Qur'an 4:163-164)[2]

All the prophets come with God's message and clear signs in order to help the people pursue justice (Qur'an 57:25). All the prophets preached the same essential message, a message that Muhammad confirms and the Qur'an codifies. Over and over again the Qur'an affirms that good Muslims do not make distinction between any of the prophets. This does not mean, of course, that all prophets did the same thing in the same way. As we saw in the text above, God spoke directly with Moses. God gave the book of Psalms to David. Apparently, this is not so with the others. The "no distinction" clause is there to safeguard God's honor. A prophet does not deserve worship; only God does. This is likely aimed at Christians who regarded Jesus as divine and worshiped him as God.

This special (but lower) place of the prophets is underscored and expanded in Qur'an 6:84-89. In no uncertain terms it affirms that God sent the prophets, guided them, rewarded them for the good they did, counted them righteous, favored them over others, and chose them for this excellent task. Allah (the Arabic word for "God") gave them the Scriptures, wisdom and prophetic office. Yet any prophet who associated other gods with Allah would undo any good that he had done. God's honor must be preserved above all.

Even if the Muslim Jesus' message is the same as other prophets, his mission is unique. The Muslim Jesus may be nothing more than a servant of God, but he came as an example for the children of Israel (Qur'an 43:59).

> When Jesus came with clear signs he said, "I have brought you wisdom; I have come to clear up some of your differences for you. Be mindful of God and

---

[1] In the Qur'an a capitalized "We" refers to Allah.
[2] All references to the Qur'an are from *The Qur'an: A New Translation by M. A. S. Abdel Haleem*, Oxford World Classics (Oxford: Oxford University Press, 2004).

obey me: God is my Lord and your Lord. Serve Him: this is the straight path."
(Qur'an 43:63-64)

Allah sent Jesus to walk in the steps of the earlier prophets and to confirm
the Torah. God also "gave him the Gospel with guidance, light, and confirmation of the Torah already revealed—a guide and lesson for those who take
heed of God" (Qur'an 5:45). The true gospel then was none other than a
restatement and clarification of the Torah. Still, the Qur'an suggests that
Jesus comes to make some things lawful that were forbidden in the past
(Qur'an 3:49-51). Again, according to Muslim tradition, God had laid down
the same message with all the prophets; but over time people went astray
and divided into factions. The prophets were sent in order to uphold the
faith and unify the people (e.g., Qur'an 42:13).

Mary and the virgin birth. One of the main titles for Jesus in the Qur'an
is "the son of Mary." For this reason, it is appropriate to consider what the
Qur'an and Muslim tradition
say about Mary. Mary is mentioned often in the Qur'an; in
fact, Sura 19 is named for her.
No other woman figures as
prominently.

Mary's story begins with
her mother, the wife of Imran.
Not long before her birth,
Mary's mother offers the fruit
of her womb to God. When
her daughter is born, she
names her "Mary" and com-
mends her and her offspring,
Jesus, to God's protection
(Qur'an 3:35-64). The Lord
accepts her gift and entrusts

SO WHAT?
. . . .

"Father Abraham Had Many Sons"

I sang this little song as a child in
church. Our Muslim friends claim
that Abraham was a Muslim. They
trace their ancestry back to Abraham (through Abraham's firstborn
son, Ishmael). Why does this matter?
Well, God made promises to Abraham.
Jews claim that they get the promises through Isaac. Muslims claim the
promises through Ishmael. Christians
lay their claim through Jesus.

Mary's care and future to Zachariah. Inspired by God's faithfulness to Mary,
Zachariah prays that he too might have a child. The angels immediately
respond to say that he will be the father of a righteous prophet; we know him
as John the Baptist.

The angels affirm that Mary is chosen by God for a special task and urge her to devote herself continually to the Lord, praying with those who pray and prostrating herself before God (Qur'an 3:42-43). One day the angels say to her,

> Mary, God gives you news of a Word from Him, whose name will be the Messiah, Jesus, son of Mary, who will be held in honour in this world and the next, who will be one of those brought near to God. He will speak to people in his infancy and in his adulthood. He will be one of the righteous. (Qur'an 3:45-46)

Mary asks a sensible question: How can she bear a child if she has never known a man? The angel answers, "This is how God creates what He will: when He has ordained something, He only says, 'Be,' and it is" (Qur'an 3:47). In another account of the announcement to Mary, Allah sent "Our Spirit . . . in the form of a perfected man" (Qur'an 19:7). This heavenly messenger told about the gift of a pure son. When Mary asks, "How can this be?" the messenger speaking for God says, "It is easy for me."

After Mary conceives, she withdraws to a distant place. In the throes of labor she clings to the trunk of a date palm even as God miraculously provides her food and drink. When the child is born, she vows not to speak (Qur'an 19:19-26). Mary takes the child and returns to her people, who immediately accuse her of wrongdoing. Since Mary had taken a vow of silence, she could not speak to defend herself. Instead, she points to the child, as if to say, "He will explain it to you." Miraculously, the infant Jesus speaks to them:

> I am a servant of God. He has granted me the Scripture, made me a prophet; made me blessed wherever I may be. He commanded me to pray, to give alms as long as I live, to cherish my mother. He did not make me domineering or graceless. Peace was on me the day I was born, and will be on me the day I die and the day I am raised to life again. (Qur'an 19:30-33)

The chastity of Mary and the virgin birth of Jesus are central to the portrait of the Muslim Jesus. Because of his miraculous birth, Jesus is associated closely with Adam. God created Adam from dust and said to him, "Be," and he was. Likewise, God created Jesus in the womb of Mary apart from natural intercourse and said to him, "Be," and he was (Qur'an 3:59).

Jesus the miracle-worker. The Muslim Jesus is a miracle-worker. The infant Jesus rebuked Mary's scornful family. On another occasion the child Jesus is said to have fashioned a bird out of clay, breathed on it, and because God permitted it, the clay bird became a real bird (Qur'an 3:49-51; 5:110).

This episode is not recorded in the New Testament Gospels; it is told in the apocryphal book known as the *Infancy Gospel of Thomas.* With God's permission, Jesus also heals the leper and brings the dead back to life.

It is important to note that the Muslim Jesus performs miracles not because he has the authority in himself; he does it only because God permits and empowers him. A good example of this is found in chapter eleven of the *Gospel of Barnabas.* On his way into Jerusalem Jesus meets a leper who happens to know that Jesus is a prophet. He requests, "Lord, give me health." Jesus rebukes him and calls him foolish. "Pray to God for healing," he says, "I am only a man." The leper confesses the truth; Jesus is indeed a man. Yet he is no ordinary man because he is the holy one of God. So he asks the Muslim Jesus to intercede for him with God, hoping of course that God will restore his health. Jesus honors his requests and prays for the man; the man is subsequently healed because it was God's

---

SO WHAT?
. . . .
Mary and the Virgin Birth

Many Christians maintain belief in the virgin birth as a pillar of the Christian faith; yet, Muslims hold, what seems at first, the same belief. But if you examine the beliefs closely, you realize an important difference. Though the virgin birth is a miracle by any reckoning, only in Christianity does the Virgin Mary give birth to the preexistent Son of God. The preexistence of the Son is exclusive to Christianity.

Protestants often accuse their Catholic brothers and sisters of idolizing Mary, but Protestants can be accused of trivializing her. Scot McKnight has argued that Protestants need to develop a greater appreciation of the sacrifice and faithfulness of the mother of Jesus.[a] She made an essential contribution to God's redeeming act in the world. As Scripture notes, she was blessed among women (Lk 1:42).

[a] Scot McKnight, *The Real Mary: Why Evangelical Christians Can Embrace the Mother of Jesus* (Brewster, MA: Paraclete Press, 2006).

will to do so. The man then bears witness to Israel that Jesus is truly a prophet of God. Thus, the Muslim Jesus is associated with miracles, but he does not perform them. In that sense, he is not a miracle-worker but rather a prophet. He has special access to God to plead on behalf of those who need him.

Unique to the Muslim Jesus' role as a prophet is the privilege he had to announce the coming of the final prophet, Muhammad:

> Jesus, son of Mary, said, "Children of Israel, I am sent to you by God, confirming the Torah that came before me and bringing good news of a messenger to follow me whose name will be Ahmad." Yet when he came to them [the Jews] with clear signs, they said, "This is obviously sorcery." (Qur'an 61:6)

The name "Ahmad," like the name "Muhammad," means "praised." Although these are different forms, they are derived from the same Arabic root and are associated closely in Muslim piety. Both names indicate that the prophet is a man of good character, righteous before God and his fellow citizens. It does not mean, though, that the one who bears the name is worthy of praise or religious devotion. Religious praise and adoration belong only to God.

WHAT'S MORE . . .

Christians Can Say, "Amen!"

The Muslim Jesus has a lot in common with the Christian Jesus:

- Jesus' mother, Mary, was uniquely chosen among women for God's purposes.
- Jesus was born of the Virgin Mary, announced by an angel.
- Jesus was like Adam.
- Jesus was sent to the people of Israel.
- Jesus was the Messiah.
- Jesus was a prophet of God; yet, he had a unique role.
- Jesus performed miracles.
- Jesus came to confirm the Hebrew Scriptures (Torah).

From the Christian perspective, much of what Islam teaches about Jesus is true, but it does not go far enough.

Even as the Qur'an is the authoritative, textual center of the Muslim gospel about Jesus, the city of Kufa in Iraq appears to have been the geographical center for later developments. Stories and sayings credited to Jesus in the tradition emerged from here and other regions where Islam was adopting and adapting many Christian traditions for its own purposes. These sayings often sound familiar to those schooled in the Christian faith. For example:

> Jesus said, "If it is a day of fasting for one of you, let him anoint his head and beard and wipe his lips so that people will not know that he is fasting. If he gives with the right hand, let him hide this from his left hand. If he prays, let him pull down the door curtain, for God apportions praise as He apportions livelihood."[3]

Any casual observer will notice that this saying is closely related to Jesus' teaching in the Sermon on the Mount regarding the right way for disciples to practice their righteousness (Mt 6:5-6, 16-18). They are not to do so to attract attention to themselves. They are to do their acts of piety for God's eyes only.

The Muslim Jesus is considered the "patron saint of Muslim asceticism."[4]

> Jesus used to prepare food for his followers, then call them to eat and wait upon them, saying: "This is what you must do for the poor."[5]
>
> Jesus used to say, "Truly, I say to you, to eat wheat bread, to drink pure water, and to sleep upon the dunghills with the dogs more than suffices him who wishes to inherit paradise."[6]
>
> Jesus said to his disciples, "You will not gain God's bounty until you wear coarse wool with joy, eat barley with joy, and make the ground your bed with joy."[7]

The ascetic impulse has been strong in several branches of Islam. Those who gravitate toward a mystical, more contemplative spirituality consider Jesus a prophet worthy of imitation. The ascetic movement has also been im-

---

[3]Tarif Khalidi, *The Muslim Jesus: Sayings and Stories in Islamic Literature* (Cambridge, MA: Harvard University Press, 2001), p. 53.
[4]Ibid., p. 34.
[5]Ibid., p. 79.
[6]Ibid., p. 76.
[7]Ibid., p. 126. The garment of wool suggests strongly that this saying arises among the Sufis, whose name means "wearer of wool." The Sufis are Muslim mystics.

portant to various groups within Christianity, particularly and early, the Desert Fathers.

As in the New Testament, the Muslim Jesus is seen as a model of good behavior:

> Christ passed by a group of people who hurled insults at him, but he responded with blessings. He passed by another group who insulted him, and he responded likewise. One of his disciples asked, "Why is it that the more they insult you, the more you bless them? It is as if you were inviting this upon yourself." Christ replied, "A person can bring forth only what is within him."[8]

Jesus' example of what to do when insulted appears to be based loosely on sayings attributed to him in the New Testament Gospels (e.g., Mt 5:11, 43-48; echoed perhaps in Rom 12:14) and other early Christian texts: "When he was abused, he did not return abuse; when he suffered, he did not threaten; but he entrusted himself to the one who judges justly" (1 Pet 2:23).

As we have seen, Muslims picked up on many aspects of Jesus' life, character and significance from Christian traditions that they encountered. They went on to develop them according to their own, unique brand of religion and piety. Jesus was, according to Islamic tradition, a true Muslim. Therefore, they revered Jesus but rejected any claim of his divinity.

How Is This Jesus Different?

Jesus was not crucified. According to Muslim tradition, Jesus did not die on the cross. Here is the key Qur'anic passage:

> [The Jews] said, "We have killed the Messiah, Jesus, son of Mary, the Messenger of God." (They did not kill him, nor did they crucify him, though it was made to appear like that to them: those that disagreed about him are full of doubt, with no knowledge to follow, only supposition: they certainly did not kill him—God raised him up to Himself. God is almighty and wise. There is not one of the People of the Book who will not believe in [Jesus] before his death, and on the Day of Resurrection he will be a witness against them.) (Qur'an 4:157-159)

The context of this statement is a series of charges leveled against the Jews for wrongdoing, including violating God's covenant, rejecting God's reve-

---

[8]Ibid., p. 39.

lation, killing the prophets, and slandering Mary. In Muhammad's day Jews were routinely blamed by Christians for killing the Messiah Jesus. Indeed, in this passage it sounds as if the Jews are accepting credit for this impious act. Yet God reveals to Muhammad that the Jews did not kill him, nor was Jesus crucified. It was all apparently a case of mistaken identity, a ruse of sorts propagated perhaps by God himself (see *Gospel of Barnabas* 214-220).

We can see some parallels to ancient Gnostic views of Jesus here. Jesus only "appears" to suffer. Yet the Qur'anic passage is not clear how this occurred. There is no consensus by Muslim scholars on what this enigmatic passage means. Some take it as a case of mistaken identity; others, like the Ahmaddiya Muslims, teach that Jesus was taken down from the cross before he died and was later revived in the tomb. Afterward he escaped from Jerusalem, traveled to Kashmir, and later died. His tomb is located in Qadian, India. But their views on this and other issues are considered outside the norm by the majority of Muslims.

Although we are not sure how the Muslim Jesus only appeared to die, the theology behind the Muslim denial of Jesus' crucifixion is straight-forward. Jesus is a great prophet in Islam, and God would not have abandoned him. Allah would not have handed over Jesus to the fury of an executioner. To agree with orthodox Christians that Jesus was crucified would imply that God had somehow failed to protect his prophet. Indeed, to deny the crucifixion of Jesus is to preserve God's honor.[9] It stands to reason that

---

SO WHAT?
. . . .
Jesus Without a Cross

Luke reminds us that the crucifixion is God's exclamation point to turning the world upside down. The last becomes first; the least is greatest; the crucified becomes the King. God's way of looking at the world is upside down from ours. But this is not so in Islam. The Muslim world stays right side up (which is, from a Christian perspective, wrong side down). The Muslim path is obedience and submission to God's will, but it is not God emptying himself and taking on the form of a servant. In Islam, God never leaves his heavenly throne.

---

[9]M. Ali Merad, "Christ According to the Qur'an," *Encounter* 69 (November 1980): 7. Otherwise, see Mahmoud Ayoub, "The Death of Jesus," *Muslim World* 70 (1980): 91-121. Ayoub argues that

if there is no crucifixion in Islam, there is also no sense of Jesus' death as an atoning sacrifice. Muslims seek atonement with God in other ways.

When the Qur'anic passage above mentions God raising Jesus, it does not mean that God raised Jesus from the dead. Rather, God raised Jesus up before he dies. Put another way, his body was assumed into heaven, where he awaits the day of judgment. According to the Hadith, Jesus will return before the day of judgment. Although there are variations on this future scheme, it is said that he will break the cross, kill the swine, destroy the antichrist (Masih ad-Dajjal), and reign over the world with peace and justice for forty years. Afterward, he will die of natural causes and be buried beside the prophet Muhammad in Medina.

Jesus is not the Son of God or divine in any sense. The Qur'an and Muslim tradition deny adamantly that Jesus is God's Son or that he is to be regarded as divine in any sense. It cites the Trinity expressly as a blasphemous doctrine that must be abandoned if the faithful are to escape judgment. Let's consider some of the relevant texts:[10]

> Yet . . . without any true knowledge they [unbelievers] attribute sons and daughters to Him. Glory be to Him! He is far higher than what they ascribe to Him, the Creator of the heavens and earth! How could He have children when He has no spouse? (Qur'an 6:100-102)

> Those people who say that God is the third of three are defying [the truth]: there is only One God. If they persist in what they are saying, a painful punishment will afflict those of them who persist. . . . The Messiah, son of Mary, was only a messenger. (Qur'an 5:73-76)

> Those who say, "God is the Messiah, the son of Mary," are defying the truth. (Qur'an 5:17)

> People of the Book, . . . do not say anything about God except the truth: the Messiah, Jesus, son of Mary, was nothing more than a messenger of God. . . . So believe in God and His messengers and do not speak of a "Trinity"—stop [this], that is better for you. God is only one God. He is far above having a son, everything in the heavens and earth belongs to him and He is the best one to trust. (Qur'an 4:171-172)

---

the man Jesus did die on the cross. What the cross could not vanquish, however, was the Word of God, who descended from God and returned to heaven.

[10]Compare Qur'an 9:30-31; 5:17, 72; 19:19-92.

Believers, those who ascribe partners to God are truly unclean: do not let them come near the Sacred Mosque after this year. . . . Fight those People of the Book who do not [truly] believe in God and the Last Day, who do not forbid what God and His Messenger [Muhammad] have forbidden, who do not obey the rule of justice, until they pay the tax and agree to submit. The Jews said, "Ezra is the son of God," and the Christians said, "The Messiah is

---

WHAT'S MORE . . .

The Christian Title "Son of God"

Muhammad's criticisms against false religion were directed origi-nally toward the pagan gods and goddesses of Mecca (Qur'an 6:101). Given the ambiguities of language, some people may have confused Christian notions of Jesus' sonship with pagan ideas. To be clear, Christians reject any notion that Jesus is the Son of God in any physi-cal sense. The Christian Scriptures are unequivocal: Jesus is not the product of God's physical union with Mary (versus pagan myths like that of Hercules). Greek allows "son of . . ." language to be used metaphorically, such as "sons of the evil one" (Mt 13:38). When Je-sus used that phrase, he was not suggesting that they were physical offspring of Satan. In the New Testament Jesus talks about "sons of this age" and "sons of light" (Lk 16:8). If the Islamic rejection of the title "Son of God" is based on some claim that God and Mary had sexual relations, then Christians reject it as well. In this understand-ing, Christians could agree with the Muslim assertion "God does not beget and He is not begotten."

What is in Mary is a new creation of God. This is why the "new Adam" language in the New Testament is appropriate. "Son of God" is rooted instead in creative, interpretive readings of Hebrew Scrip-tures and the powerful fact of the resurrection. As we have seen in earlier chapters, "Son of God" is a title and is used first as a way of describing Jesus' status as "Messiah" or "Christ" (see 2 Sam 7:12-16; Ps 2:7; Mt 16:16-18; Jn 11:27). Later, the title "Son of God" comes to relate to Jesus' unique relationship to God and his exalted status after the resurrection: "the gospel concerning his Son, who was de-scended from David according to the flesh and was declared to be Son of God with power according to the spirit of holiness by resur-rection from the dead, Jesus Christ our Lord" (Rom 1:3-4).

the Son of God"; they said this with their own mouths, repeating what earlier disbelievers had said. May God confound them! How far astray they have been led! (Qur'an 9:28-31)

Say, "He is God the One, God the eternal. He begot no one nor was He begotten. No one is comparable to Him." (Qur'an 112:1-4)

These statements speak clearly enough. Muslim tradition consistently denies that God has any equals or any partners. It refuses any notion that God has had a spouse or any sons (or daughters). This is directed specifically against the Christians' claim that Jesus is the Son of God. This means, of course, that there can be no discussion of the Trinity. To hold on to this error is to face sure and painful punishment from God. What is unclear is how the Qur'an envisions the Christian Trinity. Are the three Father, Son and Holy Spirit? Perhaps. But there is some evidence that the Qur'an is actually responding to a Trinity made up of Father, Mother (Mary) and Son (e.g., Qur'an 5:116). If so, this suggests that Muhammad and his followers were countering Christians on the Arabian Peninsula who had at the very least a robust devotion to Mary. Even as many Protestants today think that Catholics "worship" Mary, perhaps it seemed so to the early generations of Muslims. Or perhaps, the movement that Muhammad encountered was a deviation of Christianity that elevated Mary to deity. Therefore, the Muslim Jesus is nothing more than a messenger of God. Any attempt to ascribe to him a higher status or to elevate him beyond his humanity is considered blasphemy. At the same time, the Muslim Jesus is described positively in unique ways and given the titles "Word" and "Spirit"; no other person is offered those honorific titles.

WHAT IF THIS WERE OUR ONLY JESUS?

If the Muslim Jesus were the only Jesus, then the last two thousand years of world history would have gone much differently. As a prophet and reformer of the old ways and nothing more, Jesus would have never founded a movement that came to be called "Christianity"; after all, Jesus was only the next-to-last prophet, pointing the way to the coming of Muhammad six centuries later. It follows that the disciples of Jesus would have started a school and nothing like "the church." Indeed, if Jesus has not been raised from the dead, then Christianity as we know it is an empty, pointless religion (e.g., 1 Cor 15:12-19).

The Muslim Jesus would have never inspired a collection of writings like The New Testament. The New Testament requires a new covenant. With the Muslim Jesus there is no new covenant, no body broken, no blood poured out, no Eucharist. There may have been a Gospel written—like the *Gospel of Barnabas*—but probably no letters and certainly no apocalypse. When we gather together with other like-minded believers, we would study the Torah, the book of Psalms and perhaps a Gospel, but we would do so through the lens of the Qur'an and the Hadith. Arabic, not Greek, Hebrew or Latin, would be the language studied by ministers in seminary.

For her virtue Mary may well occupy a higher place in our thoughts and devotion; however, it would not likely eclipse the devotion offered her among some Catholics and Orthodox today. Prayers to Mary and the saints would undoubtedly be out of bounds. It is possible that Christmas would be on our calendars as a celebration of the virgin birth, not in commemoration of the God who was made flesh and lived among us. Since the Muslim Jesus is not the Son of God and divine, then worshiping Jesus, praying to him, and composing hymns in his honor would be considered blasphemous.

If the Muslim Jesus were the only Jesus, then Islam, not Christianity, would be the largest world religion, and most of you reading this book right now would be Muslim.

Read More About It

Khalidi, Tarif. *The Muslim Jesus: Sayings and Stories in Islamic Literature*. Cambridge, MA: Harvard University Press, 2001.

Masri, Fouad. *Connecting with Muslims: A Guide to Communicating Effectively*. Downers Grove, IL: InterVarsity Press, 2014.

Shedinger, Robert F. *Was Jesus a Muslim? Questioning Categories in the Study of Religion*. Philadelphia: Fortress, 2009.

Siddiqui, Mona. *Christians, Muslims and Jesus*. New Haven: Yale University Press, 2013.

Discussion Questions

1. Where has your knowledge of Islam come from? Based on your sources,

are you confident that you have a true sense of what the Muslim faith is about?

2. If someone came to you and said, "Muslims believe in Jesus just like Christians do," how would you respond?

3. Mary figures prominently in the faith of many Muslims and Christians. How do you assess her significance?

4. Why is it important for Christians to affirm the divinity of Jesus as the Son of God?

5. If the Muslim Jesus were the only Jesus, how would your faith be different?

11

THE HISTORICAL JESUS

"W hy does God hate our bell tower?" the villagers around St. Mark's Church in Venice might have wondered. The 325-foot bell tower took its first hit of lightning in 1388. Lightning completely destroyed it in 1417, and after they rebuilt it, no doubt dedicating it to God's glory, lightning destroyed it again in 1489. *Fulgara frango* ("I break up the lightning") was engraved on many medieval bells. Priests were trained to ring church bells and recite specific prayers during storms to ward off lightning. More strikes hit St. Mark's tower in 1548, 1565 and 1653. In 1745 the tower was reduced to rubble again by lightning. Why did God hate their bell tower? In 1766 the church installed a lightning rod designed by Benjamin Franklin, and the tower has never been damaged by lightning again. Most of us would not conclude that Ben Franklin had found a way to thwart God's wrath. Rather, we would argue that thunderstorms are the result of unstable air masses and certainly not God's anger. Most of us would applaud the medieval scholar who researched for thirty-three years what happened when bell ringers went to work during storms. His published treatise, "Proof that the ringing of bells during thunderstorms may be more dangerous than useful," showed 386 strikes on bell towers, killing 103 bell ringers.[1]

The world of the New Testament was different. Jesus was asleep in a boat when a thunderstorm came. The disciples were afraid and Jesus rebuked

---

[1]The story of St. Mark's tower and the medieval research comes from Professor Randy Cerveny (then director of the Arizona State University Laboratory of Climatology) as recorded by John Matthews, "Fear of Lightning Grounded in Myth," *ASU Research* (Fall 1994): 8.

(*epitimēsen* [Mk 4:39]) the wind, using the same word he uses to rebuke (*epitimēsen* [Mk 1:25]) the unclean spirit. So, how do we read Jesus calming the storm when Ben Franklin stands between us and the biblical story? When thunder rumbles, we don't pause to listen intently to ascertain if God is speaking (see Jn 12:29). Paul may have seen a flash of light and heard a voice (Acts 9:3-4), but most of us merely see lightning flash and hear thunder roll. The Enlightenment encouraged us to see a Jesus who could be explained rationally by the laws of science and history, producing a historical Jesus who is quite different from the Jesus whom our faith describes.

Most Americans look upon the Enlightenment positively. The very name is positive: how do you not agree with enlightening someone? During the seventeenth and eighteenth centuries in Europe a philosophy known as rationalism replaced the way people looked at the world. The Enlightenment is really about rationalism. Prior to this, people lived in a world dominated by God on a throne directing everyday events, such as illnesses, births and deaths, and lightning strikes. At the risk of oversimplifying, rationalism has three ground rules when it comes to historical research (understanding events in the past): continuity, causality, correction.

Since Christians believe that biblical events occurred in human history, these rules apply to understanding biblical events as well.[2] *Continuity* suggests that the world in which Jesus lived is the same one as ours and operates by the same rules. This makes sense. Our world is in continuity with the world that preceded it. The biblical events happened not in a parallel universe but on the same planet Earth that we live on. Jesus didn't walk in a Nazareth that was "long, long ago, in a galaxy far, far away." Jesus lived in the world of Caesar, whose statues are still around today. *Causality* tells us that all events in history are related. One event causes another. Each event is the effect of a previous cause. The concept of cause and effect is so woven into our thinking that it practically goes without being said. A knife didn't mi-

---

[2]Ernst Troeltsch is commonly credited with applying rationalism to biblical research: "Historical and Dogmatic Method in Theology," in *Religion in History*, trans. J. L. Adams and W. F. Bense (Minneapolis: Fortress, 1991), pp. 11-32. His principles were: methodological doubt, analogy and correlation, what we are calling correction, continuity and causality. For a fuller explanation of Troeltsch and the study of the historical Jesus, see the excellent analysis by Mark L. Strauss, *Four Portraits, One Jesus: An Introduction to Jesus and the Gospels* (Grand Rapids: Zondervan, 2007), pp. 348-78.

raculously appear in Julius Caesar; someone stuck it into him. Lastly, *correction* reminds us that no conclusions are final. All analyses and reconstructions are subject to further revision. We think that it was Brutus who knifed Caesar, but we realize that an archaeologist could make a discovery that would force us to change that view. Maybe it was someone else. Knowledge isn't complete; as humans, we are still learning. To use a different illustration, we are confident that ancient humans suffered from infections like we do (continuity). Ancient infections had a biological cause (causality); it wasn't "spirits." Most of us feel the modern explanation of infection is better than the ancient one (correction). These ground rules—continuity, causality, correction—seem like sound foundations for any research.

There is much positive that can be said for these principles, but the ramifications for historical understanding are vast. Using continuity, a rationalist would argue that if folks can't walk on water now, they couldn't back then. By virtue of the principle of continuity, miracles are a priori eliminated, since one has never been documented in a modern laboratory. Causality tells a rationalist that no event can happen without a prior cause (which is understood to mean a cause from within our physical world of cause and effect). The storm that Jesus encountered arose in the same way that thunderstorms happen today. Thus, God is not intervening in human history. Perhaps God knew that an unstable air mass was forming,

SO WHAT?

Should Christians Be Anti-Science?

If God is the creator of all things, then when we are studying creation, we are studying God's handiwork. Studying is a more intense form of reflecting upon the glory of the world that God has created. The life of the mind is a spiritual pursuit, since we are to love God with our mind as well our heart. We have been charged with dominion over the earth; therefore, we must study it. Christians should be the best scientists. Actually, historically most of them were, such as Francis Bacon, Johannes Kepler, Blaise Pascal, Michael Faraday, Charles Townes, and Donald Page. William Phillips (Nobel Prize for the development of methods to cool and trap atoms with laser light) is a devout follower of Christ. I but he did not interrupt the normal chain of causes to create a unique thunderstorm. Likewise, causality rules out many miracles, since many require a cause outside of space and time. Lastly, the principle of correction tells a rationalist that any historical understanding may need to be revised in the future because human understanding is growing. A biblical explanation of an event is subject to revision now (because we humans today know more than biblical writers did). Thus, we can correct the biblical explanation of Jesus verbally rebuking the spirits in the wind. If we had been there, rationalists argue, we would have seen what really happened, which those lesser-informed ancients misunderstood as supernatural. It wasn't really a demon causing the young boy to convulse, a post-Enlightenment rationalist would argue; it was epilepsy, a medical condition with a (now) known cause and treatments.

remember hearing Francis Collins (National Human Genome Research Institute) speak about his Christian faith. At the conclusion of his talk he surprised us by pulling a guitar from under the podium and leading us in a hymn. Fritz Schaefer, director of the Center for Computational Quantum Chemistry at the University of Georgia, is an outspoken evangelical Christian, and he argues that many distinguished contemporary scientists consider the truth claims of Jesus Christ to be intellectually compelling. In the previous century intellectualism became increasingly anti-evangelical; evangelicalism became increasingly anti-intellectual. Scholars such as Mark Noll have sounded the rallying cry for Christians to reengage the intellectual marketplace and Christian scientists are leading the way.

The Enlightenment took rationalism to the extreme. Reason wasn't just a good way to understand the world; it was the sole test of truth. Therefore, anything that could not be explained rationally wasn't true. Supernatural events (by definition) can't be true. Rationalism leads to the clear conclusion that the picture of Jesus in the New Testament is an image of Jesus embellished (lovingly perhaps) by his followers. This "Jesus of faith" cannot be the same as the "Jesus of history." Rationalists know this because the Jesus of faith walked on water, but the Jesus of history could not have (continuity). Rationalism had solved the mystery of lightning; it would solve the mystery of Jesus rebuking the wind (correction). The challenge of an embellished

picture of Jesus, the rationalist argues, needs to be approached systemati-
cally. Whoever Jesus actually was, he wasn't a miracle-worker. So, who was
he? And thus begins what has come to be known as "the quest for the historical Jesus."

Who Do Historians Say That I Am?

This search for the historical Jesus, the one behind the embellished picture
of the Jesus of faith found in our Gospels, should be conducted in the same
way, it is argued, that we try to understand who Julius Caesar was. Many of
us have read biographies of Abraham Lincoln or Dietrich Bonhoeffer. How
do modern scholars uncover the "real" Lincoln? Historians look at sources
and attempt to understand Lincoln as a product of his time, placing him in
the context of his culture. Thus, modern historians took the same approach
to Jesus, seeking more enlightened explanations for the (mis)reported actions of Jesus.

The principal challenge for the rationalists, of course, was the miracles.
How can we, they ask, find the real Jesus behind the clearly embellished
picture of Jesus? First, one needed to shift the focus away from the miracles; they couldn't be "signs" of who Jesus is, as John's Gospel asserted. "It
is my chief desire that my views regarding the miracle stories should not
be taken as by any means the principal thing. How empty would devotion
or religion be if one's spiritual well-being depended on whether one believed in miracles or no!"[3] Correction (from the supposedly superior
vantage point of rationalism) enabled the rationalist historian to "uncover
what really happened," giving rise to nonsupernatural explanations for the
reported miracles. These nonmiraculous activities of Jesus were misunderstood or misinterpreted by Jesus' followers (who were less enlightened
about the world than historians are). Many of the rationalist historians of
the nineteenth century were God-fearing persons who considered themselves devout Christians. Jesus is still the one they followed, but not be-

---

[3]H. E. G. Paulus, *Das Leben Jesu als Grundlage einer reinen Geschichte des Urchristentums* [*The Life
of Jesus as the Basis of a Purely Historical Account of Early Christianity*], 2 vols. (Heidelberg: C. F.
Winter, 1828), as quoted in Albert Schweitzer, *The Quest of the Historical Jesus: A Critical Study
of Its Progress from Reimarus to Wrede*, trans. W. Montgomery (New York: Macmillan, 1968), p.
51. Schweitzer's original, published in 1906, was *Von Reimarus zu Wrede: Eine Geschichte der
Leben-Jesu-Forschung*.

cause he was a miracle-worker. "The truly miraculous thing about Jesus is Himself, the purity and serene holiness of His character, which is, notwithstanding, genuinely human, and adapted to the imitation and emulation of mankind," writes H. E. G. Paulus, one of the pioneer Enlightenment historians of Jesus.[4] For these historians, the question about supernatural miracles was secondary because all of nature was under the control of an omnipotent God, and "spiritual truths" could never be attested nor overthrown by a miracle (or lack of one). Ancient humans, they argued, needed to have their minds "astounded and subdued by inexplicable facts. This effect, however, is past."[5] Modern humankind no longer needs supernatural events to validate God's working in the world. God works through the laws of nature, which, they argue, we now understand. While God is the primary cause of all things, ancients just didn't know the secondary causes. "Their knowledge of the laws of nature was insufficient to enable them to understand what actually happened."[6] All that remains for the historian is to uncover the secondary cause (the nonsupernatural one) that explains the supposed miracle.

For these early historians, the "miracle" may no longer remain, but the spiritual truth persisted. (As this movement progressed into the late nineteenth and twentieth centuries, the spiritual truth was also dismissed.) Thus, miracles of healing are simply explained. Jesus' force of personality often had impact on a person's state of mind, relieving anxiety and stress. Jesus also used medicines unknown to those from that region. Some historians suggest that he learned these in Egypt. "The disciples too, as appears from Mark 6:7, 13, were not sent out without medicaments, for the oil with which they were to anoint the sick was, of course, of a medicinal character; and the casting out of evil spirits was effected partly by means of sedatives."[7] Thus, Jesus' remark "This kind can come forth by nothing, but by prayer and fasting" (Mk 9:29 KJV [the translation that these historians would have used]) was actually instructions to the father for making the sudden calming of an epileptic seizure a permanent one, by keeping the son to a

---

[4]Quoted in ibid.
[5]Quoted in ibid.
[6]Quoted in ibid.
[7]Quoted in ibid., p. 52.

strict diet and the regiment of devotional exercises. Nature miracles may also be explained:

> The walking on the water was an illusion of the disciples. Jesus walked along the shore, and in the mist was taken for a ghost by the alarmed and excited occupants of the boat. When Jesus called to them, Peter threw himself into the water, and was drawn to shore by Jesus just as he was sinking. Immediately after taking Jesus into the boat they doubled a headland and drew clear of the storm centre; they therefore supposed that He had calmed the sea by His command.[8]

Likewise, when Jesus was asleep in the boat, the boat slipped into the shelter of a hill and was shielded from the wind, just as they awakened Jesus. Yet it was not merely coincidence. Jesus was better at reading the signs of weather: "When you see a cloud rising in the west, you immediately say, 'It is going to rain'; and so it happens. And when you see the south wind blowing, you say, 'There will be scorching heat'; and it happens" (Lk 12:54-55).

Obviously, Jesus never raised anyone from the dead. Rather, ancients, in their haste to bury the dead, were prone to bury those nearly dead. Jesus rescues them from premature burial. Jesus hastens to Jairus's daughter to save her from being buried while only in a coma. When walking into Nain, Jesus has a sense that the widow's son might not be

---

SO WHAT?
....

The Hubris of Scientism

Most of us overreach, just a little. Some overreach a lot. By that, we mean that most of us think that we can use our discipline, thesis or expertise to explain the world better than the next person. That tendency to overreach is evidence of what the ancients called "hubris" or "arrogance." Scientism (not science) claims that the inductive methods developed in the natural sciences are the only way to know anything true about the world and reality. In fact, to claim to have any knowledge that can't be confirmed by the modern scientific method is to know nothing at all. But even if science is capable of doing many amazing things, it does have its limits. It can't explain everything.

History is one of those matters that might be informed by science, but it

---

[8]Quoted in ibid.

truly dead. Fortunately, for Lazarus, Jesus orders the stone moved away so that his friend, who had revived in the tomb but was trapped, could be freed. So, it was with joy that Jesus shouted, "Lazarus, come forth!"

Other supposed miracles are also explained from our enlightened viewpoint, such as the feeding of the five thousand. Ancient people, it is suggested, did not travel without considering food and shelter. Unlike today, there were no drive-thrus where one could grab a bite to eat or ATMs where one could fetch cash for a quick meal. Most of the people at the feeding had food in their

cannot be fully explained. What really happened in the past and why can't it be understood the same way we investigate a chemical reaction or a biological process? Paraphrasing C. S. Lewis in his essay "Meditation in a Toolshed," science might be able to help us look *at* something (rationally, objectively) but not *through* something (experientially, imaginatively).[a] Science, for example, might be able to explain the depth and weight of glass in a window; it might be able to describe the composition of the chemical compounds in the glass. But it can't give me a reason to look through the window to see what may be on the other side. Often the most important things to see are found not in looking at them but through them. History provides the lens through which we can see what is on the other side.

[a]For these insights I'm grateful to my colleague Dr. Holly Ordway of Houston Baptist University.

satchels, but they were unwilling to bring it out for fear that others were less well prepared and they would have to share. Jesus' public example of a little boy sharing his small lunch stirred the selfish hearts of the crowd, and so they quietly began to share their provisions as well. The miracle, it is argued, was the miracle of turning selfish misers into gracious givers—a spiritual miracle indeed!

The second challenge for the enlightened historian attempting to rediscover Jesus was that the historian needed to find better ways to understand the actions of Jesus.

Thus, it was the fictitious "Lives [of Jesus]" of Bahrdt and Venturini which, at the end of the eighteenth and beginning of the nineteenth centuries, first attempted to apply, with logical consistency, a non-supernatural interpretation to the miracle stories of the Gospel. Further, these writers . . . endeavoured to grasp the inner connexion of cause and effect in the events and experiences of the life of Jesus. Since they found no such connexion indicated in the Gospels, they had to supply it for themselves.[9]

The challenge in reconstructing a better picture of Jesus is not just explaining what the historical Jesus was doing but why he was doing it. What was motivating Jesus if it wasn't a supernatural commission from God? Just as modern historians attempt to explain the motivations of Julius Caesar or Abraham Lincoln, these historians of Jesus worked to correct the biblical explanation of Jesus' actions. One of the first to suggest a comprehensive motive was Karl Friedrich Bahrdt (1741–1792). Originally an orthodox cleric, Bahrdt abandoned faith in divine revelation (and cast off most moral restraints) and sought to explain the Jesus movement solely on rational grounds in "An Explanation of the Plans and Aims of Jesus." In what sounds like a plot borrowed from a Dan Brown novel, Bahrdt identifies a conspiracy behind the story of Jesus, where the principal figures were actually Nicodemus and Joseph of Arimathea. These two men were not followers of Jesus but actually were members of a secret society, the Essenes.[10] With members throughout Jewish society around the Roman Empire, they also infiltrated the Sanhedrin. Committed to freeing the Jewish nation from worldly messianic hopes (of a Davidic king), they sought a messiah who would steer the nation away from militaristic goals. According to Bahrdt,

> Jesus came under the notice of the Order immediately after His birth. As a child He was watched over at every step by the Brethren. At the feasts in Jerusalem, Alexandrian Jews, secret members of the Essene Order, put themselves into communication with Him . . . inspired Him with a horror of the bloody sacrifices of the Temple, and made him acquainted with Socrates and Plato. . . . At the story of the death of Socrates, the boy bursts into a tempest of sobs. . . . He longs to emulate the martyr-death of the great Athenian.[11]

As the boy Jesus grows, various figures secretly influence him. An Essene priest, disguised as a shepherd, guides Jesus, along with his cousin John, into

---

[9]Schweitzer, *Quest of the Historical Jesus*, p. 38.
[10]Bahrdt wrote before the Dead Sea Scrolls were discovered, which did much to clarify the Essenes. Since that discovery, it would be difficult to portray the Essenes as some type of Illuminati or Bilderberg Group.
[11]Schweitzer, *Quest of the Historical Jesus*, p. 40. The rest of the reconstruction of Bahrdt's position is derived from Schweitzer.

deeper mysteries. These deeper understandings explain how the twelve-year-old Jesus is able to amaze the temple authorities. While living in Nazareth, "a mysterious Persian" gives Jesus two powerful medicines, one for eye problems and the other for nervous disorders. Later Luke the physician is introduced to Jesus, providing Jesus additional medical resources for healings. The pieces are now in place for the Order to begin the "cleverly staged drama" that we call Jesus' ministry.

The Order has three levels of members: the Baptized, the Disciples and the Chosen. The Baptized receive the teachings that we find in the Gospels. The Disciples get special teachings, as we see portrayed in the Gospels, although Bahrdt stressed that there was more not described in our stories. Lastly, the Chosen, who are also called "Angels" in the stories, are fully informed, including the secret machinations happening behind the scenes. As the church movement begins, it is run by the Apostles, who were only members of the second tier, the Disciples. Therefore, they were not privy to the secrets of the movement; hence, such details were lost in history, until the clever rationalist historians figured it out. Our Gospels were written by those not fully informed, so they wrote in good conscience, reporting as factual miracles events that were actually cleverly staged by the Order. For example, the Order had actually secretly collected a large amount of bread in a cave. Jesus stood just outside the concealed entrance. Several of the Chosen kept handing him bread to pass out to the crowd of five thousand. On the Sea of Galilee the Chosen had arranged a large floating raft on which Jesus walked. The uninformed Disciples assumed that it was a miracle.

The Order intended Jesus to be proclaimed as the Messiah in Jerusalem and then explain to the masses the proper understanding. Political events got out of hand, and Jesus was arrested and crucified. Luke the physician arranged medicines to make Jesus go into a deathlike stupor, explaining his "quick death." Joseph of Arimathea, one of the Chosen, arranged with Pilate for a quick burial. The Order later took Jesus from the tomb; several of its members apparently were mistaken for angels. After ten days of treatment, Jesus is well enough to "appear" to some of the Disciples. But after forty days, his strength is gone. He departs from them. Only the Order knows where he died and was actually buried.

The challenge for Bahrdt's imaginative reconstruction is that it doesn't result in any reasonable motive. At times, it seems that Jesus didn't know what the Order was doing. He was a stoolie, a dupe, a pigeon, manipulated behind the scenes by others. Yet, in the staging of the miracles Jesus had to have been a knowing participant, in which case he was deceiving the crowds. Holders of this view can point to select texts that suggest Jesus intended only the Chosen to understand: "The reason I speak to them in parables is that 'seeing they do not perceive, and hearing they do not listen, nor do they understand'" (Mt 13:13). Nonetheless, this reconstruction ultimately contradicts itself. If Jesus were trying to move the crowds to a "rational religion," why would he deceive them into believing in miracles? It would be counterproductive. Any "rational" explanation of Jesus' motives is better served by a sincere Jesus.

Herman Samuel Reimarus (1694–1768), often credited with beginning the quest for the historical Jesus, looked at first-century Judaism (and not the Christianity of Reimarus's day) to find a sincere motive. He argued that Jesus considered himself a human messiah (like David) who was to free his people from a foreign (Roman) empire (also like David) and to establish a political kingdom on earth (like David). He was the Son of David, just as the crowds considered him when they welcomed him to Jerusalem (in what we call "the triumphal entry"). Reimarus (whose theory was published after his death) argued that Jesus' hopes were crushed by his arrest and execution for treason against Rome. His disciples resurrected the movement by stealing his body and claiming an actual resurrection by Jesus. Effectively, the fraud is moved from Jesus to the disciples.

Reimarus's claim that the Christian faith was founded upon fraud could not stand the weight of scrutiny. Why would disciples die for a movement they knew to be a lie? They didn't profit from it; rather, they suffered for their proclamation. Scholars after Reimarus rejected his theory that the disciples were deceiving everyone. Nonetheless, following the tenets of rationalism, they continued in the approach of seeing Jesus as an ordinary human. Therefore, if Jesus' disciples didn't steal his dead body—a theory conceded as implausible—what is the rational explanation for the resurrection stories (since we "know" humans do not come back from the dead)? Well, other scholars have suggested Jesus fainted ("swooned") on the cross and was buried prematurely. The coolness of the tomb revived him, and he escaped.

Although the "swoon theory" for Jesus' supposed resuscitation was possible (resurrection is a completely different matter), others argue that it is also implausible. It simply doesn't make sense. No one was requiring or even expecting a resurrection. Where did Jesus go after he left the tomb? If he had died nearby, his body would have been found. If he were still alive, his disciples would have celebrated his "miraculous" escape from the Romans. If the stolen body or swoon theories don't make muster, the way forward was not to go back. Scholars were not going to return to the premodern world, where the miraculous was celebrated as divine and ignorant superstitions ruled daily life. We know better, they argue.

In the subsequent decades of studying the historical Jesus other theories have arisen, all seeking to find a rationalist reconstruction of a very human Jesus. Scholars have initiated other quests of the historical Jesus, all producing various results with no consensus—not even a majority opinion. Recently, one group decided they would sort out what the historical Jesus actually said and did, since the Gospels were (in their estimation) little more than propaganda written to inspire faith. The renowned Jesus Seminar produced a color-coded "Gospel" that diminished practically all of the "red letter" sayings of Jesus to pink (probable), grey (possible), and black (certainly not). Other scholars dismissed these findings as pretentious and arbitrary. How could someone know for certain what anyone said last year much less two thousand years ago?

Some scholars decided to look for the key that unlocks the historical Jesus by refining more clearly our understanding of the first-century world. Since Jesus was a man of his time, it is argued, reproducing a more accurate picture of Jesus' world should yield a better understanding of his life. The problem, of course, was not only settling on the best description of first-century life in Galilee (was it more or less Jewish than Judea?), but also determining where Jesus belonged. And, even if we could agree on where Jesus came from, scholars still couldn't agree on what he was trying to do. After all, he wasn't a man confined by his own context; he was out to change the world. So, was he a social revolutionary, a political activist, a reformation prophet or a subversive sage? Did Jesus intend to start the religion "Christianity" or not? Did he ever claim to be a divine, Son of God, someone to be worshiped as God? Did he plan for his death on the cross to be the sacrifice that would take away the sins of the whole world?

WHAT'S MORE

A Historical Harmony of the Gospel

In certain respects, every quest for the historical Jesus is another attempt to present a "harmony of the Gospels." The difference, of course, is that the historian is not trying to harmonize every verse of the four Gospels into one coherent story. Rather, these scholars are trying to harmonize their understanding of the first-century world and Jesus with the parts of the Gospels that they choose to use, ignoring the parts that don't fit. It would be like taking six different thousand-piece puzzles of Jesus (four Gospels, historical background, historian's imagination), dumping only part of each box on the floor, then recreating a composite picture of Jesus out of the remaining pieces. One might suggest this is what even the more conservative, "evangelical" scholars do, such as N. T. Wright.[a] He presents his version of Jesus (which is really a Matthean Jesus with bits from Luke and Mark, and barely any from John), filtered through the lens of his theological reading of the Old Testament, as the "real Jesus." We may prefer Wright's Jesus over, say, John Dominic Crossan's Jesus,[b] but the point remains: like any "harmony" of the Gospels, much material has to be ignored in order to get all the pieces of the "historical Jesus puzzle" to fit.

---

[a]See N. T. Wright's three-volume work on Jesus, *The New Testament and the People of God, Jesus and the Victory of God* and *The Resurrection of the Son of God* (Minneapolis: Fortress, 1992, 1996, 2003).

[b]See, for example, John Dominic Crossan, *The Historical Jesus: The Life of a Mediterranean Jewish Peasant* (San Francisco: HarperSanFrancisco, 1991).

Scholars during these quests may have moved beyond the question of miracles, but they were still trying to provide a rational explanation for how whatever Jesus did and said gave birth to a new religion, and even on that question they couldn't agree. Consequently, with all the diverse opinions built on the firm foundation of "rationalism," the human invention called "the historical Jesus" never materialized. Every scholar constructed a different Jesus depending upon his or her own reasonable preferences.

How Is This Jesus Different?

In certain respects, this is an entirely believable Jesus. He operates solely within the same space-time continuum in which we do. He may fall within the rarified category of amazing human beings, like Moses, Muhammad and Gandhi, but he had no supernatural abilities, and he certainly wasn't divine. His teachings were inspirational but not inspired.

The critique by Albert Schweitzer in 1906 of the so-called first quest for the historical Jesus was accurate, but one may suggest that it remains true of all the others. The researcher often produces an image of Jesus that looks more like the researcher than any biblical image. In the nineteenth century Reimarus, Paulus and Adolf von Harnack painted a picture of a "modern philanthropist preaching an inoffensive message of love and brotherhood."[12] When the principles of rationalism are applied to the search for Jesus, the results are, perhaps inevitably, a mirror of the character and values of the historian.

After looking at the various reconstructions of the historical Jesus, we can ask, "Why would crowds follow this Jesus?" The answer, historians have argued, is "For the same reason, crowds followed other great teachers." The classic liberal picture of Jesus casts him as a great moral teacher, encouraging the fatherhood of God and the brotherhood of all humanity. More recently, historians have suggested other explanations for why crowds would follow Jesus. Geza Vermes (1973) suggested that the historical Jesus was a Jewish miracle-worker, such as others described in Jewish writings. Similarly, Morton Smith (1978) painted Jesus as another example of a first-century magician, working wonders to amaze the crowds. Both would grant Jesus no more supernatural ability (if any) than other such wonder-workers of the time. The historical Jesus drew crowds just as these other men did. Other historians have described Jesus as a leader of a social movement. Richard Horsley (1987) casts Jesus as the head of a peasant revolt, objecting to the injustices suffered by the poor. John Dominic Crossan (1991) portrays Jesus leading a broader social movement. Crowds followed the historical Jesus like they have followed other revolutionaries.

A nonsupernatural Jesus is difficult to explain and harder to understand.

---

[12]Strauss, *Four Portraits*, p. 350.

Why was Jesus traveling and preaching? The various nonsupernatural explanations of Jesus struggle to suggest any convincing motive.

If people were burying their (nearly) dead prematurely, why wouldn't Jesus correct their misunderstanding? Why would he allow them to think that it was a miracle? If Jesus suspected that Lazarus had revived in the tomb, why all his talk about being the resurrection and the life? Why not just tell Mary and Martha, "Your brother has not yet died!" In the case of healings, why not share the medicines that he had? His "miracles" did not bring him fame and fortune. Even his notoriety was rather limited. As Schweitzer notes, "the hypothesis condemns itself."[13] Attempts to explain the motives of Jesus find no support in what the followers did afterwards. While each individual explanation is dubious at best, the die had been cast. The quest to explain Jesus as a mere human being remains.

It might not surprise us that the application of continuity, causality and correction to the life of Jesus produces a Jesus much like other great leaders. What might be more surprising is that the rationalist

---

SO WHAT?
. . . .
Jesus in Our Own Image

The Christian call is to imitate Christ, so how are we supposed to perform miracles? Well, one answer that some historians gave is that he didn't perform them. Therefore, we end up creating a Jesus who was motivated by the same things that we care about and has the same abilities that we have. So, the Jesus whom historians describe often look likes the person they see in the mirror. The end result is often that we don't imitate Christ; rather, Christ ends up imitating us. Or, on the other hand, we tend to imitate the Christ we create, as in the case of Albert Schweitzer. He created a historical Jesus—a man who threw himself before the unjust wheels of history to force God's providential hand—and then imitated him by giving up a cushy job teaching theology, studying medicine, and spending most of his life helping the poor in Africa. Either way, the historical Jesus ends up becoming the imitable creation of human beings.

---

[13]Schweitzer, *Quest of the Historical Jesus*, 53.

quest to rediscover Jesus also resulted in skepticism about ever really knowing who Jesus was. In fact, thoroughgoing skeptics claim Jesus never existed at all.[14] Ironically, then, the historical Jesus—the product of rationalism—remains a mystery.

WHAT IF THIS WERE OUR ONLY JESUS?

For most modern people, the historical Jesus *is* their only Jesus. The two centuries of skepticism have resulted in a population that immediately dismisses suggestions of miracles. The principle of "correction" is so ingrained in our culture that we arrogantly view ourselves as able to critique and correct all the inferior viewpoints of the past. The Gospels aren't reliable. Supernatural events can't happen in the modern world. We must be suspicious of ancient sources because we can see historical events from our superior vantage point. Unlike us, we argue, biblical writers were racist, sexist oppressors who manipulated the real stories of Jesus to say what they wanted. Only we modern historians can objectively see the past. The only Jesus we should have is the improved one re-created by enlightened modern scholars who have freed themselves of the influences of ancient Christians. The irony is too obvious to miss. The lure of Gnosticism seduces those who believe that they know more. Again, the established church, with its Gospels, has it wrong, whereas this or that historian has the secret to unlocking the real Jesus.

What would our preaching look like? This is a Jesus worth living for but probably not worth dying for. This Jesus is inspirational. What would our churches be doing if this were our only Jesus? We would be getting along with other religions because we would not be constrained to maintain exclusivity claims. Followers of this Jesus would be able to hold hands with imams, rabbis and Buddhist monks as we all talked about the fatherhood of God and the brotherhood of humankind. We could joyfully sing with all religions,

> Thou the Father, Christ our Brother,—
> all who live in love are Thine:
> Teach us how to love each other. . . .

---

[14]See James K. Beilby and Paul Rhodes Eddy, eds., *The Historical Jesus: Five Views* (Downers Grove, IL: IVP Academic, 2009), especially the chapter by Robert M. Price, "Jesus at the Vanishing Point."

Father-love is reigning o'er us,
brother-love binds man to man.[15]

This Jesus inspires us to help out the less fortunate, to love one another, to be tolerant and inoffensive.

Since we are able to read and correct the Bible from our superior vantage

---

WHAT'S MORE . . .

Was Jesus Married?

From time to time a claim is made that Jesus of Nazareth was married. Usually the scenario is put forward that Jesus had a relationship with Mary Magdalene and children resulted from their union. In 2003 Dan Brown popularized the notion in his bestselling novel *The DaVinci Code*. A film adaption was released by Sony Columbia Pictures in 2006. Brown's own plot bears certain similarities to assertions made in the controversial nonfiction book *The Holy Blood and Holy Grail* (1982), by Michael Baigent and Richard Leigh. An entire cottage industry of Christian books sprang up to challenge Brown's revision of history, denouncing its historical inaccuracies. Since then others have made similar claims that Jesus was married based on a variety of evidence. Some, for example, read the patchy Gnostic *Gospel of Philip* to imply Jesus had a relationship with Mary Magdalene, but the date is centuries after Jesus' time and the document is very fragmentary.

In the end there is no credible evidence from any ancient source that Jesus of Nazareth was married. But even if he were, there would have been no reason for his contemporaries to hide the fact. After all, there is no shame in marriage or bearing children. The Jewish tradition is clear that marriage is an institution ordained by God, a normal state of human affairs, and bearing children is a blessing from heaven. Nevertheless, the claim that Jesus was married will continue to surface occasionally, as long as it sells magazines and books and can even produce a blockbuster film.

---

[15]Henry van Dyke, "The Hymn of Joy," in *Book of Poems* (1911). According to Kenneth Osbeck, the hymn was written to be sung to the melody of the "Ode to Joy," the final movement of Ludwig von Beethoven's final symphony, Symphony No. 9 (*101 Hymn Stories* [Grand Rapids: Kregel, 1982], p. 145).

point of having been enlightened, we would be regularly tweaking our image of the historical Jesus. Yearly televisions specials would uncover more "hidden" facts about Jesus. We can shake off those silly premodern superstitions about spirits. In fact, the entire notion of "evil" is probably antiquated. We should perhaps rid ourselves of unenlightened views of morality and sexuality. Jesus inspires us to find the noblest traits of humanity. If there is a god (or gods), we will find him or her most likely by looking inward. The historical Jesus, like Moses, Buddha, Confucius and Muhammad, motivates us to achieve the highest level of goodness that we can. If they could do it, then we can (continuity). If they are able to rise to greatness, we should be able to control ourselves and our environments (causality) to do the same. Celebrating this Jesus is celebrating humanity. Since Schweitzer is probably correct that the Jesus created by rationalist historians is like looking in a mirror, one might even suggest that worshiping this Jesus is self-worship.

Read More About It

Beilby, James K., and Paul Rhodes Eddy, eds. *The Historical Jesus: Five Views.* Downers Grove, IL: IVP Academic, 2009.

Brown, Colin. "Quest of the Historical Jesus." In *Dictionary of Jesus and the Gospels*, edited by Joel B. Green, Jeannine K. Brown and Nicholas Perrin, pp. 718-56. 2nd ed. Downers Grove, IL: IVP Academic, 2013.

Keener, Craig S. *The Historical Jesus of the Gospels.* Grand Rapids: Eerdmans, 2009.

Schaefer, Henry F., III. *Science and Christianity: Conflict or Coherence?* 2nd ed. Watkinsville, GA: Apollos Trust, 2013.

Schweitzer, Albert. *The Quest of the Historical Jesus: A Critical Study of Its Progress from Reimarus to Wrede.* Translated by W. Montgomery. New York: Macmillan, 1968.

Discussion Questions

1. Many Western worldviews are dominated by an "either-or" mentality; thus, viewpoints are right or wrong, yes or no. When brought to this issue, we may find ourselves subconsciously thinking, "So, was the Enlightenment a good thing or a bad thing? Are continuity, causality and correction good or bad principles?" How does this discussion change when we stop dividing into two extremes? What happens when ask in-

stead, "How, like every cultural movement, has the Enlightenment both helped and hurt our faith?"

2. Many rationalists sincerely sought to follow Jesus. They just whittled Jesus down until he fit into their worldview. How might we be guilty of the same?

3. We critique the rationalists for their hubris, feeling superior to ancients and thus better able to understand Jesus. How might we be guilty of hubris today?

4. If your local church took seriously the rationalist's historical Jesus, how might it be different?

12

The Mormon Jesus

They are easy to spot. They travel in twos, often on bicycles, sporting white shirts and dark slacks, carrying backpacks. Clean-cut young men in their twenties, they canvass neighborhoods hoping to be invited into homes to share their faith. They are always polite, respectful and irenic. Rarely ones to argue, these missionaries say their piece and move on, never overstaying their welcome. And yet, for all their endearing qualities, the reputation of their strange ways precedes them. They are known to abstain from caffeine. There was a time when they avoided the title "Christian" and believed that black people couldn't become priests. Their religion was started by an American teenager in 1820. They baptize for the dead. They maintain careful genealogical records and believe that all humans can become gods. Their scriptures say that America is the Promised Land and that the New Jerusalem will be established in Independence, Missouri. Most outsiders call them "Mormons." Many Mormons prefer to be called "Latter-day Saints" (LDS). There are over two hundred different groups of Mormons, but the largest and best-known sect settled in Utah. Tourists flock to see the magnificent temple in Salt Lake City and to hear the Mormon Tabernacle Choir. Even though they maintain a squeaky-clean public image, they have been labeled as a "cult" by some Christians. Most people, however, see Mormons as just another Christian denomination, mainly because LDS members talk a lot about Jesus Christ. In fact, their church is named after him, "The Church of Jesus Christ of Latter-day Saints." So, do Mormons believe in the same Jesus whom Christians believe in?

WHO DO MORMONS SAY THAT I AM?

Here's a surprising discovery: there's nothing unorthodox about Jesus in the Book of Mormon. To be sure, Christians will see as pure fiction the story of Jesus Christ appearing shortly after his ascension to the indigenous people living on the North American continent (3 Nephi 11:1–28:12). In fact, the entire story in the Book of Mormon sounds preposterous: before Nebuchadnezzar destroys Jerusalem, some Jews leave the country and sail to North America, establishing new tribes of Israel (Nephites and Lamanites); there are ongoing conflicts between these tribes of Israel and predictions regarding the coming of Jesus Christ to America; cataclysmic events in America coincide with the death of Jesus in Jerusalem; Jesus appears in America in A.D. 33, followed by Pentecostal events that mirror the book of Acts; the story ends with the eventual dissolution of the two tribes and predictions regarding the production and preservation of the Book of Mormon. To those unfamiliar with Mormon scripture, these fanciful tales read like the fill-in-the-gaps stories typical of ancient apocryphal literature. What happened in America during the "silent years" of the Protestant canon (between Malachi and Matthew), and especially after the ascension of Jesus? Well, the Book of Mormon supplies the answer to such an American-centric question. And yet, despite all of these peculiar stories, Jesus is presented in rather orthodox terms; he doesn't say or do anything heretical in the Book of Mormon.

The reason Jesus sounds like himself in the Book of Mormon is that he quotes himself. During this postascension visit to North America, most of the sermons sound very similar to what Jesus said in the canonical Gospels. For example, Jesus repeats, nearly word for word, the King James Version of the Sermon on the Mount (3 Nephi 12:3–14:27). And, nearly everything that Jesus does is a repeat of what he did according to the Gospels. When Jesus appears to the Nephites, he invites them to "thrust your hands into my side, and also that ye may feel the prints of the nails in my hands" (3 Nephi 11:14). When Jesus preaches his "doctrine" of salvation, it sounds like the sermons we read in Acts: "And whoso believeth in me, and is baptized, the same shall be saved; and they are they who shall inherit the kingdom of God" (3 Nephi 11:33). He implores them to "repent, and become as a little child, and be baptized in my name" (3 Nephi 11:37). Jesus is seen establishing the Lord's Supper, laying down the requirements of baptism, and giving commandments similar to ones found in John's Gospel. There are even stories of Jesus choosing twelve disciples, performing several miracles of healing, and blessing little children brought to him (3 Nephi 17:1–18:39). In other words, compared to the canonical Gospels, there's very little that is new here. The Mormon Jesus seems to be assembled from the canonical Gospels and is, therefore, rather familiar.

That's why whenever Mormons talk about Christ, especially salvation in Christ, it sounds like the gospel. Indeed, the articles of faith written by Joseph Smith could be mistaken as the Apostles' Creed by those who are unfamiliar with both:

> We believe in God, the Eternal Father, and in His Son, Jesus Christ, and in the Holy Ghost. We believe that men will be punished for their own sins, and not for Adam's transgression. We believe that through the Atonement of Christ, all mankind may be saved, by obedience to the laws and ordinances of the Gospel. We believe that the first principles and ordinances of the Gospel are: first, Faith in the Lord Jesus Christ; second, Repentance; third, Baptism by immersion for the remission of sins; fourth, Laying on of hands for the gift of the Holy Spirit.

When the contemporary Mormon scholar Robert Millet describes his faith in "the Christ of Latter-day Saints," we could easily believe it was offered during the typical "personal testimony" time at a Billy Graham crusade:

> Jesus suffered and bled in the Garden of Gethsemane and submitted to a cruel death on the cross of Calvary, all as a willing sacrifice, a substitutionary atonement for our sins. That offering is made efficacious as we exercise faith and trust in him; repent of our sins; are baptized by immersion as a symbol of our acceptance of his death, burial, and rise to newness of life; and receive the gift of the Holy Ghost. . . . I know the power that is in Christ, power not only to create the worlds and divide the seas but also to still the storms of the human heart, to right life's wrongs, to ease and eventually even remove the pain of scarred and beaten souls. There is no bitterness, no anger, no fear, no jealousy, no feelings of inadequacy that cannot be healed by the Great Physician. He is the Balm of Gilead. He is the One sent by the Father to "bind up the brokenhearted, to proclaim liberty to captives, and the opening of the prison to them that are bound" (Isaiah 61:1).[1]

---

[1] Robert L. Millet, *A Different Jesus? The Christ of Latter-day Saints* (Grand Rapids: Eerdmans, 2005), pp. 69, 177.

So, after considering the way Jesus talks and acts in the Book of Mormon, and especially after hearing LDS members describe their faith in Christ in such orthodox terms, who would doubt that Mormons are Christians? They may have their peculiar ways and strange religious ideas, but the same could be said of any number of Christian groups. In fact, although they may not know it, some Christians even hold to uniquely Mormon, and therefore unorthodox, ideas about Christ.

When it comes to the Mormon Jesus, the unorthodox part doesn't show up until later, in the Mormon scriptures that were written after the Book of Mormon, like the Doctrine and the Covenants and the Pearl of Great Price. It's in these books (as well as other writings, such as the King Follett Discourse) where the distinctively Mormon Jesus is found. That is to say, one wonders whether a new religion would have been established if Joseph Smith had merely stopped with the Book of Mormon. Christians may have considered the story of Jesus visiting America years ago a nice idea and left it at that. But, because he claimed continuous revelations, Smith kept writing Mormon scripture that would contain even more foreign ideas. And, it's in these heterodox teachings where Mormons find their unique identity—something they relish. In fact, they are quick to point out that they know their ideas about Jesus are not orthodox.[2] They believe that orthodoxy, especially the doctrines of the church established during the great christological councils of the fourth century, was so heavily influenced by Greek philosophy that Christian doctrine is a perversion of the true doctrine of Jesus Christ. That's why Joseph Smith received visions and eventually produced Mormon scripture. As a fourteen-year-old boy, he sought the Lord earnestly as to which Christian denominations were true. God the Father and God the Son showed up side by side and told him "that I must join none of them, for they were all wrong; and the Personage who addressed me said that all their creeds were an abomination in his sight; that those professors were all corrupt" (Pearl of Great Price, Joseph Smith—History 1:19). To the Mormon way of thinking, then, God had to start over with Joseph Smith in order to recover the gospel of Jesus Christ that had

---

[2]See Craig L. Blomberg and Stephen E. Robinson, *How Wide the Divide? A Mormon and an Evangelical in Conversation* (Downers Grove, IL: InterVarsity Press, 1997); see also Millett, *A Different Jesus?* pp. 39-58.

been lost to the corrupt influence of Christian ministers and theologians for over seventeen hundred years.

Because Mormons recognize the New Testament as scripture, it should come as no surprise that their view of Jesus from his birth to the resurrection and ascension is no different from that of most Christians. In other words, Mormons add nothing to the story of Jesus from Bethlehem to Jerusalem. In fact, they hold to a very high view of the canonical Gospels, taking exception to scholars who question whether Jesus said everything attributed to him. And, they fiercely defend the miracles performed by Jesus according to the four Gospels. What sets Mormons apart, however, is their view of Jesus before Bethlehem and after the ascension; this is where all the significant differences appear. What was Jesus like before he was born to Mary? What did Jesus do after the ascension? It's their beliefs about Jesus outside the New Testament, before Matthew and after Revelation, that reveal the unorthodox teachings of the LDS church.

Jesus is Jehovah. Mormons believe that the God of the Old Testament is Jesus (Doctrine and Covenants 38:1-6). Therefore, Jesus is the subject of the stories from Genesis to Malachi. He created the world in six days (Pearl of Great Price, Abraham 3:24; 4:1-31; Doctrine and Covenants 29:30-34). He established the covenant with Abraham and commanded him to take Hagar as his concubine (Doctrine and Covenants 132:29-35). It was Jesus who appeared to Moses in the burning bush and gave the law on Mount Sinai (3 Nephi 15:5). He ordained the priesthood (Doctrine and Covenants 132:28). Indeed, Jesus is described as "the God of Israel" even at his death: "And as for those who are at Jerusalem, saith the prophet, they shall be scourged by all people, because they crucify the God of Israel" (1 Nephi 19:13).

Jesus is an individual God. Because Joseph Smith saw two beings during his first divine encounter—God the Father and God the Son—Mormons believe that Jesus is a separate God from the Father. In other words, they do not affirm a trinitarian view of God (three persons, one being). In fact, they believe that there are many gods, but the preeminent Gods are three beings: God the Father, God the Son, God the Holy Ghost. They are one in purpose, one in mind, but they are three distinct Gods. Two of them have bodies "of flesh and bones" like humans (the Father and the Son); the Holy Ghost is immaterial (Doctrine and Covenants 130:22). Furthermore, according to Joseph Smith, "God himself was once as we are now, and is an exalted man, and sits enthroned in yonder heavens. . . . God himself, the Father of us all, dwelt on an earth, the same as Jesus Christ himself did" (King Follett Discourse).

Jesus was born twice. Jesus was the first spirit child born of God. As the Firstborn of God, he is eternally subordinate to the Father. There was a time when Jesus was not fully like his Father; he had to grow and become like God the Father, even before the incarnation (Doctrine and Covenants 93:13-17; Pearl of Great Price, Abraham 3:24). As the story goes, before Genesis 1:1, God the Father met with all the good souls/gods and asked for a volunteer to do his will. Satan stepped forward and promised to "redeem all mankind, that one soul shall not be lost," but the Father chose Jesus to be the Savior, who then created the earth according to God's purpose (Pearl of Great Price, Abraham 3:24-27; Moses 4:1-2). Angered by the Father's rejection, Satan led a rebellion on earth to destroy humankind, tempting Adam to sin; therefore Jesus had to be born of a woman to come to earth and finish God's plan of redemption (Pearl of Great Price, Moses 4:3–5:15; 7:53-57).

SO WHAT?
. . . .
The Preexistent Me

Christians believe that Jesus existed before he was born in Bethlehem; we refer to this as "the preexistent Christ." But Mormons believe that all of us existed before we were born here on earth. Oddly, many Western Christians, perhaps influenced by Plato via Hollywood, believe that we lived in heaven (as angels?) and then came to earth to be born. A funeral can then be described as "returning to heaven." This Greek idea of an eternal soul found its way into Mormonism and, unfortunately, into some branches of Christianity.

There are several other Mormon teachings that are unorthodox: the preexistence of all human souls, that Satan and Jesus are spirit brothers, that the dead can be saved through proxy baptism.

The most radical difference between Mormon doctrine and historic Christian doctrine has to do with their teachings about the essence of God(s), especially as it relates to the story of redemption. Indeed, Mormon doctrine seems to have taken the narrative of salvation and turned it upside down. Christians celebrate the story of incarnation: how God became a man; Mormons celebrate the story of deification: how man becomes a God. And yet, ironically, both LDS members and members of Christian churches point to Jesus as the centering reality of that story.

How Is This Jesus Different?

Is it possible to get Jesus mostly right but God completely wrong? Or, to put it in theological terms, should Christology (doctrine of Christ) trump theology (doctrine of God); can soteriology (doctrine of salvation) eclipse ecclesiology (doctrine of the church)? That is to say, if Mormons believe the essential parts of the gospel—Jesus was God in human flesh, he lived a perfect life, he suffered and died for the forgiveness of sins, he was raised from the dead, he's coming again to set up his kingdom on earth—then shouldn't our differences about God be consigned to the oversized folder in the filing cabinet of Christian history labeled "Things Christians Don't Agree About"? Indeed, when Mormon missionaries come to my house, when we talk about Jesus, it seems like we're discussing a shared faith. But, that can't be the case because the LDS keep sending their missionaries to my house. They are still trying to convert me. And, I'm still convinced that the Mormon Jesus is different from the Jesus I have always believed in. In other words, it's quite apparent to all three of us—the Mormon missionaries in my living room and me—that we're not talking about the same Jesus.

The first and most obvious difference is that the Mormon Jesus visited North America shortly after his ascension. Why not South America, or Southeast Asia, China, Russia or even Australia? The answer, according to the Book of Mormon, is that Jesus needed to appear to these pioneer Jews (the faithful remnant of Israel) who fled to the continent in their Christopher Columbus–like adventure. That may answer the question "Why America?" but it still doesn't answer the question "Why did Jesus need to make another postascension appearance on another continent?" The answer is embedded in the prophecies in the Book of Mormon. Jesus knew that the postapostolic church would corrupt his teachings. He knew that he needed to get his "true doctrine" to a faithful people before it was completely lost. But, even those people (the Nephites) were eventually destroyed, leaving only the record of this fantastic tale in the form of gold plates, buried in the hills of New York, to be discovered and translated by Joseph Smith.

Again we hear the lure of Gnosticism: the established church has it wrong, but someone had the secret knowledge needed to set things straight. In this case, Joseph Smith had the knowledge to unearth the buried treasure of the real gospel. Salvation can be found only by knowing the real truth about the real Jesus—the Mormon Jesus.

The Mormon Jesus isn't very Jewish either, and that is rather surprising since he is supposed to be Jehovah, the God of Israel. The Mormon scriptures contain several theological ideas that are contrary to foundational Jewish beliefs; the two most obvious ones are that God was once a human being and that humans can become gods (the stuff of Greek mythology). Furthermore, Jesus seems to have switched his loyalties; the land of promise is no longer Israel but America. Jerusalem is replaced by Independence, Missouri, as the center of God's eschatological work. In fact, the whole story of Israel is folded into the story of America. God will gather the lost tribes of Israel in America. The truth of the gospel of Jesus Christ was recovered by an American. Jesus will come back to America to establish his kingdom on earth. The new temple will be built in the New Jerusalem, fittingly located at a place called "Independence"—something that Americans prize more than anything else. This is not the story of a Jewish Messiah restoring the glory of Israel. The Mormon Jesus is an American messiah come to save the rest of the world. Indeed, it could be said that the Mormon Jesus is the first American Jesus. No wonder Joseph

SO WHAT?
. . . .
The Mormon Jesus Seems to Be a Chronic Failure

Despite all of his efforts—through the apostles, through the New Testament, through the Nephites, through the Book of Mormon—Jesus can't seem to get his message out. Indeed, the Mormon Jesus becomes completely dependent upon one man, Joseph Smith, to accomplish what he couldn't do: tell the truth about God and humankind to the whole world. Without Joseph Smith, Jesus would be lost.

Smith was inspired to write "Another Testament of Jesus Christ." This American Jesus needed a completely different story.

WHAT IF THIS WERE OUR ONLY JESUS?

This is an easy question to answer. If the Mormon Jesus were the only Jesus, then all Christians would be Mormons. And, since Mormons recognize only their version of the King James Bible, there would be no modern versions, such as the NIV, NASB, ESV or NRSV. Furthermore, we wouldn't even refer to it as the "King James Version." We would simply call it "the Bible," and it would be much thicker, with all the scriptures under one cover: the Old Testament, the New Testament, the Book of Mormon, the Doctrine and the Covenants, and the Pearl of Great Price. Our premier Christian holiday might be "Joseph Smith Day," sometime during the month of April. And we would be gearing up for a massive bicentennial festival in 2020.

Of course, all our churches would be tabernacles. More temples would need to be built, not only in America but also especially around the world, to accommodate all the liturgical needs of the priesthood, especially the increased demand for proxy baptisms. There would be no seminaries because Mormons do not have professional clergy. The tourist trade in Israel would dry up. Coca Cola probably would go out of business. Without pressure from orthodox Christianity, polygamy might be American law by now. And the reputation of all who confessed Jesus as

---

SO WHAT?

Shame on Us

Mormons are admired, and rightly so, for their strong family values, high ethical standards, work ethic and discipline. They meet the conservative expectations for Christian morality. Regardless of one's political loyalties, Mormons should be admired for living what they believe. That's why unbelievers even say, "I may not care for their Jesus, but I really like those Mormons." Of course, Mormons aren't perfect. But, shouldn't it bother us that Christians have a reputation for being hypocrites—not holding to high ethical standards—leading unbelievers to say, "I may not care for those Christians, but I really like their Jesus"?

their Lord might be significantly improved by their morality, which is sparkling clean.

Ultimately, if the Mormon Jesus were the only Jesus, we would say that Joseph Smith was right, that everything he claimed was true. He did see God the Father as a human. He was visited by an angel and given directions to find the gold plates. He did translate the Book of Mormon with the help of the divine stones, Urim and Thummim. Jesus did continue to speak through him words of prophecy and direction for the church. And therefore, most importantly, everything in the Mormon scriptures would be true: six centuries before Christ Jews traveled by ship to America, Jesus preached the gospel to them after his ascension, the Christian church is completely corrupt, the only true gospel was preserved by Joseph Smith. It all depends upon him, every bit of it, which leads to the inevitable question: What if Joseph Smith was wrong? What if he made up the whole thing? Would we still say that the Mormon Jesus is worthy of faith? Would we still wonder whether Mormons are Christians? And, therefore, wouldn't we continue to engage Mormons—even their well-dressed, kindhearted missionaries—in conversation about the truth of the gospel of Jesus Christ?

Read More About It

Blomberg, Craig L., and Stephen E. Robinson. *How Wide the Divide? A Mormon and an Evangelical in Conversation.* Downers Grove, IL: InterVarsity Press, 1997.

Millet, Robert L. *A Different Jesus? The Christ of Latter-day Saints.* Grand Rapids: Eerdmans, 2005.

Millet, Robert L., and Gregory C. V. Johnson. *Bridging the Divide: The Continuing Conversation Between a Mormon and an Evangelical.* Rhinebeck, NY: Monkfish Book Publishing, 2007.

Millet, Robert L., and Gerald R. McDermott. *Claiming Christ: A Mormon-Evangelical Debate.* Grand Rapids: Brazos Press, 2007.

Mouw, Richard J. *Talking with Mormons: An Invitation to Evangelicals.* Grand Rapids: Eerdmans, 2012.

Discussion Questions

1. Why is it important to Mormons that they hold unorthodox ideas about Jesus?

2. What is distinctive about the Mormon Jesus?

3. Why do Mormons maintain such a high moral standard? What does that reveal about their faith?

4. Why is it crucial to the Mormon faith that Joseph Smith was a true prophet of God?

5. Are Mormons Christians? Why or why not?

6. Does the Mormon Jesus trouble you? If so, which part and why?

7. Does it bother you that Mormons believe that America is the new Israel? Why or why not?

13

THE AMERICAN JESUS

Americans love conspiracy theories and superheroes. And, when these two obsessions collide, the perfect storm of an irresistible fascination is born. Throw Jesus into the mix, and the media have their feeding frenzy, which explains why every Christmas and Easter "shocking, new revelations" about Jesus appear in the news and tabloids. The same thing happens whenever a new Superman movie comes out: the story of conspiracy to keep Clark Kent's identity a secret despite his miraculous abilities often inspires talk about Jesus. So, it's not surprising that a recent film about the *Man of Steel* (2013) included a marketing strategy aimed directly at ministers and churches. Surely Christians would see the obvious parallels between the son of Jor-El and the Son of God coming to earth to save humankind. Predictably, Superman's ship crashed in the heartland of America. We don't question that part of the story. Where else could he have been raised? After all, Superman is to fight for "truth, justice and the American way." Had he landed in Nigeria, it would have been awkward, not least because Superman is white. But it is more than race; the Superman-Jesus myth is built upon the bedrock American conviction that the center of God's saving work for the world is the United States of America. Without blushing, therefore, churches celebrate Independence Day by singing patriotic songs as worship to God, by hearing sermons about "freedom in Christ," and by displaying crosses draped with the American flag. We pretend that the Fourth of July is a Christian holiday. So, it's no wonder that Superman reminds us of Jesus. To

American ears, the "gospel" story of the mission and purpose of both of them sound the same.

Who Does America Say That I Am?

For a country that emphasizes the separation of church and state, we sure have a hard time keeping Jesus out of American ways. Jesus shows up in our politics, in our schools, in our businesses, in our entertainment, in our history. He appears on billboards and bridges ("Jesus Saves"), in advertising and speeches, on jewelry and monuments, for Democrats and Republicans. He is everywhere and for everyone. Indeed, Jesus seems to be the person everyone wants on their side. Name any political or social issue, and Jesus is there. Jesus supports the war in Afghanistan and promotes world peace. He inspires revolution and requires obedience to the government. He's for gay marriage and encourages traditional marriage. Jesus sides with the poor, and the wealthy are "blessed." He protects the vulnerable and advocates for the rights of the individual. Jesus defends the powerless and empowers the rulers. Even though the apostle Paul claimed it, Jesus seems to be the one to have pulled it off: he's become all things to all people so that by all means he might save some (see 1 Cor 9:22).

Hebrews claims, "Jesus Christ is the same yesterday and today and forever" (Heb 13:8). But that's difficult to believe when we consider the many manifestations of the American Jesus. From the founding fathers to our postmodern world, Jesus seems to conform to the image-making preferences of every generation. In fact, that is one of the first things that happened to the American Jesus: stripped of his Jewish history, the Gospel story of his life was rewritten by the story of America. Or, as the historian Stephen Prothero so aptly puts it, "Jesus has an American history. To hold Jesus up to the mirror of American culture is to conduct a Rorschach test of ever-changing national sensibilities."[1] During every stage of the American experiment in democracy, a revised Jesus supported the cause. In the beginning, with the help of Thomas Jefferson, Jesus was edited down to a proverb-spitting rationalist, encouraging colonists to live by the higher law of "love thy neighbor." During the Great Awakenings of the eighteenth century Jesus was cast as

---

[1]Stephen Prothero, *American Jesus: How the Son of God Became a National Icon* (New York: Farrar, Straus & Giroux, 2003), p. 9.

the friend of sinners and savior of souls. With the industrial revolution, Jesus was called into the service of big business, the ultimate entrepreneur according to Bruce Barton's book *The Man Nobody Knows*. And yet, at the same time and on the other side of the fence, Walter Rauschenbusch held up Jesus as the champion of factory workers when he attacked the industrial prisons known as "sweatshops" that treated employees like slave labor. During the two World Wars and the Great Depression between them, a manly Jesus appeared to guide Americans through troubled times, epitomized by Warner Sallman's painting *Christ Our Pilot*, depicting Jesus with his hand on the human pilot's shoulder (but not on the wheel), pointing to where the pilot ought to steer the ship. After Vietnam Jesus was touted as the original "flower child," promoting peace and love. By the end of the century Jesus had become a hot commodity that could sell almost anything: necklaces, bracelets, bumper stickers, breath mints, diet plans, t-shirts, music, films, videos, paintings. In light of his stratospheric rise to iconic status, it could be argued that Jesus was the first "American Idol."

When John Lennon claimed in 1966 that the Beatles were more popular than Jesus Christ, he unknowingly set off a fierce competition in the marketplace for the battle of American loyalties. Not only did Christians gather to smash phonograph records made by the Fab Four, but also a flood of merchandise to challenge Beatlemania accompanied the modern "Jesus Movement." Ironically riding the wave of music inspired by the Beatles, "Jesus rock" took to the airwaves and infiltrated music stores. Jesus music festivals drew devoted fans to re-create Christian versions of Woodstock. And all kinds of "merch" (as those in the business call it)—what singer Keith Green notoriously railed against as "Jesus junk"—was made available to a souvenir-hunting fan base. So-called secular artists rode the wave of Jesus' celebrity, as the Doobie Brothers sang, "Jesus is just alright with me," and James Taylor asked Jesus to help him make a stand in "Fire and Rain." Catching the spirit of celebrity endorsement, Billy Graham began to feature famous people (actors, athletes, musicians) giving personal testimony of their faith in Jesus Christ during the massive crusades that filled sports arenas and convention centers. Christian television networks were launched, and Christian theme parks were built in order to give entertainment options to those committed to "hold up the name of Jesus." Fame and fortune, popularity and money enshrined Jesus as a cultural phenomenon in America.

For the most part, none of these things happened anywhere else. No other country has seen the likes of such megatrends. Why did it happen in America? Prothero thinks that it's because America was born without a history. The colonies were trying to get away from their puritanical past; in order to create the new world, they cast off their Calvinistic theological moorings, trading their reformation heritage of *sola scriptura* for the existential *solus Iesus*, making room for the American ideals of individual freedom and rationalism. Jesus became the "go-to guy" to justify the interpretation of events that shaped a country, creating a "history-in-the-making" tradition that forged America's identity. Personal piety eclipsed theological creeds. Knowing Jesus became more important than going to church. America replaced Israel in the sweeping story of redemption. Consequently, as America was creating its own history, Jesus was stripped of his, turning him into the poster boy of the latest development in the ever-changing landscape of this social revolution. This new free enterprise of religion also explains why the first American-made religion was Mormonism, a faith that blossomed in the new frontier because it so capably blended the stories of Israel, Jesus and America into one.[2]

The theologian Stephen Nichols finds the syncretistic ways of a people formed in a "melting pot" as the best explanation for the culturally fashioned Jesus. The fact that orthodox Christians, known for a robust Christology, have welcomed an acculturated Jesus from the beginning highlights the religious syncretism that is part and parcel of American history. So, like Prothero, Nichols shows how Americans took Jesus with them as they went forth and conquered, establishing a brave new world. Early in the republic, Jesus blended into the fabric of American civil religion as founding fathers such as Thomas Jefferson mixed threads from the Gospels with the yarn of the Enlightenment.[3] A rugged Jesus accompanied those who explored

---

[2]Ibid., especially pp. 43-85, 161-99. See also Richard Wightman Fox, *Jesus in America: Personal Savior, Cultural Hero, National Obsession* (San Francisco: HarperSanFrancisco, 2004).

[3]Nichols writes, "Christianity, in any orthodox sense, demands that Jesus is more than a teacher of morals and an exemplar of virtue, that the Bible is more than a helpful resource, and that God is more than a benevolent Deity" (*Jesus Made in America: A Cultural History from the Puritans to "The Passion of the Christ"* [Downers Grove, IL: IVP Academic, 2008], p. 71).

westward, but later the Victorian ethic that turned pioneers into settlers also turned Jesus into a sweet and gentle Savior, domesticated for home and hearth. During both World Wars Americans needed a hero, so Jesus was extolled as a "man's man." By the end of the twentieth century we were looking for a rock idol and a movie star, for the age of consumerism had turned Jesus into a product that made life better. In other words, the Jesus we have today, even in the evangelical world, is, as the title of Nichols's book suggests, a *Jesus Made in America*.[4]

What historians help us to see is that there's nothing new to the latest manifestations of the American Jesus among evangelicals. When a famous pastor on the West Coast rails against a "wimpy" Jesus and thunders with great bravado that he'd never believe in a Savior whom he could beat up, we're actually going back in history, revisiting old terrain (1865: "Onward, Christian soldiers . . . Christ, the royal Master, leads against the foe"). Or, when a female singer croons in a contemporary Christian music song that Jesus is her boyfriend, she's simply conjuring up images of Jesus that were popular during the Victorian era ("He walks with me and he talks with me, and he tells me I am his own," 1912). In other words, most current versions of the evangelical Jesus are reincarnations of one form or another of an American Jesus who has been around for a long time. Because we have a short view of history and inhabit a culture that constantly celebrates the latest and greatest, we act as if the most recent "made in America" Jesus is novel, exciting, even spiritual. But these current "American Jesuses" have been around for a long time. Let's look at six of them.

The politically correct Jesus. This is Jefferson's "rational" Jesus. The politically correct Jesus has been edited until everything that we find offensive has been taken out. This is the Jesus of the mainstream media. He's the Jesus that is left over after the Jesus Seminar finished eliminating all the embarrassing things that he said, like claiming to be the only way to God. We can't handle a Jesus who is so narrow-minded about salvation, distinguishing between those who get eternal life and those who go to hell. Rather, the politically correct Jesus would get along with everyone, would affirm every faith and every religion, saying that everyone who is sincere makes it to God.

---

[4]Nichols thinks that the only way out of our self-absorbed, self-deceived mess is to recover a holistic Christology and a historical Christian tradition (see ibid., pp. 37-45, 95-97, 144-45, 222-27).

The politicized Jesus. This is an odd variant on, perhaps even the opposite of, the politically correct Jesus. In this case, Jesus doesn't get along with everyone because he is offensive. The members of a political movement press Jesus into the service of their cause. Everything that their political movement would find offensive about Jesus has been edited out, but what offends their opponents' movement is highlighted. A popular anti-Republican bumper sticker reads, "Like Jesus would own a gun and vote Republican." While not as witty, the counter anti-Democrat bumper sticker, sporting a cross, reads, "Pro God, Pro Gun, Pro Life." Thus, I have a black friend who suggests that the white evangelical church has sold its soul to the Republican Party, and a white friend who retorts that the black evangelical church has sold its soul to the Democratic Party. Indeed, complex issues tend to be reduced to us-versus-them realities in the world of politics, so Jesus ends up for one side or the other. And yet, in the midst of this tug-of-war over Jesus for political gain, many seem to ignore the real problem: the kingdom of God has been co-opted by the etiology of American politics, and Jesus gets a bad name.

The Prince Charming Jesus. This Jesus is like the "romanticized" Jesus of the Victorian age. The Prince Charming Jesus tells us to wait passively until he shows up (in worship) and capti-vates us. After all, he's the darling of heaven, the lover of my soul, the only one we have eyes for, the dashing groom riding in to sweep his bride off her feet—at least for some of the women among us. Men (and many women), though, don't want to be swept off their feet; such worship songs make them

---

SO WHAT?
. . . .
Which Kingdom Are You Seeking First?

Jesus said, "Strive first for the kingdom of God" (Mt 6:33). When I was a missionary in Indonesia, my permission to remain in the country expired. I applied for Indonesian citizenship as a way to remain in the country to serve the kingdom of God. Many American friends were appalled. "I would never give up my US citizenship," they exclaimed. My application was eventually denied, and my friends were relieved because they were certain that God would never have expected me to give up my American citizenship for the kingdom.

uncomfortable. That's why the masculine Jesus doesn't show up too often in church services. We find him mostly in sports arenas and around campfires, where he calls males to be "manly men."

Just as the romanticized Jesus of the Victorian era provoked a backlash, inspiring the "rugged Jesus" of Billy Sunday, who bragged about Jesus fighting the devil like a boxer and who sometimes would shadow box as he preached about the crucifixion, so today the Prince Charming Jesus has been countered by the manly Jesus of the so-called Masculinity Movement. David Murrow, author of *Why Men Hate Going to Church*,[5] suggests that the current message of loving, nurturing relationships creates a church environment that doesn't appeal to men. Brandon O'Brien, in a well-argued critique, notes that champions of this movement want more testosterone in modern Christianity.[6] Men are turned off by church, they argue, largely because of its image of Jesus. Men want, according to this movement, a more masculine Jesus, one with big biceps and a more aggressive demeanor. A prominent American pastor champions the need for this kind of Jesus, not a "Richard Simmons, hippie, queer Christ" but an "Ultimate Fighting Jesus."[7] O'Brien gives a vignette that characterizes this movement:

> In a 2002 GodMen meeting, this experience included videos of karate fights, car chases and songs like "Grow a Pair!" whose lyrics read:
>
> We've been beaten down
> Feminized by the culture crowd
> No more nice guy, timid and ashamed . . .
> Grab a sword, don't be scared
> Be a man, grow a pair!
>
> It's *not* sung to the tune of "In the Garden."

As O'Brien notes, "sweet and sentimental, nurturing and nice" are considered expletives that characterize the church's abandonment of radical discipleship for mere moralizing. While not stated so crassly, manly traits

---

[5]David Murrow, *Why Men Hate Going to Church*, rev. ed. (Nashville: Thomas Nelson, 2011).
[6]Brandon O'Brien, "A Jesus for Real Men: What the New Masculinity Movement Gets Right and Wrong," *Christianity Today* 52, no. 4 (April 2008): 48.
[7]As stated by Mark Driscoll in a sermon titled "Death by Love," 2006 Resurgence Theology Conference (available at TheResurgence.com), quoted in O'Brien, "Jesus for Real Men," p. 48.

are considered inherently godly. Thus, to be a good follower of Jesus requires one to act manly. As O'Brien observes,

> I'm not sure where a man like me fits when the only categories for masculinity are "metrosexual" and "Ultimate Fighting champion." Like Jesus, I've worked as a carpenter, and I've sweated in a lumber mill. But I don't gauge my masculinity by the girth of my neck, and I'd rather not sweat for a living. I'm happiest when I'm reading and writing. I like lattes.[8]

The Church by the Glades is a leader in baptisms among Florida Baptist churches. Some friends attended in 2013. I marveled at the video they took. The lights were bright, the sound was nearly deafening, and the stage had been reconstructed to look like a fighting ring. The pastor, David Hughes, a graduate of the denominational seminary, spoke from inside the ring. Vitor Belfort, a Brazilian mixed martial artist and former UFC Light Heavyweight Champion, gave his testimony. But, what does this mean for women who want to "follow Jesus"? Do they have to enter the ring and "fight like a man"? What about short, little bald guys? Does everyone have to become an "ultimate fighter" to follow Jesus?

The pragmatic Jesus. Here is a Jesus with a clear purpose, who should drive everything his church does. Like Barton's Jesus from *The Man Nobody Knows*, Christ is the CEO of the kingdom industry. He is the model expert for everything: how to manage a company, how to create a business, how to improve marriages, how to raise children. He inspires books with titles like *What Would Jesus Eat?* and *What Would Jesus Drive?* The pragmatic Jesus has an opinion about everything, and he knows how to do it efficiently. Big is always better. More is always greater. And, above all he wants things to work well. If it's broken, it must be fixed. If we're failing, we must improve. The pragmatic Jesus wants his kingdom to run like a well-oiled machine. Consequently, as long as we get the desired results, we know that we're doing things right. Therefore, those who promote the pragmatic Jesus say things like, "Statistics never lie" and "What is your desired outcome?" and "You only hit what you're aiming for." They are always quick to interpret the latest poll and diagnose the current dilemma facing the church.

---

[8]Ibid., p. 49.

Indeed, modern disciples of the pragmatic Jesus demand quantifiable results because hard data reveal success or failure. But, what are we to make of the times when Jesus celebrates failure (the least, the last, the lost) as the essential requirement of the kingdom of God?

The radical Jesus. This is the "subversive Jesus." He is antiestablishment, the Jesus of Rauschenbusch and the more recent "Jesus freak" hippies of the 1960s and 1970s. Cast as the ultimate "zealot," the radical Jesus had nothing more than political aims for the kingdom of God.[9] The last thing he wanted was for Christians to start a church in his name and worship him. In fact, the church itself needs to be subverted. Disciples of this radical Jesus must doubt all authority and become "orthodox heretics." For, just as Jesus questioned the religious establishment, followers of the radical Jesus must always question the church down the street.

But there's another radical Jesus, one who supports the local church. In fact, church members who follow him are required to go to extreme lengths to demonstrate their crazy love for him. They can't just join a church; they must take a vow. They can't simply help the poor among us; they must take a weekend and live like a homeless person. Everything about following Christ must be intense and passionate. No one should want to live a normal, boring, traditional Christian life.

SO WHAT?

Pragmatism in Ministry

We are often encouraged to invest our ministry energies where the greatest potential lies. A "rich young ruler" lives morally, is interested in Jesus, and has a lot of money. This person could have been a very effective help in Jesus' ministry. Yet Jesus runs him off. Jesus wasn't effective in reaching this man (Mt 19:16-22; Mk 10:17-22; Lk 18:18-23). In fact, Jesus seems to invest a lot of time in disciples who don't amount to much. What ever came of Bartholomew, James son of Alphaeus, or Thaddaeus? I wonder if Jesus would get fired from many megachurch staffs for inefficiency. He squandered ministry opportunities and often didn't capitalize on crowds when he had them.

---

[9]The radical Jesus is the darling of academic types who like to portray him as a first-century rebel, the leader of subversive movement against Rome that resulted in his crucifixion.

Rather, disciples of this radical Jesus must always do radical things, such as taking annual mission trips to far-off places, holding Bible study groups in bars, and getting tattoos in Hebrew or Greek. The radical Jesus inspires an outrageous life. So, Paul must have missed the mark when he encouraged his converts to "aspire to live quietly" (1 Thess 4:11) and to "hold fast to the traditions that you were taught by us" (2 Thess 2:15) because those who follow the radical Jesus are loud and proud.

The Superman Jesus. The Superman Jesus does for us what we can't do for ourselves. This Jesus is reduced to a soteriological idea, a Super Savior who always rescues and never makes demands. The comic book Superman never called upon the people to "follow him" because they can't. So also, the Superman Jesus doesn't demand discipleship because he knows that no one can be like him. He's perfect in every way: perfect body, perfect hair, perfect teeth, perfect life. All that we're required to do is admire him through our hero worship.

How Is This Jesus Different?

It shouldn't surprise anyone, but the American Jesus really isn't about Jesus at all. With a Superman Jesus, it's really about Lois Lane and what she wants or needs. With a Prince Charming Jesus, it is actually about Cinderella. The pragmatic Jesus is the marketable Jesus who is getting the results I want. A politically correct Jesus needs to conform to our expectations. Most Americans wouldn't want to admit it, but these images of Jesus reflect whatever we need. And we will flock to the voices that proclaim the Jesus we want to hear. If they throw in a conspiracy theory suggesting that the established church has it wrong but they can share the knowledge, unearth the secrets of following the real Jesus, then the lure of Gnosticism will strengthen the case.

The politically correct Jesus appears in the sermons of Joel Osteen. Here we find a gospel without the offense of the cross. What we hear is what will make us feel better about our faith. Another version of the politically correct Jesus was portrayed in the popular television series *Touched by an Angel*. God has an angel wandering around, doing social work, and helping people to love one another, and there is no need to even refer to Jesus. The weekly drama was celebrated among church folk as a "Christian show."

Yet there was nothing uniquely "Christian" about *Touched by an Angel*; its story line told the "good news" without Jesus. The series lasted for several years because it is impossible not to like the politically correct Jesus. And yet, one cannot help but wonder: would the politically correct Jesus have been crucified?

The Prince Charming Jesus is really about Cinderella. God has to pursue me. He does all of the work. Cinderella offered no help at all; she didn't even intend to drop her slipper. She hides when the prince visits her house. It is only the (unrealistic) persistence of the prince that results in the discovery of Cinderella. (It would have been stalking, if she hadn't been interested.) In this image of Jesus there is no prodigal son who comes to senses and makes every effort to return home. Like Prince Charming, God loves us by pursuing us, carrying us away to his kingdom to live happily ever after.

This meek, mild, wimpy (Prince Charming) Jesus can't appeal to men. Men need a different Jesus, one who isn't afraid to offend.[10] Fortunately, America is able to help us again find the real Jesus, who in this case models, even champions, masculinity. He urges us to never "kill the true *man* within us," never "to get rid of those deep desires for battle and adventure and beauty."[11]

SO WHAT?
. . . .
Good News Without Jesus

Everyone is talking about the work of the kingdom these days. But what is "kingdom work"? There is a growing movement among young American Christians to see any good deed done for the common good as advancing Christ's kingdom. Yet, can you have the good news of the kingdom without Jesus? Good deeds are wonderful (and should be encouraged), but they are good deeds, not the kingdom reigning in our lives. Kingdom work is advancing the reign of Christ in our individual lives, communities and the world. We must *be* the work of the kingdom in order to *do* the work of the kingdom.

---

[10]Paul Coughlin, *No More Christian Nice Guy: Why Being Nice—Instead of Good—Hurts Men, Women, and Children* (Minneapolis: Bethany House, 2005). See the critique in O'Brien, "Jesus for Real Men."

[11]John Eldredge, *Wild at Heart: Discovering the Secret of a Man's Soul*, rev. ed. (Nashville: Thomas Nelson, 2011), p. 147 (italics added). This was a *New York Times* bestseller.

The pragmatic Jesus is interested in results—actually, only in results that can be measured and evaluated. So Adam Hamilton, pastor of one of the fastest-growing churches in the country, writes, in *Selling Swimsuits in the Arctic: Seven Simple Keys to Growing Churches*,[12] all of life is about sales. The pragmatic Jesus isn't a prophet; he's a salesman peddling wares. Since the church seems to be struggling today in America, apparently this salesman needs some consulting help. Fortunately, consultants can be found. The subtitle of a book by George Barna tells the real story: *Marketing the Church: What They Never Taught You About Church Growth*.[13] The secret to numerical church growth is not the Holy Spirit but good marketing, and we simply need to be taught the methods. "The unspoken message of target marketing is that the church need not be different from the world; it simply needs to package itself differently, position itself properly, and enjoy the benefits that come from engaging in mutually beneficial exchanges with its target market."[14] Church marketers insist that marketing is neutral and has no effect upon the church's mission. Yet the emphasis upon measurable objectives filters out personal impact or societal influence that cannot be neatly weighed. The goal of genuinely transforming the world or even an individual's life is lost among the numbers and charts of what can be measured.

The radical Jesus leads a movement in which having doubts is the only way to have faith. This emerging Jesus must question his church because faith is grounded in thoroughgoing skepticism, which self-negates since it insists that there are absolutely no absolutes. So if the norm is subversion, how do we subvert the norm? Indeed, the radical Jesus ends up being purely reactive. He is always anti–status quo. If he wins, he loses, because he becomes acculturated to the new status quo. As Hannah Arendt cleverly noted, "The most radical revolutionary will become a conservative the day after the revolution."[15] As soon as we all become "radical Christians," we are the new

---

[12]Adam Hamilton, with Cynthia Gadsden, *Selling Swimsuits in the Arctic: Seven Simple Keys to Growing Churches* (Nashville: Abingdon, 2005).

[13]George Barna, *Marketing the Church: What They Never Taught You About Church Growth* (Colorado Springs, CO: NavPress, 1988).

[14]Philip D. Kenneson and James L. Street, *Selling Out the Church: The Dangers of Church Marketing* (Eugene, OR: Cascade Books, 2003), p. 93.

[15]Quoted in *The New Yorker*, September 12, 1970.

status quo, no longer radical, so that we will always need a new spokesperson to show us a newer, even more radical Jesus.

The Superman Jesus really builds off our Lois Lane mentality. Like Lois, we are fiercely independent until we need to be rescued, and then Superman is supposed to swoop in and save the day. As soon as I'm safely on the ground, though, he is supposed to fly off and leave me alone. He is not supposed to be making daily demands on me. He's there to rescue and then leave. He is captured well in this popular bumper sticker: "God is my co-pilot." I'm still the pilot. He is there to help when I need it.

What If This Were Our Only Jesus?

The answer to this question depends on which American Jesus we are talking about. And that depends upon which book you read, which seminar you attend, which need you have. For that reason, let's use the act of preaching to flesh this out. What is preached reveals their gospel, which tells us who they say Jesus is.

Sermons about the politically correct Jesus remind us to be nice to people and not to offend. Well actually, he can offend those I don't care about, but he cannot scandalize me. This Jesus hates only the things that I hate. In any case, we wouldn't preach the cross. Our message should be about helping people deal with the everyday challenges of life. Marriage crisis, debt struggle, raising children, handling retirement—these are the subjects of our sermons. When this Jesus encourages ministry, we are to help those in need, but, like the Red Cross, we need to keep personal religious views out of it. This Jesus would never claim that he is the only way to the Father (Jn 14:6), or that there is salvation in no one else (Acts 4:12). Rather, he is a personal life coach to his followers. Sermons, then, should motivate not rebuke, comfort not convict. We need to feel good about ourselves in order to feel good about this Jesus. It is not so much that we are following him as that we are all headed the same direction.

Sermons about the Prince Charming Jesus often take two directions. When he is the feminized Jesus, he tends to show up in our worship songs. Consider the popular song "How He Loves," sung by David Crowder. He tells us Jesus loves me like a hurricane. We sing, "how beautiful you are" and about Jesus' affections for me. When John Mark McMillan first wrote the song, he spoke of a "sloppy, wet kiss." It was changed to an "unforeseen kiss." Although I personally enjoy this song, which is used frequently in my church, I have always felt a bit uncomfortable with the romantic overtones especially the kiss. In Sonicflood's song "I Want to Know You," they sing about wanting to touch and "to see your face." Are they singing about Jesus or a girlfriend? Songs like "Your Love Is Extravagant" may cause some of us to squirm in our seats. "Your fragrance is intoxicating" is a bit much for me. I am also uncomfortable with Jamie Grace's song, where she knows she should be working but she is thinking of him all the time. She loves the way he holds her in his arms. Personally, I would love my wife to say those things about me. This was the problem with the romanticized Jesus who showed up when the pioneers were domesticated. The television series *Little House on the Prairie* (1974-1983) portrayed the women liking church and the men not wanting to go. So also today, there is a similar backlash.

One can argue that a feminized Jesus always gives rise to a masculinized one. Since the Prince Charming Jesus produces "a bunch of nice, soft, tender, chickified church boys," we are fortunate that the masculine Jesus can save us (at least the men). No doubt the biblical Jesus was willing to challenge authorities and even offend. Unquestionably, the Jesus of the Gospels was no milquetoast, spineless pansy. Yet, the response to an emasculated Jesus seems to be, as O'Brien says, "to inject the church with a heavy dose of testosterone," suggesting that the task of "regaining a biblical image of Christ is as simple as re-masculating him."[16] So a popular preacher describes Jesus, Paul and, by implication, real Christian men as "heterosexual, win-a-fight, punch-you-in-the-nose dudes," asserting that this Jesus is clearly not a "limp-wristed, dress-wearing hippie."[17] Sermons encourage us to be self-reliant, brash, competitive, even offensive. Where are the fruits of the Spirit: peace, patience, kindness, gentleness? Worse, leaders in this movement commonly suggest that the feminization of the church leads it off purpose. Attributes common to males, such as aggression, assertiveness and even physical force, are by definition godly, as if untouched by the fall of humanity. One of the problems with this manly Jesus is that he doesn't appeal

---

[16]O'Brien, "Jesus for Real Men," p. 48.
[17]Mark Driscoll, quoted in ibid.

to every kind of man. But the deepest danger of this message is what it says
to women:

> This [Jesus] totally excludes women from real discipleship. To begin with, it
> blames them for neutering the gospel. . . . Perhaps worse, if Christ is the
> model of masculinity, then women can't imitate him. They can pursue him
> as the lover of their souls. . . . But they can't become like him in any essential
> way.[18]

Paul's message "there is no longer male and female" (Gal 3:28) seems lost.

What about the pragmatic Jesus? These sermons work best on a Gnostic
foundation. Christians have unhappy marriages not because of sin but because they don't know the secrets. If we have the special knowledge (usually
held only by ministers and select Bible teachers), then we can find happiness.
If I attend their special marriage enrichment weekend, I will learn the "Five
Secrets to a Successful Marriage." Sermons about the pragmatic Jesus are
straightforward, like the seven keys to church growth. This appeals to Americans. We can quantify it, make a list, check it off, and see if we are getting it
done. This is why we need data; polling groups to tell us what percentage of
church members are doing this or that. We need cold hard facts. (What we
often don't hear is much about the Spirit.) We need methods that deliver the
results. We are not even troubled by Jesus losing disciples from five thousand
down to a few, because we can draw pragmatic lessons from it. Sometimes
it is necessary to prune, Jesus teaches us, to trim down the hedge before it
can grow.

Sermons on the radical Jesus easily fall into the pattern of guilt-trip
preaching. The message is "You are never doing enough." Terms such as
"deep," "true," "committed," "significant," "passionate" and "reckless abandon"
are common parlance in sermons urging us to be more radical in following
Jesus. The enemy is not the world or even the devil, but actually the average,
normal (undercommitted) Christian. "Does something deep inside your
heart long to break free from the status quo?" asks the opening line of
crazylovebook.com (accessed April 10, 2015). The greatest threat to the gospel
is to be boring, predictable—even worse, reliable. The marks of a true disciple
are not to be meek, mild, submissive, obedient, but edgy, showy, maverick,

---

[18]O'Brien, "Jesus for Real Men," p. 48.

even a little abrasive. This Jesus isn't the one who gives rest to the weary; he is the one who overturns tables in temples.

Sermons on the Superman Jesus stress that he is ready to show up when we need him, especially during an extraordinary crisis. Only in desperation do we discover the Superman Jesus: "I find Jesus when I come to the end of myself. When I couldn't fix it, that's when I found Jesus." We don't thank Jesus for the way of he takes care of us daily. What is heroic about that? Who needs a Superman Jesus for the everyday, mundane realities of life? The hero

---

WHAT'S MORE . . .

American Religion of the Twenty-First Century

The sociologist Christian Smith recently studied the religious and spiritual lives of American teenagers and discovered they held five basic beliefs: (1) God created the world and watches over it from a distance; (2) God basically wants everyone to be nice to each other; (3) the main goal of religious faith is to help us feel good about ourselves; (4) God gets involved in our lives only when we need him to solve a problem; (5) good people go to heaven when they die.[a] He called this new American religion "Moralistic Therapeutic Deism" (MTD)—the faith that they received in current Catholic, Protestant and evangelical churches, as well as in Mormon tabernacles and Jewish synagogues. No creed was more evident, no convictions were more pervasive. MTD has effectively infiltrated American Christianity, where faith is reduced to morality, church is therapy, and God shows up only when we can't help ourselves—which sounds like all the American Jesuses rolled into one.

[a]Christian Smith, with Melinda Lundquist Denton, *Soul Searching: The Religious and Spiritual Lives of American Teenagers* (New York: Oxford University Press, 2005), pp. 162-71.

---

we worship on Sundays only has a flair for the dramatic. In fact, this Jesus isn't a part of ordinary life. Just as Superman wasn't seen in the grocery story, so this Jesus lacks relevance for the regular routines. If this were our only Jesus, we would talk about Jesus rescuing the perishing, but not about Jesus in my daily life.

Current arguments among American Christians about the essence of the gospel are really arguments over who we want Jesus to be. We want a Jesus who conforms to the message that we preach (and want to hear). We think that we're defending the "truth" of the gospel when in fact we're arguing for our version of the American Jesus. The problem, of course, is that there have been and will continue to be many reincarnations of the American Jesus because he keeps morphing into what we need. And, as long as Americans continue to believe that we are the center of the world, we will presume that the American Jesus is the Savior of the whole world.

Read More About It

Fox, Richard Wightman. *Jesus in America: Personal Savior, Cultural Hero, National Obsession.* San Francisco: HarperSanFrancisco, 2004.

Nichols, Stephen J. *Jesus Made in America: A Cultural History from the Puritans to "The Passion of the Christ."* Downers Grove, IL: IVP Academic, 2008.

Prothero, Stephen. *American Jesus: How the Son of God Became a National Icon.* New York: Farrar, Straus & Giroux, 2003.

Richards, E. Randolph, and Brandon J. O'Brien. *Misreading Scripture with Western Eyes: Removing Cultural Blinders to Better Understand the Bible.* Downers Grove, IL: InterVarsity Press, 2012.

Setzer, Claudia, and David A. Shefferman, eds. *The Bible and American Culture: A Sourcebook.* New York: Routledge, 2011.

Discussion Questions

1. Why have there been so many different versions of the American Jesus?

2. If it's obvious to us that Jesus would be neither a Democrat nor a Republican, why do we assume that he would support our particular political platform?

3. Which version of the American Jesus do you prefer? Which one offends you the most? Why? What does it say about us?

4. If our preferences for certain versions of the American Jesus are divided along gender lines, are there other social groupings that form around other versions? For example, what kind of people would prefer the radical Jesus to the pragmatic Jesus?

5. Are there certain theological traditions that are better represented by a particular American Jesus? For example, would it surprise us to find that Calvinists prefer the Superman Jesus, or that those who belong to the Wesleyan tradition are drawn to the pragmatic Jesus, or that Baptists gravitate toward the radical Jesus?

14

The Cinematic Jesus

"Have you seen the video where Jesus is smiling all the time? That's my favorite of all the Jesus films. Most of them treat Jesus as if he were serious all the time, as if he never smiled. But this one shows a radiant Jesus. In nearly every scene he has this wonderful, happy face. That's the way I've always pictured Jesus."

The middle-aged woman was grinning from ear to ear as she offered her recommendation. As her pastor at the time, I was always struck by her pleasant disposition; in fact, whenever I saw her, she often was smiling. Few of her fellow church members would have known that she battled depression. So, it didn't surprise me that the "the video with the smiling Jesus" was her favorite. There she stood, beaming with her usual smiling face, awaiting my affirmative response. I didn't have the heart to tell her what I really thought. I had seen the video and was rather put off by the "smiling Jesus" played by an American actor. To me, he didn't seem real at all precisely because he always had a silly grin on his face, even when he was berating the Pharisees or clearing the temple. I liked the sober Jesus. In fact, my favorite Jesus film at the time was Franco Zeffirelli's *Jesus of Nazareth*, which featured a brooding, pensive Jesus. To this day, when I visualize the stories about Jesus in the Gospels, Robert Powell's face appears on my mental screen. And, in the sound track running through my head, Jesus speaks with a slight British accent—just like Powell. After all, Jesus has serious things to say, and everyone knows that words spoken in a British accent sound more important.

So, in my mind I was thinking, "I don't care for the smiling Jesus who talks like an American." But, what I said was, "Yes, I've seen that video. It's an interesting portrayal of Christ, isn't it?" To which she predictably replied, "Yes, it certainly is because it's so *realistic!*"

WHO DOES HOLLYWOOD SAY THAT I AM?[1]

Here's the problem: all of us have a visual library in our heads that informs the way we read the Gospels. Whether we realize it or not, we have a mental image of Jesus, the way he looks, the way he talks, even the way he walks. Our picture of Christ is subconsciously constructed from a mishmash of several sources—from Warner Sallman's ubiquitous painting *The Head of Christ*, to the picture of Jesus in a chair with the multiracial group of children around him, to the first Jesus film we saw or especially our favorite actor's portrayal of Christ. Everyone has created a mental image of Jesus that didn't come from the Bible, because nowhere in the New Testament are we ever given a physical description of Jesus. John the Baptizer, yes. We know that John looked like Elijah because the Gospels describe him. But, not Jesus. Nowhere do the Gospel writers feel obliged to tell us what Jesus looked like. Was he tall or short? Skinny or portly? Did he have a beard, sharp features, kind eyes? Was he missing several teeth? Did he have an overbite? Was he soft-spoken? Did he speak with dramatic gestures? Was he a baritone or a bass? Did he have large hands? Was he a fast walker or did he saunter about like a man with all the time in the world? Did he wear shoulder-length hair and loose-fitting clothes? The Gospels cannot help us with any of these details. Indeed, much of what we think about Jesus' physical appearance is inferred, either from well-informed historical studies (Jesus probably wore a beard, had dark hair, and was skinny because he was a first-century Galilean Jew) or from fanciful feature films that derive as much from inherited perceptions (don't all Jesus actors look the same?) as from the imagination of the director and actor.

Readers bring all kinds of assumptions to the text without realizing their presence or influence. Think about the weather. When we're reading the Sermon on the Mount, was it bright, warm and sunny or cold, dark and rainy? Most of us assume that it had to be a beautiful day for such a mar-

---

[1]Using "Hollywood" in terms of a guild, not a place.

velous sermon. Or, consider the unwritten cues that we give to the vocal tone or facial expression of Jesus when he said, "Foxes have holes, and birds of the air have nests; but the Son of Man has nowhere to lay his head" (Mt 8:20). Most would assume that Jesus said it with a grim look on his face, in somber tones. But, perhaps Jesus was celebrating the anxiety-free life of following him—that disciples don't have to worry about things like where they are going to bed down for the night (Mt 6:25-34). Maybe he had a big grin on his face and a light-hearted tone when he invited this would-be disciple to join him in counting on the open-ended hospitality of God (in the very next episode Jesus certainly seemed unbothered by the storm as he slept in the boat [Mt 8:24]). Think about how the meaning of Jesus' saying changes in light of the nonverbal cues that we bring to the text—in this case from solemn warning to carefree declaration. In other words, what if the smiling Jesus shows up more often than we suppose? Who's to say?

Well, directors and actors are the ones to say when the cinematic Jesus smiles and when he doesn't, when he shouts and when he whispers, when he speaks and when he remains silent. They have the nearly impossible task of bringing Jesus to life on the screen, having to make thousands (even millions?) of interpretive decisions that automatically go beyond what is written because the Gospels are so vague about these minor details that are crucial to the visual Jesus. In fact, of all the "Jesuses" we've considered, both those from the Bible and outside the Bible, the cinematic Jesus is the only one that has to deal with the question that no one can truly answer: What did Jesus look like, and what did Jesus sound like? And, in an age that places so much importance on image—what you see is what you get—one wonders how any Jesus film could deliver the goods, matching the expectations of our collective mental pictures of Jesus. But, that hasn't stopped filmmakers from trying.

Since the beginning of cinema, every twenty years or so, the film industry gets the hankering to produce the life of Jesus for the screen, both in theaters and on television. The more prominent feature films were *From the Manger to the Cross* (1912), *The King of Kings* (1927), *King of Kings* (1961), *Jesus Christ Superstar* and *Godspell* (both 1973), *Jesus of Nazareth* (1977), *The Last Temptation of Christ* (1988) and *The Passion of the Christ* (2004).[2] Anyone watching

---

[2]For an excellent overview, see W. Barnes Tatum, *Jesus at the Movies: A Guide to the First Hundred Years*, rev. ed. (Santa Rosa, CA: Polebridge, 2004).

these movies cannot help but notice how each film is a product of its own time, a reflection of the society and culture of its decade. Of course, the art and science of filmmaking has changed drastically from 1912 to 2004. But looking beyond the aesthetic differences, these films present Jesus in such a radically different way that one might be tempted to say that "the Christ" is

---

WHAT'S MORE . . .

Major Jesus Films

1905	*The Life and Passion of Jesus Christ,* Zecca and Nonquet (France)
1912	*From the Manger to the Cross,* Olcott (United States)
1916	*Intolerance,* Griffith (United States)
1927	*The King of Kings,* DeMille (United States)
1961	*King of Kings,* Ray (United States)
1965	*The Gospel According to Saint Matthew,* Pasolini (Italy)
1965	*The Greatest Story Ever Told,* Stevens (United States)
1973	*Jesus Christ Superstar,* Jewison (United Kingdom and Canada)
1973	*Godspell,* Greene (United States)
1977	*Jesus of Nazareth,* Zeffirelli (Italy and United Kingdom)
1979	*The Jesus Film,* Sykes and Krisch (United States)
1979	*Monty Python's Life of Brian,* Jones (United Kingdom)
1988	*The Last Temptation of Christ,* Scorsese (United States)
1989	*Jesus of Montreal,* Arcand (Canada)
1999	*Jesus,* Young (United States)
1999	*The Miracle Maker: The Story of Jesus,* Hayes (United States)
2003	*The Gospel of John,* Saville (Canada and United Kingdom)
2004	*The Passion of the Christ,* Gibson (United States)
2006	*The Nativity Story,* Hardwicke (United States)
2014	*Son of God,* Spencer (United States)

(Taken primarily from Jeffrey L. Staley and Richard Walsh, *Jesus, the Gospels, and Cinematic Imagination: A Handbook to Jesus on DVD* [Louisville: Westminster John Knox, 2007].)

not the same character. Whenever I show college students clips from Nicholas Ray's *King of Kings*, they roar with laughter during the parts that aren't supposed to be funny. It seems what was considered reverential in the late 1950s (when the film was made) is now comical. I can imagine what the World War II generation would say to my students, "Well, that says more about you than it does about the film." And they would be right because Jesus films function more like mirrors of our world than windows into the world of Christ. How we see Jesus may say more about us than it does about him.

To illustrate the point, try to imagine a film like *Jesus Christ Superstar* being produced in the 1950s. A "hippie" version of Christ would be completely foreign to people then, but it makes sense for the 1970s. Or, picture Nicholas Ray's *King of Kings* digitally remastered to bring it up to modern standards; would it have any chance at today's box office? To put it another way, why was Cecil B. DeMille's *The King of Kings* such a blockbuster back in the 1920s and 1930s, or why would a man like Martin Scorsese make *The Last Temptation of Christ* in the late 1980s? Every Jesus film is a reflection of the era; filmmakers produce movies to be seen by their contemporaries. So, it shouldn't surprise us that the cinematic Jesus of the 1920s would be a mere shadow of himself at the beginning of the twenty-first century. The cinematic Jesus keeps changing because we are not the same people. What Shakespeare counted on for his plays is especially true for Jesus films: the "invisible" wall separating the

---

SO WHAT?
. . . .
What Does It Mean to Say That Jesus Is Perfect?

In our visual image of Jesus, to be "perfect" (especially for the camera) means that he must look like a Greek god. He can't be short or squatty or have a limp. When he smiles, his teeth have to look like a box of Chiclets. It seems sacrilegious to suggest that he might be missing teeth, even though we know that ancients didn't brush their teeth. If we say that Jesus was perfect, then in our minds he had to look more like Brad Pitt than Danny DeVito; yet, both men were created in the image of God. Should Hollywood decide for us what perfection looks like?

audience from the performance is really a mirror. Indeed, the way we picture Jesus tells us a lot about ourselves.[3]

Do we want to see a divine Christ or a human Jesus? In the first half of the twentieth century the sacredness of Christ is preserved on film. Reverence is the theme. Careful lighting insures the halo effect; Christ's transfigured face glows with a heavenly aura. He speaks with a calm, lofty voice; the Son of God is never rattled, always walking confidently from one scene to the next. Even the agony of Gethsemane is staged more like a deeply pious prayer than the tortured struggle during a dark night of the soul. And, compared to Mel Gibson's *The Passion of the Christ*, the crucifixion scenes are rather tame, romanticized versions of Christ's death. Obviously, back then we wanted a knight-in-shining-armor hero who was prepared to save the world. So, "Thy will be done" (divine presence) is the operative script for Jesus films prior to the revolutionary times of the 1960s.

During the last half of the twentieth century we seem to want another kind of hero: a very human Jesus, who struggles with his calling, his identity and, especially, his destiny. In *Jesus Christ Superstar*, *The Last Temptation of Christ*, and the made-for-television movie *Jesus* by Roger Young (1999), Jesus is a conflicted man, trying to make sense of his own place in the world. It's difficult to tell whether his "divinity" is a blessing or a curse. Irreverence is the theme. In *Jesus Christ Superstar*, Jesus is troubled by his celestial celebrity, which eventually leads to his downfall, a destiny that he embraces as God's will.[4] In *The Last Temptation of Christ*, Jesus agonizes over his mortality, wondering at the last minute whether life as a husband and a father would have been more promising than the martyr-for-God destiny that he has chosen.[5] And, in the ultimate "I-can't-figure-out-who-I-am-because-I'm-a-mixed-up-young-adult" story, *Jesus* is a fittingly self-titled film (he's nothing more and nothing less than his name) that pictures the plight of a man who can't make up his mind about who he is or what he's supposed to do. (To say he has "father issues" is an understatement.) So "Young's Jesus

---

[3]For an insightful explanation as to why and how this happens, see Richard Walsh, *Reading the Gospels in the Dark: Portrayals of Jesus in Film* (Harrisburg, PA: Trinity Press International, 2003), especially pp. 1-39.

[4]Richard Wightman Fox, *Jesus in America: Personal Savior, Cultural Hero, National Obsession* (San Francisco: HarperSanFrancisco, 2004), pp. 376-80.

[5]Staley and Walsh, *Jesus*, pp. 112-13.

empties himself of divine power, thereby becoming a joyously carefree in-dividual—one who invites all kinds of people to follow him on a direc-tionless journey."[6] In all three films, Jesus' death is a tragic end to a good story. Indeed, "My God, my God, why have you forsaken me?" (divine ab-sence) is the haunting refrain that moves the script along in the cinematic Jesus' quest of self-awareness.[7]

Of course, not all Jesus films fit easily into these two trends that divide the twentieth century. For example, both *Jesus of Nazareth* and *The Passion of the Christ* feature a resolute Jesus. And yet, it's still easy to see why Jesus

---

WHAT'S MORE . . .

Jesus the Actor: "What's My Motivation?"

- The optimist in *King of Kings*
- The rebel with a cause in *The Gospel According to Saint Matthew*
- The lone ranger in *The Greatest Story Ever Told*
- The troubled celebrity in *Jesus Christ Superstar*
- The serene sage in *Jesus of Nazareth*
- The tortured soul in *The Last Temptation of Christ*
- The happy-go-lucky seeker in *Jesus*
- The stoic victim in *The Passion of the Christ*

---

films are cultural products, reflections of the social convictions of the times. It's more complicated than this, but what mattered to us in the 1920s must be seen in Christ. Those who endured the Great Depression longed for a hero with steely resolve when facing the uncertainty of desperate times. For the generation of hippies and yuppies, the introspective struggle of the human condition—godlike potential in vulnerable frames—must be seen in Jesus, the quintessential über-male (powerful, single, unique) who is tor-tured by the same dilemma. The early films appeared to follow the market

---

[6]Ibid., p. 130.
[7]Paul V. M. Flesher and Robert Torry, *Film and Religion: An Introduction* (Nashville: Abingdon, 2007), p. 142.

strategy of "comforting the afflicted," while most of the latest Jesus films seem bent on "afflicting the comfortable." Whatever the artistic/ideological intent, market pressures that come with spending millions of dollars in film production created a cinematic Jesus whom moviegoers will want to see. Indeed, Jesus films "fail if we expect them to reject prophetically the culture that produced them."[8] A movie that critiques culture must still appeal to the masses. If we ever question whether we create Jesus in our image, film erases all doubts. That's why critics dismiss movies about Jesus as "follower films."[9] Mel Gibson's *Passion of the Christ* proved the point: the only people who want to see films about Jesus are those who already know him, and therein lies the rub. We decide whether Hollywood gets him right; success at the box office will tell "the truth." But, who's to say that we recognize "the truth," since his story tends to look and sound a lot like our story?

How Is This Jesus Different?

Seeing our favorite literary characters come to life on the big screen is fraught with excitement and disappointment all at the same time. For us, producers never seem to get it right. Films hardly do justice to books because they can't; there's too much stuff in a good book to capture on film. Besides, films can never live up to our imaginations—the very skill that books require. Rather, films stifle imagination. Once we've encountered an imaginary literary character, such as Gollum in J. R. R. Tolkien's *The Hobbit* and *The Lord of the Rings*, and then see that same character in a film version, it's hard to remember the original mental image that we formed from the literary depiction. The same applies to Jesus films. Of course, we don't have the same emotional attachment to Sméagol as we have to Jesus. But to carry the analogy further, even though some fans thought that director Peter Jackson got Gollum right, his attempts at creating the cinematic version of Gollum were never hampered by "multiple" versions of the same character. Gollum is essentially the same in both *The Hobbit* and *The Lord of the Rings*. But when it comes to Jesus, as we have already noted, we have four literary versions of the same character (not counting the rest of the New Testament), and Jesus is different in each of them. That's one of the reasons why no one

---

[8]Walsh, *Reading the Gospels*, p. 13.
[9]Ibid., p. 25.

can create an adequate "harmony" of the four Gospels; Matthew, Mark, Luke and John defy homogenization (Tatian, with his *Diatessaron*, tried but failed like all of his successors). In fact, as it happens in the movies, the only way to cast one Jesus from four Gospels is to leave out mountains of information.

WHAT'S MORE . . .

Modern Harmonies

Scholars and publishers today produce books that set the four Gospels in parallel columns so that their episodes and sayings can be easily compared. This is a useful tool for anyone who is trying to understand how each evangelist told his particular story of Jesus. By studying the similarities and differences, we can know something of the evangelists' audiences and purposes in writing. These parallels also provide a kind of harmony to the life of Jesus.

There is a growing interest today too in putting the Scriptures in chronological order. So Bible publishers are creating chronological study Bibles. There are many benefits; they can provide a more harmonious picture of the life of Jesus for the reader. After all, behind the four Gospels is the life and ministry of a single person. The problem, of course, is that the only way to harmonize the four Gospels is to leave parts of each Gospel out, especially the unique parts, which is the same thing that directors and producers do to create the cinematic Jesus.

What's different about the cinematic Jesus? Everything. This is why we tend to be critical of Jesus films, because they're so very different from what we read in the Gospels. In fact, most Jesus films operate like a "fifth" Gospel. Vital information is ignored, some of our favorite stories about Jesus are left out, bits of information are added, fictional characters are created, and before you know it, the Jesus story on film is barely recognizable to our Gospel-sensitive eyes and ears. "They didn't get Jesus right at all," we say with righteous confidence. But this is where all of us—church people, biblical scholars, film critics, moviegoers—are hypocritical in our judgments. As we pointed out in the introduction, all of us have a smorgasbord Jesus, picking and choosing the parts that we like. Whether we admit it or not, we operate with a "fifth" Gospel, a hodgepodge of information that we've collected from a variety of sources. The "Jesus in our heads" is a patchwork, made up of scraps of material sown together in our minds, giving us the mistaken impression that what we've created is the "real" Jesus.

Several yards from Matthew's bolt of cloth here, some of Mark there, knitting our favorite parts of Luke around the edges, adding John where we need him, using rags from films, plays, music and paintings to fill in the gaps, and before long our hand-stitched blanket is a homespun quilt created by our preferences and designed for our comfort. Indeed, after a while, the quilted image of Jesus becomes a religious heirloom that must be handled with care. It's no wonder, then, that the cinematic Jesus is barely recognizable. He will never match the mental image that we've stitched in our minds because every single one of us has created our own homogenized Jesus.

What the cinematic Jesus forces us to do is recognize

SO WHAT?
. . . .

Is the Cinematic Jesus Really a Gnostic Jesus?

Well, a Jesus on film isn't flesh and blood; he only "appears" real. The ancient Gnostics suggested that they had a fifth Gospel that had it right. Film can often suggest the same thing. Like the ancient Gnostics, a film can pick parts of the canonical Gospels that it likes, add "insights" from other sources, and produce the "real Jesus." The cinematic Jesus can have the same lure of the ancient Gnostic Jesus. You have to have the knowledge that it provides to make sense of the biblical story. Toss in a conspiracy idea, salt with some new titillating "never heard before" details (like a last temptation), and you have a blockbuster that the crowds will flock to see.

the influence of our imaginations. What we see when we read the Gospels— our vision of Jesus—can lie comfortably in the shadows of presumption until we watch a movie about Jesus. It's a scary thing to ponder: the Gospels themselves encourage us to create an imaginary Jesus because reading is not a benign activity. Why didn't the Gospel writers create picture books? Imagine how helpful it would have been to have "The Illustrated Bible" from the very beginning. Because we didn't have a picture book, it is easy to assume that our mental image of Jesus is the "real flesh-and-blood" Jesus. But, Jesus films won't let us. Ironically, the cinematic Jesus brings us face to face with the problem of history—his and ours, especially since we can't keep the two from mingling together. For example, prior to the Holocaust, Jesus films appeared to have no reservations about placing the blame of the crucifixion on "the Jews" while Roman executors lurked in the background. Since World War II, however, directors are far more inclined to implicate the Romans in the execution of Jesus, highlighting the political tensions between Pilate and the Jewish leadership.[10] Film reveals our cultural sensitivities; the cinematic Jesus story is shaped by our story. And yet, even though we know that Jesus films are projections, we pretend that we're going to see the "real" Jesus at the movies, knowing that we'll be disappointed. Why? Because we operate with

---

WHAT'S MORE . . .

Jesus Films and the Gospel Script

There are a few versions of the cinematic Jesus that rely less upon imaginary dialogue and stick more closely to the Gospel narratives. For example, *Jesus* (1979), also known as "the Jesus film," was funded by supporters of Campus Crusade for Christ, an evangelical parachurch organization that targets university students for evangelism. From start to finish, the film relies exclusively on Luke's Gospel for dialogue, chronology and setting. Therefore, some might claim that this cinematic Jesus is more biblical than what is usually produced by Hollywood. But the truth of the matter is that even "the Jesus film" included a lot of material that isn't in the Bible: music, camera angles, costumes, geographical settings, facial expressions, actors speaking in English, and so on. All of this proves that Campus Crusade's *Jesus* version is not a strictly "biblical version" of the life of Jesus. Even this film is a highly interpretive picture of Jesus. Besides, "the Jesus film" is a cinematic portrayal of only Luke's Jesus. As much as the director kept to one Gospel as his script, *Jesus* certainly isn't the whole gospel on film.

---

[10]Walsh, *Reading the Gospels*, pp. 4-9; Staley and Walsh, *Jesus*, p. 171; Fox, *Jesus in America*, pp. 315-16. For a fuller treatment of the sociopolitical forces at work in Jesus films, see Adele Reinhartz, *Jesus of Hollywood* (New York: Oxford University Press, 2006), pp. 51-63, 198-250.

the presumption that the Jesus we've imagined is the gospel truth, and no film will convince us otherwise.

What If This Were Our Only Jesus?

Sex and violence sell films. And, since Jesus' story includes both, films about him should be automatic blockbusters. Jesus was a friend of prostitutes, and his death certainly came by one of the most violent means of execution in human history. Predictably, these episodes are featured in every Jesus film (imagine what we would say about the film if they weren't). But there are certain chunks of the Gospel story that don't make it onto the big screen because they have little to no cinematic value. In other words, parts of Jesus' story are visually boring; indeed, some of the major features of Jesus' life never make it into a feature film about him. Take, for example, the teaching material. Jesus is known for being one of the greatest teachers of all time. And yet, we never get to hear him offer a lengthy discourse, like the Sermon on the Mount or the Olivet Discourse. A dramatic reading of Matthew 5–7 would take about thirty minutes. Would audiences used to action-packed films that coddle our short attention spans sit through a half-hour monologue? Even though the material is brilliant, varied camera angles of Jesus' face and constant shots of the crowd's response might hold our interest for about two minutes. Or, why hasn't a single Jesus film included the Olivet Discourse? It seems that Hollywood is embarrassed by a Jesus who predicts the end of the world. And yet, even the more popular teaching of Jesus—his parables—sneaks into the film only as remarks laid over a particular scene. In other words, as long as Jesus is doing something interesting, we'll watch. If all we had were the cinematic Jesus, we would never know that he was such a great teacher.

Miracles don't fare very well in Jesus films either, and that's surprising, given the visual nature of both. There are a few miracles that always seem to make the director's cut, such as the feeding of the five thousand, the miraculous catch of fish, walking on the water, and raising Lazarus from the dead. But these stories are sprinkled throughout the film as asides. Even though miracle stories provide great drama, they come few and far between. Furthermore, some miracles are completely ignored, like the exorcism of the demon Legion, the cursing of the fig tree, the healing of Peter's mother-in-law, the coin in the fish's mouth, and the feeding of the four thousand. Even though the Gospels are saturated with signs and wonders performed by Jesus (the author of John's Gospel lamented that no library could contain all the stories [Jn 21:25]), Jesus films marginalize the miraculous. But why? Could it be that certain miracles are easier to replicate on film, especially in light of the fact that some "must see" scenes involving the supernatural come off as cheesy imitations (like the Holy Spirit baptism of Jesus, the transfiguration, or especially the ascension)? Or, is it that some miracles make better sense to our way of thinking? That is to say, when Jesus heals the blind and the lame, feeds the masses, or even raises the dead, his compassionate work tends to match our humanitarian efforts for people with the same disadvantages. In other words, as long as we can understand Jesus' intent, whether in miracles or teaching or challenging Jewish and Roman leaders, we can identify with his mission. And yet, it's the climax of the story, the meaning of his death, where we seem to have the most trouble making sense of the cinematic Jesus.

Why did Jesus die? The question is loaded with all kinds of implications, not only for making sense of Jesus' identity and mission but also for sorting out the main conflict of the story, identifying Jesus' opponents. These two ideological forces—the intentions of Jesus and his enemies—dominate the plot of the Gospel story, but are they related? In other words, if we could identify who wanted Jesus dead and why, would that necessarily uncover the purpose of Jesus' mission as he understood it? The connection is difficult to sort out in the literary Gospels because Jesus had several enemies who act like villains in the story: Judas Iscariot, the Pharisees, Caiaphas and the Sanhedrin, Herod, Pilate, the Roman soldiers and Satan/the devil. Different Gospels heighten or minimize the role of each "villain" to tease out the dynamics of the social, political and spiritual forces at work in the execution of Jesus. But, films require a unified plot without complexities so that the audience isn't confused about "whodunit."

Therefore, regarding the cinematic Jesus, the purpose of Jesus' death depends upon the villain featured in the film. In DeMille's *The King of Kings*, Jesus fights against the lust for power (Caiaphas) and money (Judas) in order to establish a peaceful kingdom seemingly built on the moralistic ideals of middle-class America.[11] But in Zeffirelli's *Jesus of Nazareth*, Judas doesn't betray Jesus on purpose. Rather, he thinks that he's helping Jesus by arranging a meeting with the Sanhedrin, only to find out that he's been duped by Zerah, a fictitious character who plays the role of the betrayer. And, even though Judas is remorseful for unwittingly setting up the execution of Jesus, in a roundabout way he did help Jesus fulfill his destiny because, for Zeffirelli, Jesus' singular mission was to die for the sins of the world.[12] In *Jesus Christ Superstar* Jesus dies as a victim of celebrity. According to Young's *Jesus*, Jesus is crucified to break the vicious cycle of violence in the world: love overcomes hatred. Likewise, even though it seems that the primary purpose of Gibson's *The Passion of the Christ* is to validate Catholic traditions, it takes a saying from the apocalyptic Jesus, spoken on the Via Dolorosa, to explain his gruesome death: "See, mother! I make all things new" (ironically, the best line in the film comes not from the Gospels but from Rev 21:5). Consequently, the purpose of Jesus' mission depends upon what film we are watching at the time. And, the time when the film was made determines the kind of Jesus we are watching. Indeed, when it comes to the cinematic Jesus, perhaps more than any other, seeing is believing. For many moviegoers, then, the words of Jesus to his first disciples still resonate: "Come and see."

SO WHAT?
The Power of Film

Human beings are hardwired to tell stories, remember them, pass them on, and draw life lessons from them. In the past storytellers gathered in small groups around tables and campfires to share. Film adds a powerful new dimension to the ancient art of storytelling. Filmmakers are storytellers who can reach millions with a well-written and well-financed script.

Ministry today involves more than answering a call to preach or lead worship. Some today are hearing a call to make films, tell the greatest stories, and bring Jesus to life in fresh and daring ways.

---

[11]Fox, *Jesus in America*, pp. 318-19; Walsh, *Reading the Gospels*, pp. 8-9.
[12]For the evolving portrayal of Judas in Jesus films, see Walsh, *Reading the Gospels*, pp. 34-39.

Read More About It

Flesher, Paul V. M., and Robert Torry. *Film and Religion: An Introduction*. Nashville: Abingdon, 2007.

Reinhartz, Adele. *Jesus of Hollywood*. New York: Oxford University Press, 2006.

Staley, Jeffrey L., and Richard Walsh. *Jesus, the Gospels, and Cinematic Imagination: A Handbook to Jesus on DVD*. Louisville: Westminster John Knox, 2007.

Tatum, W. Barnes. *Jesus at the Movies: A Guide to the First Hundred Years*. Rev. ed. Santa Rosa, CA: Polebridge, 2004.

Walsh, Richard. *Reading the Gospels in the Dark: Portrayals of Jesus in Film*. Harrisburg, PA: Trinity Press International, 2003.

Discussion Questions

1. What is your favorite film about Jesus? Why? How has it influenced your view of him?

2. Why does it take more imagination to read the Gospels than to watch a Jesus film? Does that make "our Jesus" an imaginary character?

3. Where do some Christians get the idea that Jesus had to have a perfect body? And, even if we believe that, what should a perfect, first-century Jewish man look like?

4. Why do we believe that most Jesus films get him wrong? What does that reveal about us? Could there ever be an R-rated film about Jesus that is biblical?

5. Why are films so important today? Should that make us more or less determined to produce and see Jesus films?

6. What role should the consumer market play in the production and success of a film about Jesus?

Conclusion

"Our Jesus"

So what? In light of all these images of Jesus, we are kidding ourselves
if we think that we have Jesus figured out. In many of our churches we
have a Jesus drawn largely from Paul and John, ignoring most of the New
Testament. While Matthew is a "go and tell" Gospel, Paul and John offer a
"come and see" message. Perhaps this is one reason why Paul's and John's
Jesus appeals to us. Really, what else do we need but Paul's and John's Jesus?
Paul tells us what Jesus did for us on the cross. John tells us that we need to
be born again. So what do we talk about in our churches? We need to be
born again (based upon what Jesus did on the cross). Our focus is on the
by-and-by. Yet, this leaves us struggling to decide if Jesus makes a difference
at home or at work. How should I live as a Christian today? Once we are
born again (as John's Jesus commands), what should we do at home? Well,
we should tell our family and friends to be born again. How does Jesus show
up at work? We need to tell our co-workers to be born again. But is that all?
Surely the kingdom of God announced by Mark's Jesus is more than getting
people to make a decision for Christ.

Every generation has the task of rediscovering Jesus. Jesus, of course,
hasn't been lost, but we often lose sight of him. In the pursuit of other things
we can neglect him and perhaps even forget him. Yet he has been there all
along waiting to be (re)discovered by the next generation of seekers. Also,
we need some humility, and we need to look over our shoulders, back into

history. We are not the first followers of Jesus to come along, and we won't
be the last. Maybe my Jesus isn't the real Jesus. In order to rediscover Jesus
we need to find *our* Jesus, the one whom followers all over the world see and
whom followers throughout history have adored. When Jesus came to Caesarea Philippi and asked the Twelve about his identity, we might mistakenly
think that he asked two separate, unrelated questions. When he asks, "Who
do people say that I am?" he is not asking an unimportant question in order
to get to the real question, "Who do you say that I am?" Jesus knew that we
need both questions. We can't answer one without the other. What others
think influences us. If we are not aware of it, we can end up picking and
choosing from the various images (like a smorgasbord) to suit our tastes. If
Christians err by assuming that only the second question matters, non-
Christians err by pretending that it's possible to answer only the first
question. The latter group tries to objectively answer the question of who
people say that Jesus is without having to be involved themselves, as if what
they think about Jesus doesn't influence their interpretation of the material
that we have about him.

So how do we rediscover Jesus? We need a biblical Jesus. This is a two-
edged sword. First, it means that we consider the biblical texts to present an
authoritative voice about Jesus. Not every answer to the question of who is
Jesus is equally valid. Some are mutually exclusive, such as the Muslim Jesus
and the Mormon Jesus. While we can learn from the Gnostic Jesus or the
American Jesus, we do not consider these images to be on par with the biblical texts. Yet the other edge of the sword is that a biblical Jesus must include
voices from the entire Bible. A canonical Jesus is not a truncated one. We
need to let Matthew tell us about Jesus. But we also need to let John and Paul
and Hebrews complete the image of Jesus.

Mark's Jesus is a man of action. Right out of the chute, he is curing dis-
eases and casting out demons. Jesus is a healer and exorcist. The kingdom
of God is a war, and its general has stormed onto the scene. Here we have a
leader who can take us into battle. As with most generals, though, we are
left to guess what Jesus is thinking, inferring that from his actions. Matthew's Jesus, however, lets us know exactly what he is thinking. We are reminded that God has been at work saving his people Israel, and now this
salvation is being culminated in the promised son of Abraham, the son of

David. Although he is the consummate rabbi, he is not what many in Israel were expecting. Matthew's Jesus picks a fight with the Jewish leaders, accusing them of not truly understanding what God was doing. While not one jot or tittle of God's law will pass away without Jesus fulfilling it, God's people haven't correctly lived the law. Jesus' followers were guiltless even when they seemed to be breaking the Law (Mt 12:1-8), taking the true message to the lost sheep of Israel first (Mt 10:5-15), with the inclusion of Gentiles later (Mt 28:18-20).

Luke's Jesus is subversive, turning the world upside down. Actually, Jesus insists, it only looks upside down; his is actually right side up. It is the way the kingdom truly is. It is Lazarus, not the rich man, who is actually blessed. It is the approach of the tax collector, not the Pharisee, that pleases God. The kingdom of God is found on the margins, not where we are. Zacchaeus up in a tree is on the margins; yet, he is the one invited to supper with Jesus and who enters the kingdom. The subversive nature of the kingdom, where the last are first and the least are greatest, is seen most decisively in the cross. It is God's final act to show that we have the world upside down. The act that looks most clearly like the defeat of Jesus is when he gets his kingdom— "today" (Lk 23:43).

John's Jesus answers the question of what happened to the Wisdom of God. The Word that created the cosmos has come to dwell among human beings. Yet, the world that he created didn't recognize or accept him. But those who believe do become children of God; and he loves them, takes care of them, prepares a place in his temple for them, and will return for them. How do we know that Jesus is this Word? We should see the signs that point to who he is. He is the true light, the bread of life, the good shepherd, the resurrection. He is God-among-us. For John, the cross is the sacrifice of the Passover lamb to save his people.

Paul's Jesus explains why the Messiah had to suffer and die. While John's Gospel tells us that Jesus was the Lamb of God, Paul explains how he was so. Paul's Jesus is the propitiation, the atoning sacrifice for our sins. While the Synoptic Gospels talk about the kingdom, Paul reminds us that it's all about the King. While John's Gospel invites true believers to eternal life, Paul understands that life in the Spirit begins now in this world.

Even though the King has left, he has given his followers the Spirit. Indeed, he is coming back for us, and the kingdom seems real enough now, but there is more to come. So what do we do in the meantime? The Jesus of exiles described by Peter, James and Jude shows us how to live as aliens while we are awaiting our restoration.

The Jesus of Hebrews is our Great High Priest. As modern Westerners, we commonly react by saying, "I don't need a high priest." The ancient recipients of this letter would have reacted by saying, "Jesus doesn't have the pedigree to be a high priest." While this might not be our first question, the answer still clarifies who Jesus is. He is not born a Levitical priest, but he is installed as a priest in the order of Melchizedek by God's oath. Thus, the need for the right kind of priest predates any law. Modern Westerners like to have things set out in black and white, with no gray areas, but not all the world thinks as we do. My Chinese friend says, "Buddhism taught me so much about living in harmony with the world. But Jesus is better." To my ears, this statement of faith in Jesus seems lacking. It is not black-and-white enough. If Jesus is right, then my friend needs to say that Buddhism is "wrong." The way to make Jesus superior is to denigrate the rest. Right? Wrong. Hebrews shows us another way. It is not necessary to say that the old covenant was bad or that the law was worthless. Rather, the priestly Jesus is better. It is not necessary to find the old priestly system faulty. The cross in Hebrews is God's better sacrifice, bringing together the priest (the sacrificer) and the lamb (the sacrificed).

The apocalyptic Jesus reminds us that he is the King. We may call him friend (Jn 15:15) and teacher, but he is far more. He may well be our elder brother in the family of faith, but Revelation reminds us he is also a fearsome sovereign. Here the kingdom has come, and so there is no reason to live in fear of evil powers of this world. While the Lamb of God is described as "slaughtered," he is alive and powerful. This is our King. And, the apocalyptic Jesus shows us how to reign with him by offering ourselves as living sacrifices.

When we consider the biblical Jesus, we seek to hold all these images in our minds, allowing each to clarify and augment the other. Yet to rediscover Jesus, we also need to recognize what has also crept into our consciences from images of Jesus outside the Bible.

The Gnostic Jesus calls us to come learn the "secret," hidden knowledge. Some leaders today promise that if we will follow their teachings, learn their secrets, then we can discover who we truly are. We can have successful marriages and fat bank accounts. Yet, as Gnosticism had many forms, so also does the Gnostic Jesus. For many, salvation has nothing to do with this life; it is an escape from this world. There is no kingdom of God to see here. Move along. Focus on the life beyond. Often, then, our actions here have no implications for the kingdom, allowing many followers of a Gnostic Jesus to discount ethics. For most versions of the Gnostic Jesus, however, the cross plays little to no role. It is all about me gaining the knowledge that I need.

The Muslim Jesus is primarily concerned about God. His followers discover peace by submitting to God the creator and master of the world. This lofty God has no equals: there is no God but God, and Muhammad is his prophet. Thus, the Muslim Jesus must disclaim any ties. He belongs squarely with humanity. He may be one of God's elite prophets, but he is human only. God gave him a message much like the message that Muhammad delivered, but Jesus' followers distorted it and made Jesus out to be someone he was not, the Son of God. Muslims do not believe that Jesus died on the cross. He was assumed to heaven and will come again at the end. After his return, Jesus will die and be buried beside Muhammad. The cross has no function in the story of the Muslim Jesus. It was a deception.

The historical Jesus, the Jesus left after the rationalists are done, is a very believable Jesus. It requires no real faith to believe in this Jesus. Naturally, his actions are reasonable, his deeds explainable. Yet, the cross becomes the mystery. The historical Jesus is a man worth commending, not crucifying. He often isn't someone worth killing. In the story line for most descriptions of the historical Jesus, the crucifixion is the tragic result of someone misunderstanding what Jesus was really doing. The cross is not the plan of God but rather the unfortunate misdeed of a few misguided persons. The cross marks the end of a human's life, providing whatever inspiration the noble death of a human can provide us fellow humans.

The Mormon Jesus is a very orthodox Jesus slipped into a very unorthodox framework. A sense of "manifest destiny" drove Europeans westward, conquering the Americas. So likewise was it for the Mormon Jesus. It was necessary for John's Jesus to go through Samaria (Jn 4:4), and so also the Mormon Jesus had to go to North America. God had a plan for moving his kingdom from Jerusalem; therefore, the King by necessity needed to go there as well. Between a birth in Bethlehem and a death in Jerusalem, the Mormon Jesus differs little from the New Testament one. His backstory and his plans for the future, however, are very different. The cross becomes the key to humanity's door to divinity.

The American Jesus is what we need. Just as you can "have it your way" when you order your burger, so also you can tailor a Jesus to fit your desires. Americans are experts at improving whatever comes our way. Jesus is no exception. The American Jesus, though, takes many forms, depending upon who is doing the ordering. Likewise, the cross has different meanings. For the Prince Charming Jesus, the cross is the ultimate sign of how much Jesus loves me (personally). For the Masculinity Movement, the cross is the sign of just how manly Jesus was. He took all that suffering without running away (he didn't ask God for "twelve legions of angels" to rescue him [Mt 26:53]). For others, the cross indicates that God has a plan for my life, and it must be important because it cost the cross. The cross indicates to others how radical God is. The old status quo under the old covenant wasn't enough. The Superman Jesus must face the cross because in all hero stories the villain "nearly" defeats the hero before the hero rallies back and saves the day.

The cinematic Jesus challenges our generation to recognize that we all have a "fifth" Gospel. Since films cannot tell every story from our Gospels

SO WHAT?
....

Why Does Our Theology Matter?

"Theology" is not simply a technical word and a formal field of study. Whenever we think about God or talk about God, we are doing theology. In that sense, all of us are theologians—perhaps not in a professional sense, but in a sense that truly matters. In simplest terms, it might be said that Muslims get God right and Jesus wrong, while Mormons get Jesus right and God wrong. It is becoming popular when emphasizing worship to denigrate theology. "As long as I love Jesus, who cares about theology?" Well, what we think about God matters. For what we think determines what we believe and how we feel and thus how we act. The path is this: believing to behaving to becoming. Theology matters.

and must also add backgrounds, dialogue and other incidentals, viewers are presented with a Jesus who doesn't match the Jesus of their imagination. Human characters cannot look like I imagined them to appear. Films never get Jesus right because they don't show him the way I see him. Worse, a film can show only one Jesus, so we are back to the problem of Tatian, who blended our four Gospels into one. Yet, in a generation that watches rather than reads, the risk runs high of creating another *Diatessaron*, another harmony of the Gospels. In film, as with the historical Jesus, the cross becomes the tool of the "villain," but the villain varies from film to film, and thus the villain's motive shifts the meaning of Jesus.

The Jesus outside the Bible can on occasion help us rediscover some aspect of Jesus that has been ignored or sidelined. More commonly, though, these nonbiblical images influence and color our biblical image. Understanding these images helps to reveal ideas that need to be expunged from "my Jesus." While I found themes and emphases from the various biblical images of Jesus that needed to be reintroduced into my picture of Jesus, I also found other themes and emphases from nonbiblical images that needed to be extracted from my portrait of Jesus. Both of these processes help me to rediscover Jesus.

Finally, although it is beyond the purview of this book, we also suggest that in order to rediscover Jesus we need the Jesus seen in the community of faith, worldwide and down through the ages. Somewhat ironically, Christianity is often viewed as a religion of white Americans, as noted in a famous statement made by Booker T. Washington: "No white American ever thinks that any other race is wholly civilized until he wears the white man's clothes, eats the white man's food, speaks the white man's language, and professes the white man's religion."[1] Moreover, Christianity is often distinguished from "Eastern religions." Yet it began in the Middle East, founded by a Galilean peasant. How did a Mediterranean movement come to be seen as a Western religion? Unquestionably, the Western world has left its mark on modern Christianity and, one must admit, upon our image of Jesus. Gratefully, the English-speaking church is developing a more global understanding in at least two ways. First, we are rediscovering historical expres-

---

[1]Booker T. Washington, *Up from Slavery* (1901; repr., New York: Dover, 1995), p. 47.

sions of Christianity from Africa and Asia. Second, modern non-Western Christians are finding ways to express themselves and their understandings of Jesus to the English-speaking market. We believe that this will help us to rediscover Jesus. Initially, we had proposed to write a chapter on the "global Jesus." We quickly realized that there is no global (meaning non-Western or non-American) image of Jesus. There is no "African Jesus." A Cameroon portrait of Jesus is not the same as an Ibo one. There is no "Asian Jesus." Even attempts to find an East Asian (Chinese), South Asian (Indian) and Southeast Asian (Indonesian) picture of Jesus quickly reveal that there is no consensus. In the chapter on the American Jesus we discovered a Superman Jesus, a Prince Charming Jesus, and a politically correct Jesus. So likewise, we would find a similar diversity in Africa or Asia. Nonetheless, such a conversation helps us clarify our own image of Jesus.

What you think about Jesus is the dividing issue. There is a great deal of commonality in the ethics, lifestyle and religious perspective of a Western Mormon, a Western Muslim and a Western Christian. The real dividing issue is what they think about Jesus. Jesus himself said, "Do you think that I have come to bring peace to the earth? No, I tell you, but rather division!" (Lk 12:51). Jesus asked his original disciples, "Who do you say that I am?" We believe that he is still asking. Rediscovering Jesus is a necessary task for each generation. Just as Peter's response was influenced by their current struggle against the Roman occupation, so each generation answers with an image colored by its own concerns and agendas. Jesus' question, however, is not a futile one. He was not and never will be undiscoverable. We believe that each generation and culture adds a bit of clarity to the task of rediscovering Jesus. Like a spiral, the picture of Jesus will become clearer when we hear from "every nation, from all tribes and peoples and languages" (Rev 7:9). Most extrabiblical answers about Jesus have positive contributions to make. Nonetheless, most of these answers about Jesus are ultimately inadequate in light of the biblical texts. The clearest picture of Jesus is found in his community, across the globe and down through the ages: our Jesus.

SUBJECT AND NAME INDEX

SCRIPTURE INDEX